George Clarke Musgrave

Under Three Flags in Cuba

George Clarke Musgrave

Under Three Flags in Cuba

ISBN/EAN: 9783337379155

Printed in Europe, USA, Canada, Australia, Japan

Cover: Foto ©ninafisch / pixelio.de

More available books at **www.hansebooks.com**

UNDER THREE FLAGS IN CUBA

A Personal Account of the Cuban Insurrection and
Spanish-American War

BY

GEORGE CLARKE MUSGRAVE

AUTHOR OF "TO KUMASSI WITH SCOTT," "WEST AFRICAN
FETISH," "THE CUBAN INSURRECTION."

BOSTON
LITTLE, BROWN, AND COMPANY
1899

TO

M. J. L.

A SLIGHT TOKEN OF APPRECIATION FOR HER SYMPATHY
AND MINISTRATION TO ME WHEN SICK
AND WOUNDED.

Introduction

"UNDER TWO FLAGS IN CUBA" was to have been published in the spring of 1898; but the manuscript, together with three hundred photographs illustrative of Weyler's régime in Cuba, and some historical letters that had passed between the Captain-General and Premier Canovas, were seized in Havana with my effects when I was deported to Spain at the beginning of the war. Thus the circulation of that work was limited to General Blanco and those of his officers who understood English.

After witnessing the triumph of the American army at Santiago, I prepared the present work, "Under Three Flags in Cuba," during a prolonged attack of fever contracted in the campaign. But again fate, acting now through the pistol of an incensed Spanish officer, delayed publication. During my convalescence from the wound, a number of books on Cuba

Introduction

were issued from the pens of gifted writers. In each work the primary cause of the war is omitted, and frequent criticism of the Cubans, based entirely on misconception, has tended to raise doubts of the justification of American intervention in the Island.

Landing in Cuba, a warm sympathizer with Spain, to write upon her military failure for a British service organ, and enjoying at various times exceptional opportunity to study the question from both a Cuban and Spanish standpoint, my heart went out to Cuba in her struggle. While I held a commission in the Cuban army, stories of my fighting prowess that appeared in various Spanish papers were absolutely false. When travelling across Cuba, my escort was at times involved in skirmishes, and participated in larger fights when visiting other commands, but I was an observer rather than a warrior. I have endeavored to write the simple story without bias. Thrice a prisoner in the hands of the Spaniards, they treated me with a surprising consideration; and now that Right has triumphed and Wrong is overthrown, we can feel

Introduction

sympathy with the humiliated nation that, blinded by traditional pride and patriotism, cloaked and defended the policy of a corrupt faction, to its own undoing. But by that policy thousands of innocent women and children have been starved to death, and a bloody era of history has been achieved.

On the ashes of a glorious country the United States stands as foster-parent to a new nation. Russian aggression liberated Bulgaria; American aggression, if you will, freed Cuba. But under the present régime, the Cubans have fears of the curtailment of the freedom they have given their all to achieve. As a people, they are not ungrateful; they do not ask for the Cisalpine independence guaranteed at Campo Formio. But they have seen motives of patriot husbands and brothers impugned by descendants of Washington's followers, they have been condemned for the effect of environment from which they have been lifted. Thus they fear that the heterarchy of General Brooke is permanent, and joy at their release from Spain's mailed hand is marred by the dread of a rule by American bayonets.

Introduction

Thus I venture to hope that a plain story of the sufferings and sacrifices of the Cubans for their freedom may be of interest. A knowledge of their struggles will create an appreciation of their aspirations, and I would that an abler pen than mine had pictured them.

GEORGE CLARKE MUSGRAVE.

October 1, 1899.

Contents

	PAGE
INTRODUCTION	xiii

CHAPTER I
LANDING IN CUBA. — THE CAUSE OF THE INSURRECTION. — WEYLERISM 1

CHAPTER II
THROUGH THE SPANISH LINES. — THE RECONCENTRADOS. — SANTA CLARA. — THE INSURGENT ARMY. — CAPTURED AND RELEASED 30

CHAPTER III
HAVANA. — THE VOLUNTEERS. — THE EXECUTION OF MOLINA. — GENERAL WEYLER. — THE RAID OF MARIANO 58

CHAPTER IV
EVANGELINA CISNEROS 92

CHAPTER V
THE DOWNFALL OF WEYLER. — FAILURE OF AUTONOMY OBVIOUS. — GENERAL BLANCO. — THE DE LOME LETTER. — SPAIN'S FINANCIAL DISABILITIES . . 109

CHAPTER VI
A TRIP ACROSS CUBA. — REJECTION OF AUTONOMY. — CROSSING THE SPANISH LINES. — A DEVASTATING COLUMN. — A NIGHT OF HORROR. — THE ATTACK ON ESPERANZA 127

Contents

CHAPTER VII

PAGE

THE INSURGENT GOVERNMENT. — PRESIDENT MASO. — HIS VIEWS OF THE SITUATION. — MINISTERS OF THE CABINET. — AN OFFER TO SPAIN 157

CHAPTER VIII

A MODERN DON QUIXOTE. — A FAIR PATRIOT. — GENERAL ROLOFF. — AN EFFECTIVE DEMONSTRATION. — A HORSE THIEF. — GUAIMARO. — A FRIGHTFUL INCIDENT. — COLAZZO AND HERNANDEZ. — LAS TUNAS. — THE ENEMY. — A MINE. — AMBUSHED. — GARCIA AT LAST 176

CHAPTER IX

PANDO'S FAILURE. — GARCIA'S STAFF. — BARACOA. — OVER THE SIERRAS. — A FRIGHTFUL STORM. — A NIGHT ATTACK. — UNEXPECTED SUPPER. — BEFORE SANTIAGO. — THE GUERILLA. — I ENTER THE CITY. — CIENFUEGOS. — OUTRAGES AGAINST BRITONS 206

CHAPTER X

THE "MAINE" DISASTER. — THE SENATORIAL COMMISSION — TO HAVANA AGAIN. — CAPTURED AND DEPORTED TO SPAIN. — WAR DECLARED. — RECEPTION OF THE NEWS IN SPAIN 224

CHAPTER XI

FORMING THE EXPEDITION FOR CUBA. — THE VOYAGE. — LANDING IN CUBA 253

CHAPTER XII

THE FIGHT AT GUASIMAS. — THE ENEMY REPULSED. — DISEMBARKATION AT SIBONEY. — COMMISSARIAT SHORT-COMINGS. — GARCIA'S ARRIVAL. — A GENERAL ADVANCE ORDERED 267

Contents

CHAPTER XIII

THE ATTACK BEGINS. — THE ARTILLERY DUEL. — A RECKLESS ORDER. — THE STORMING OF SAN JUAN. — AGUADORES. — CANEY FALLEN 287

CHAPTER XIV

THE AFTERMATH OF SAN JUAN. — THE WOUNDED. — THE SIEGE OF SANTIAGO. — HORRORS OF CANEY. — CAPITULATION OF TORAL. — SANTIAGO AFTER SURRENDER. — CLOSE OF THE CAMPAIGN . . . 321

CHAPTER XV

SANTIAGO AFTER CAPITULATION. — A RETROSPECT OF '99. — CONCLUSION 354

List of Illustrations

AN INSURGENT STRONGHOLD IN OCCIDENTE . *Frontispiece*

COLONEL CARRERA'S GUERILLAS AT SAGUA . . . *Page* 40
With bloodhound used for tracking fugitives.

CIVIL GUARDS SHOOTING UNARMED SUSPECTS CAP-
TURED BEYOND THE LINES, HAVANA, JUNE 13,
1897 . . . . " 75
From actual photograph of the execution.

SEÑORITA COSIO Y CISNEROS . . . . " 101
As I first saw her in prison.

A FLANKING PARTY OF CASTELLANOS' COLUMN EN-
GAGED WITH FORCES OF THE CUBAN GOVERN-
MENT AT ESPERANZA . . . . " 155
From a photograph by a Spanish officer, taken during the en-
gagement.

EX-PRESIDENT SALVADOR CISNEROS, MARQUIS OF
SANTA LUCIA; GENERAL GOMEZ, AND GEN-
ERAL LACRET . . . . " 185

CUBAN CAVALRY AT LAS TUNAS . . . . " 197

A STREET IN LAS TUNAS SHOWING HOUSES DE-
MOLISHED BY COLONEL FUNSTON'S ARTILLERY " 197

GENERAL GARCIA AND STAFF . . . . " 208

CAPTAIN GEORGE CLARKE MUSGRAVE . . . . . " 240

COLONEL THEODORE ROOSEVELT . . . . " 270

MELGAR'S HALF-BATTERY OF PLASENCIA'S, LOADING
AT SAN JUAN, JULY 1, 1898, AS THE BATTLE
OPENED . . . . " 298

GENERAL JOSÉ TORAL . . . . " 347

Under Three Flags in Cuba

CHAPTER I

LANDING IN CUBA. — THE CAUSE OF THE INSURRECTION. — WEYLERISM.

WHEN we first sighted Cuba, the sun was setting in tropical suddenness, like a globe of fire extinguished in the sea. The declining rays, scintillating in multicolored beams across the water, revealed a low-lying coast, fringed with palms and backed by distant hills. Bathed in crimson light, the land appeared a paradise, and it seemed impossible that in such magnificent setting a tragedy of two nations was being enacted, and a whole people were writhing in the throes of despair, oppression, and bloody death.

In speedy transformation, as the stage limelight is shut off to turn the day scene to night, a black veil seemed drawn across the heavens, and darkness supervened. A faint sprinkling of stars shone feebly down, and then gradually the face of the heavens became bespangled with constellations, and the luminous beauty of a clear night in the tropics was revealed. On the distant coast lights flickered, while blazing above the horizon rose the Southern Cross, typical of

Under Three Flags in Cuba

the sacred emblem to which the struggling Cubans had so long appealed.

Suddenly a long beam of light quivered across the sky and swept to right and left along the coast, and we were awakened with a shock to the dangers of our enterprise. A Spanish warship was watching for filibusters, and we well knew the summary justice meted out by Spain to those taken in the act. We had left the Florida Keys in the tight little schooner, but not as a regular expedition. Ostensibly on a fishing-trip, we were carrying a few cases, stores, and ammunition to Pinar del Rio, where I expected to effect a landing. We did not forget the "Virginius" massacre nor the treatment of the "Competitor" crew. There was no distinction in those precedents, — sailor and Cuban, armed or unarmed, were treated alike, and our faces blanched at the thought of capture. We sprang to the tell-tale boxes, ready to hurl them overboard; but the cruiser held to her course, the blinding glare still searching but never resting on our craft, and as the distance widened between us we breathed more freely.

It was eight bells when we drew in near shore and prepared to land just west of the Bahia Honda Point. José, the practico, or guide, was a coal-black negro born in slavery in Cuba, but he had lived years in Jamaica, and proudly asserted he was an Englishman. As he spoke both languages fairly, and knew western Cuba like a book, I gladly reciprocated his assurances of friendship and brotherhood, and a true friend did

Landing in Cuba

he ultimately prove. He had piloted the ship to a nicety, and after the cases had been handed over to the gig, we took our seats and rowed silently ashore.

A flash and loud boom to westward forced us to ply our oars rapidly, and at first we thought the ship was discovered. Probably it was the night gun from the warship in the Bay, for nothing transpired to confirm our fears. We ran into a sandbank and, braving sharks, were forced to drop over and haul the boat across; but finally, wet and tired, we had everything on shore. The boat returned to the ship, and José and I struck out for the interior, to find a Cuban camp and warn the guardia costa of our advent.

I was in no enviable frame of mind when we plunged into the bush. This was a venture of my own choosing; but I had heard stories of these Cuban insurgents, — "Negro and half-bred cut-throats, a scum gathered for loot, murder, and robbery, under the guise of patriotism," said my Spanish friends, — and even allowing for their prejudice, I was extremely apprehensive. "Would they steal my effects? How would they treat me? Probably my good clothes would excite cupidity, and they would hang me as a spy to legalize the murder. It had been done in Central America, and why not here?" Such were the forebodings that flashed before me that night, for of the Cuban question I was absolutely ignorant. Far from civilization, in Darkest Africa, I had not been aware of a Cuban revolution until reaching the Canary

Under Three Flags in Cuba

Islands. Here I saw weedy conscripts dragged from sunny valleys and driven to the transports for Cuba, their arms shipped on separate vessels to prevent mutiny. Weeping mothers told in awed whispers of their boys murdered by these ferocious insurgents, whom, in their misled innocence, they believed to be fiends incarnate; and even the kindly old Commandante of Las Palmas told me such a history of the ungrateful colonists that my sympathies were awakened for Spain. When Canovas, in his leonine power, issued his fiat, "last peseta, last man," before he would grant reforms to the island, she had shipped an army of 200,000 men across the Atlantic. In proud assent the Spanish nation continued to expend blood and treasure, though the result was as water poured on the Sahara.

After describing the raising and equipment of the conscript hordes in Spain, I was asked simultaneously by the editors of a London daily and review to outline the military situation and method of warfare in Cuba. Such a mission guaranteed interest and adventure, and finding that under no circumstances could I join the Spanish forces in the field, I was now en route for the insurgents. I was warned previously that even if the rebels did not eat me, — for the ignorant Spaniard even credits them with cannibalism,[1] — I must expect

[1] In Cuba and Hayti a few of the negroes in the mountains keep up the "voodoo" practices of their African ancestors, and a society called the "nanigoes" still exists secretly, though it is almost stamped out. Murders have been traced to these miscreants, and in Hayti, at least, the true fetish medicine of virgin's blood and herbs

A Rebel Vedette

no quarter if captured by the Imperial troops, so enraged were they against the insurgents and those who cast in their lot with them.

José and I marched painfully up a rocky track in the darkness, stumbling at every step. From the row of forts around Bahia Honda rose the shrill "Alerta!" of successive sentries, a few campfires gleamed fitfully in the distance, and tolls of the cracked bell of the little chapel, merry laughter, and the strains of a hand-organ in the city were wafted over on the still night air. Around us all was silent as death.

"Alto! Quien va?" came the sudden challenge.

"Cuba!" responded José, with alacrity; and in a moment two dark figures sprang at him. My revolver was out in an instant, but they were only embracing my guide and vigorously patting him on the back, a mark of deepest affection among the Cubans. The two sentinels brought their horses from the field, and courteously insisted that I should mount, while one rode forward to apprise the camp of our arrival and send men to the beach for the stores.

I was loath to rob the soldier of his horse; but he insisted, marching ahead on foot, and cautioning us to keep absolute silence. I scrambled into the saddle, and we jogged along for perhaps a league, when we reached the Cuban outposts. Round the campfires were grouped picturesque-looking bandits, negroes to

was recently mixed and drunk, a girl being killed for this purpose. In Cuba the "nanigoes" were a band of negro ruffians who murdered for plunder only; but the stories of cannibalism can be traced to this source.

a man. By the flickering light they did not look prepossessing, but they greeted me effusively, and gave me a palmleaf shelter to sleep under. Being worn out, I gladly crawled in, and keeping my revolver handy, was soon asleep.

A hand on my shoulder, a strange voice — the robbers, I thought. I sprang up only to be blinded by brilliant sunlight, to find a ragged asistente had brought a cup of delicious coffee, and stood grinning at my confusion. José came soon after, and said we must be moving, for we were too near the city for safety, and I found the outpost had waited an hour rather than wake me. The officer, a commandante or major, was a half-caste named Gonzales, and through the medium of José, he welcomed me to Cuba libre, adding that General Rivera would be glad to see me. He was sorry he had no breakfast then to offer, but the Spaniards had been very bad there and nothing was left in the country. Later, however, we would reach a prefectura and perhaps find food. He insisted on my keeping my mount, and the owner thereof tramped along gayly, telling me he, his house, his horse, and his all, were at my service. These rebels were certainly interesting fellows, and apprehensions as to my reception soon vanished.

Crossing hills and skirting woods, we reached a wilder district and finally the insurgent camp. The colonel was a black of gigantic proportions, with one of the finest faces I have ever seen. His features were small and regular, of the Arab or Houssa

A True Patriot

rather than the negro type. He was a veteran of the ten years' war, bore numerous wounds, and was one of the most trusted officers in the brigade of General Ducasse. His manly bearing was impressive, and he neither boasted of his prowess nor related horrible massacres by the Spaniards that could not be verified, — two common failings in west Cuba.

I had been sitting in camp but a few minutes when I was addressed in perfect English, and met my first white rebel gentleman, Major Hernandez by name, a graduate of an American college and a law student. He explained that he was on a commission and had stayed in camp for the night.

Friendships ripen quickly under such circumstances, and we were soon exchanging confidences. In half an hour I had received some new ideas of the Cuban revolution. " Todo mambi negro," laughed my friend, "just here and in some other places, yes, but members of the best white families in Cuba are in the woods." And as I talked with that young patriot who had given up a good home and pleasant surroundings for a rough life of danger and privation, I began to realize there was something in the cause of Cuba libre. I had been given to understand that no white colonists of repute, no true Cubans were engaged in the uprising, that it was simply an extensive brigandage, — a western " Francatripa " or " Cincearotti." How soon I found it was the whole Cuban race writhing and struggling against a fifteenth-century system!

Under Three Flags in Cuba

The winter campaign of '96 was just closing, and the insurgent army of the West was never in a worse condition. Antonio Maceo had been killed but a few days previously, and the province was flooded with guerillas, and soldiers flushed with this success. Rivera crossed the Mariel Trocha early in December, and was in command near Artemisa, toward which Hernandez was going. I was anxious to accompany him, but he persuaded me against it, pointing out the innumerable dangers and hardships of travelling poorly mounted through a district so strongly invested by the enemy. He advised me to go to a certain prefectura in the hills, where I could secure a guide and good horses, and join some force when things grew more settled. There were a few Americans in Pinar del Rio, he said, two correspondents, and some artillerymen. I met but one, some time later, a man named Jones, in the last stages of consumption; the correspondents, Scovel and Rea, had gone to visit Gomez. I reluctantly said farewell to Hernandez, and later reached the prefectura.

The prefect was a white man of considerable intelligence, a guajiro, or farmer. His house had been destroyed by Maceo's order, to prevent its conversion into a fort, and the Spaniards had looted his cattle; but with true Cuban philosophy he explained that boniatos (sweet potatoes) were easy to raise, and when Cuba was free all again would be well. His residence was now in the hills near La Isabella, a mere bohio of clay, thatched with palm. In the deep

Pinar del Rio

ants gorges below, the Guardia Civil, the local guerilla, and sometimes columns operated, but fearing ambuscades, the hilly trails were usually given a wide berth by the Spanish regulars. To the west lay the fertile valley of La Palma, now simply a blackened desert right up to Pinar del Rio City. The valleys to the south were in even a worse condition; many residences had been destroyed by Maceo, and later Weyler with his columns had swept the country with fire and sword until it was a desert of ashes, the towns unfruitful oases.

I had a sharp attack of fever in the prefect's house, and was exceedingly well treated. When, after several days' hospitality, I moved on, he was grossly insulted because I offered him money. Many days had passed uneventfully in the district. I rode around occasionally, but in the valley the columns were operating, and guerilla raids took place too close to us to be pleasant. I had a narrow escape one day, several shots being fired after me by a marauding party, and I soon witnessed many phases of the horrible warfare Spain was waging. No important insurgent force came in our district, only small rebel bands; and becoming impatient we finally marched across country toward the Trocha, a mule having been secured for José and my own sorry steed exchanged advantageously.

After crossing the hills to the once glorious valley to the south, Weyler's brutal measures were in evidence on every side. Following Maceo's death, he had redoubled his efforts to subdue Pinar del Rio, and each day we came across smouldering houses, rotting carcasses of cattle, wantonly slaughtered, and blackened stalks of burnt crops. For miles we rode without meeting a living soul; but later, striking the woods again, we found Cuban families camped in the thickets, subsisting on roots, and living in constant terror of the guerilla. These cut-throats raided and looted at pleasure, driving into town the fugitives they captured, killing the men and frequently outraging women.

Raid followed raid, the pacificos, or non-combatants, being ruthlessly slaughtered if captured too far from the town for convenient transportation, or upon attempting to escape from the soldiery. Five miles from Mariel, not twenty feet from the camino Real (Royal highroad), the bodies of two women and four men, all killed by the local guerilla, lay for three weeks unburied, and probably the remains are there yet. In the hills just north of Candelaria I was shown the ruins of a field hospital, and the charred remains of sick men, butchered and burned therein.[1] Later in the mainroad, near Artemisa, we found the body of an aged pacifico, his head split in twain with a machete. Sylvester Scovel, who had spent weeks in the province before I landed, personally investigated the cases of over two hundred non-combat-

[1] From this hospital Delgado, a young New Yorker, alone escaped capture, all his sick comrades being butchered. He was taken prisoner later, and died from the treatment of his captors en route to Havana. His body was claimed by General Lee.

Atrocities

ants murdered by Weyler's orders, in Pinar del Rio. This was but a fraction of the atrocities, and from the bodies I actually saw, and the cases brought to my notice in a regular journey through this district, I have no hesitation in saying that I believe Scovel's investigations to be correct, regardless of the attempts of others to impugn his veracity in these reports.

Exaggerated stories of Spanish atrocities have flooded the American press, until responsible persons are inclined to doubt the authenticity of every case reported; but in those early weeks I saw evidences of sickening horrors that turned me from a strong sympathizer with Spain to a bitter hater of everything connected with her brutal rule in Cuba. True, I also heard and verified stories of oppression and cruelty by individual insurgents in Pinar del Rio, notably of one Bermudez, a blackguard given a command by Maceo when officers were scarce. . He, a Cuban, instituted a reign of terror in his district, equalled only by Weyler's rule. But Bermudez was soon disgraced, and finally hanged by Gomez, while the butchers in Spanish uniform were but obeying Weyler's implicit orders by the perpetration of outrages.

A number of desperadoes had joined the insurrection for loot, and in the rich West, Gomez and Maceo found constant crimes committed by their followers, — stealing from farmers, and other lawless acts that terrorized the pacific Cubans. False leaders arose, and by carrying on a war of rapine under the guise of patriotism, greatly damaged the Cuban cause. These men were dubbed plateados, or plated Cubans; and Gomez for many weeks warred only against them, hanging some convicted of flagrant outrage. So severe were the measures instituted by the old leader, that men were executed for petty theft, and false patriots deserted in dozens.

Several miscreants in Pinar del Rio, under Burmudez, and Colonel Murgado, who had also obtained a regular commission, were simply brigands. When Maceo broke up the gang, most of them reached Havana, and re-enlisted in the Spanish guerilla, where they could loot at will without the risk of being hung. Maceo then put his personal friend, the brave young Ducasse, in command of the perturbed district, and he gradually won back the confidence of the distracted pacificos.

Another colonel, named Nunez, was deprived of command and reduced to asistente rank for executing five Spanish cavalrymen whom he declared were caught burning a house. Lieutenant Castillo and Prefect Gonzales were shot for looting. These severe examples had a very salutary effect upon the insurgent army. Gomez claimed that a revolution that became a refuge for those who wished conveniently to follow criminal and disorderly lives would not be justified, even for the cause of liberty. With such in their ranks, the Cuban cry, "Viva nuestra bandera sin mancha" (Long live our unstained banner), would be of none effect.

The insurgent forces were composed of all classes

An Historical Retrospect

and shades of society, — once wealthy planters, farmers, farm laborers, and ignorant negroes from the canefields formed the bulk of the Army of Deliverance, students from Havana College, clerks, cigarmakers, and a tatterdemalion scum from the slums adding a considerable contingent from the cities. Diverse as were these elements of the revolution, they were but local factors in the universal struggle of mankind for emancipation from the dominant creed, "Might is Right." A glance at Spain's history is indeed significant. Once the honored province of the Roman Empire, but later a country submerged by centuries of barbaric invasion, Spain, by a sudden acquisition of wealth and power during the rule of Isabella, proudly lifted her head as a united nation. She was soon proclaimed supreme mistress of the New World. The country became demoralized, and was ruled by a shameful tyranny of religion exerted for revenue and political ends, a corruption cloaked behind the Cross of Christ. Decadence speedily supervened. The policy inspired by Borgia and Torquemada proved reactive, Portugal and the Netherlands threw off the Spanish yoke, the Hapsburgs lost the Italian possessions. Wars and losses at home followed in quick succession, and the attempts to stay the tide of misfortune by colonial spoliation finally led to the loss of Venezuela in 1810, and a spread of the spirit of independence until not an inch of territory remained to Spain on the mainland of the Western Hemisphere.

Under Three Flags in Cuba

Cuba and Puerto Rico, however, proved loyal, despite the constant friction of home-appointed officials and the colonials. Early this century, realizing the exceptional educational facilities in the United States, Cuban parents commenced to send their sons to American schools. It soon became a universal practice among the better classes, and the rising generation drank in the early ideals of the young Republic. They returned to criticise their government at home, and in 1828 a Royal decree was issued from Madrid ordering all Cubans in American colleges to return forthwith; the parents were heavily fined, and foreign education prohibited. But the seed of liberty was already sown, and many of these young students founded reform societies, from the chief of which, "The Souls of Bolivar," sprang one of the earliest uprisings, and seven subsequent attempts to throw off Spanish yoke. In late years the educational law has not been enforced.

Cuba in 1837 had been deprived of her right of representation in the Cortes, by General Tacon, who, as Captain-General, used every means to place an absolute monopoly, political and mercantile, in the hands of Spaniards born in the Peninsula. Thus they were able to direct everything to the benefit of Spain, diverting a considerable portion of the spoils to their own pockets, and completely enslaving the colonials, who had naturally supported measures for the direction of the revenue to the betterment of their Island. Protests of the Cubans against extortion

An Historical Retrospect

were unheeded, the powers of the Spanish Captain-General were made absolute, and he held his position securely, provided he extracted enough from the unhappy country to satisfy the treasury and greedy officials in Madrid, and incidentally to fill the pockets of his chief supporters and himself. Cuba was looked upon as a possession to provide cash for the depleted treasury, regardless of the Island's development or future.

In 1865 revolution was imminent, and a commission of sixteen prominent Cubans went to Madrid to recommend reforms to satisfy the people. These commissioners were ignored, and next year taxes were further increased. Discriminating tariffs directed all imports through Spanish markets, and by this monopoly the colonists were forced to pay exorbitantly for the necessaries of life. The prohibitive duty on foreign flour placed bread beyond the reach of ordinary pockets. At the end of '67, a further tax was imposed on internal products; disaffection then rapidly spread, and the Carlist revolution in the Peninsula gave the colonials the looked-for opening for organized revolt.

A wealthy Cuban named Cespedes proclaimed the independence of the island on October 10, and twenty thousand men rose at once, electing him President. Señor Palma, the Marquis of Santa Lucia, and many prominent Cubans supported the movement, and the eastern half of the island was practically in the hands of the rebels, though they were poorly armed. Vic-

Under Three Flags in Cuba

tory followed victory. Maximo Gomez, a colonial-born Spanish colonel, joined the insurgents, and General Quesada landed with arms and ammunition. Count Valmaseda hurriedly left Havana with the Imperial army, but received severe checks and fell back; several towns then capitulated to the Cubans. Cespedes was betrayed and murdered, but Quesada led the army victoriously across Camaguey. Valmaseda, finding that he could not suppress the rebellion by force of arms, followed Torquemada's Netherland policy. He issued a proclamation, ordering no quarter to be given to any males above fifteen, found away from the towns, and instituted the systematized devastation that subsequently made Weyler infamous.

That revolution lasted ten years. It cost 45,000 Cuban lives, and saddled the island with an enormous debt; 60,000 Spanish soldiers were killed, or died of fever. Many officials and officers retired to Spain millionaires, chiefly on the proceeds of thirteen thousand Cuban estates confiscated by the government and only partially accounted for. There were 2927 Cuban prisoners executed; thousands of political suspects were seized and deported to Africa. The island was completely devastated, and the people were starving.

General Martinez Campos arrived in 1878 with full powers to end the revolution, and seeing the failure of his brutal predecessors, he made overtures to the insurgent leaders, and finally met them for a confer-

The Zanjon Treaty

ence. Both Spaniard and Cuban were forced to admit the struggle hopeless, and the Cubans agreed to submit if certain liberal reforms were granted.

They finally accepted his terms of peace, which gave them a restricted self-government, and the franchise so long denied. The treaty was signed at Zanjon in February, 1878. When the Cubans had surrendered their arms and disbanded, Polaveija succeeded Campos. He soon instituted a reign of terror, executing or deporting a number of the revolutionists. The reforms promised by the treaty were never instituted save on paper; the power of the Captain-General remained, and he could veto every proviso at will. Discontent was soon rampant, but the resources of the Cubans were so depleted that no armed protest was made until the abortive revolution of 1885, "The short war," when the leaders surrendered to Blanco under promise of reform and amnesty, both of which were then repudiated by Canovas. This last breach of faith destroyed all remnant of trust in Spain.

Thousands of Cubans, to escape tyranny, found homes in the United States. In 1893, one Fraga gathered his expatriated countrymen living in New York, and founded the Independientes Club; similar organizations were formed throughout the country. At this time arose the patriot Marti, who travelled from city to city, organizing the Cuban League, establishing newspapers, and generally advocating an active propaganda to liberate the island. Every Cuban abroad promised to subscribe weekly to the

Under Three Flags in Cuba

cause in case of revolution. Secretly also preparations were made in Cuba.

In 1894 the Spanish Government was arranging to redeem the bonds of the Cuban debt, mortgaging the island for $300,000,000 to fill the sadly depleted treasury. The European financial magnates, fearing revolution might arise, had demanded that self-government and reforms should be introduced to satisfy the people, before the loan was consummated. Minister Maura advanced a just and liberal scheme of self-government for Cuba, that would have insured peace. Minister Abarzuza presented a different plan of government by a Council of Administration of thirty members, one-half to be appointed by Madrid, and one-half elected in the island, the Captain-General to be president, with power of veto and the casting vote. On the face of this scheme the preponderance of power lay with Madrid, and with their juggled franchise, the Cubans would have had practically no representation, even among the members elected in the island.

The colonials were watching affairs closely but silently, — it was the crisis. Spain refused the Maura reforms and adopted the sham Abarzuza decrees. Her duplicity cost her the loan and the island.

The news of the rejection of the genuine reforms was cabled to New York. All was ready there. Messengers sailed at once to Cuba; and two weeks later the wily Spanish statesmen — congratulating themselves at the successful hoodwinking of finan-

The Last Revolution

ciers without loss of their power over the Cubans — were struck dumb with amazement and dismay by the news that eastern Cuba was in a blaze of revolt. Spanish diplomacy, as usual, had defeated its own ends.

Bartolome Maso, an aged and wealthy planter, raised the Cuban flag on his estate near Manzanillo on February 24, 1895. Three hundred patriots rallied round him, and the formal declaration of the independence of Cuba was read. His address to his followers is worthy of comparison to Garibaldi's speech to the remnant of his army in '49.

"Brother patriots! You know for what we fight. We have tasted the trials and perils of war in the past, and must be prepared for even greater sacrifices in the future, — famine, thirst, fatigue, and the renunciation of all dearest to us, that Cuba may be free. I am old and may not live to the end; so let me exhort you — No Surrender! Independence or Death."

Waving their machetes on high, the Cubans took up the cry, "Independencia o Muerte! Viva Cuba Libre!" and it has been their sworn motto to the end.

When the Spanish commandante at Manzanillo started out to capture Maso's little band, hundreds of men seized the best weapons they could find, and rallied under the lone-starred banner. Another Cuban gentleman, Moncada, also gathered a force, and four weeks later Antonio and José Maceo, Crombet, Cebreco, and twenty-two other veterans of the last war landed at Duaba, and joined the party. On April 11 Marti and Maximo Gomez crossed over safely. Plans were at once formulated, Gomez marched to Camaguey, Maceo waited in Santiago Province. Both mobilized considerable armies, and the revolution started in earnest.

On May 19 Marti and an aide became divided from the Cuban forces during a fight at Dos Bocas. In attempting to rejoin Gomez, they were ambushed and shot down by the Spaniards. Thus the founder of the revolution was among the first to perish in upholding it.

General Santoscildes attempted to head off Maso at Bayamo. A terrific engagement ensued, in which both sides lost heavily, but, led into a trap by the poorly armed Cubans, the Spaniards were routed in a fierce machete charge, the insurgents capturing many rifles and cartridges. Santoscildes' column retired to El Caney, now of historic fame; but the tireless Cubans, under Garzon, advancing under cover of the darkness, rushed the town and fort, routing out the garrison. Flushed with success, they then crossed to the Santiago Railroad, and captured a train with 250 rifles and 50,000 cartridges, en route to soldiers in San Luis. Thus they obtained their arms, and in July three large expeditions from the United States arrived under Sanchez, Roloff, and Rodriguez, with rifles, cartridges, and stores, that placed the insurgents on a formidable footing. Maceo defeated Salcedo's heavy columns at Jarahuca; Cuban victo-

Defeat of Campos

ries at Los Negros, Cristo, Juraguanas, and El Jobito followed. Thoroughly alarmed by the rebel successes, General Martinez Campos was ordered to take the field in person by Premier Canovas, who had just assumed power. Gathering all available forces, he met Maceo at Peralejo, and his partially raw army was completely routed. His horse was killed; he escaped capture by tumbling into a litter, being carried off the field with the wounded, which Maceo allowed to pass through his lines. General Santoscildes and four hundred and thirty Spaniards were left dead on the field.

By the end of the year, Gomez and Maceo were marching west, and on Christmas Eve, Campos, defeated again at Coliseo, retired into Havana and prepared to defend the capital. His panic was needless, for the Cubans had exhausted their ammunition, and were hardly in condition to attack such a city; but when the ultra Spaniards, long misled by false despatches, awakened to the fact that the rebels were camped but ten miles away, and the brave Spanish volunteers realized they might have to fight, their rage and terror were unbounded, and were vented upon Campos. The volunteers mutinied, the Spanish party backed them, and on Christmas Day Campos cabled his resignation to Madrid to escape forcible deposition.

Gomez's policy was to wear out Spain by destroying her revenue. To accomplish this, he had issued an order prohibiting the grinding of sugar cane.

Under Three Flags in Cuba

Finding it non-effective, and that, while patriotic owners abstained, others, especially on plantations controlled by foreign capital, had persisted to grind under Campos' protection, he applied the torch to the sugar crops throughout Matanzas and Havana. His orders and methods were harsh, and the wholesale destruction excited great indignation among the Spaniards and foreign capitalists. It was a hard test of patriotism to see one's wealth go up in smoke, but I never heard a true Cuban planter complain. They greatly regretted the necessity and longed for the end.

This policy caused great distress, but there was no starvation, for the laboring class of Cuba live entirely on their own products, and the loss of employment on the plantations deprived them chiefly of luxuries, though many of the proprietors were placed in straitened circumstances. The method was harsh, if justified by the exigencies of the situation. Cuban leaders believed "Liberty and all sentiment must be suspended temporarily to gain liberty permanently." A frequent saying of Gomez was, "What even if the whole generation perish, when countless generations will benefit so greatly." "Cuba's wealth is the cause of her bondage. Destroy that wealth and the bondage goes," was another of the many original aphorisms of the old general. In tacit obedience to this, Cuban leaders destroyed their own property to prevent reversion of the crops to Spain.

When Gomez felt the planters would respect his

Arrival of Weyler

orders to cease grinding, he decided to stay further devastation. On January 12, 1896, at the Ingenio Mi Rosa near Havana, he issued a general proclamation, staying the further burning of cane-fields, ordering his forces to respect property, and assuring all persons, irrespective of nationality, that they could live safely on their lands and cultivate crops as usual. But he prohibited the manufacture of sugar to add to Spain's revenue. Some planters with strongly fortified estates continued to grind with impunity. Their crops were then destroyed, and in some cases the whole factory burned down as a warning. Grinding then generally ceased.

Trade was thus at a standstill; and the enraged Spaniards in Havana, who naturally suffered loss of spoil, demanded that Premier Canovas should despatch a man to Cuba who would stamp out the rebellion at all costs. Campos had dared to suggest that genuine reforms would alone restore peace, but to this they would not listen. The old cry, "No quarter," was raised, and to satisfy the frenzy General Weyler was appointed.

Valeriano Weyler was but General of Cataluna, but he had the reputation of being absolutely unscrupulous, and was thus the man for Cuba. When he arrived in Havana, the intransigeants tendered him an effusive welcome, especially the volunteers. Raising his effeminate and neatly gloved hand as he harangued the populace, he announced that Spain's enemies would find his hand gloved with steel. He came to make a pitiless war upon them, and pledged himself to speedily restore peace to the island.

His first policy was to strengthen the Trochas, or fortified barricades, — one built across the narrow portion of the island from Mariel to the south coast, the other across Puerto Principe from Jucaro to Moron. Thus he hoped to shut Maceo in Pinar del Rio, Gomez in the Central provinces, the forces under José Maceo in the extreme east, and deal with each in turn. The Cubans showed their contempt by cutting their way through the Trochas repeatedly, though the barriers certainly hindered easy and frequent communication.

All cities and towns of consequence, and the railroad tracks, were fortified. Reinforcements also poured over from Spain, thousands of wretched conscripts being torn from their homes and shipped to Cuba. They were equipped with Mauser rifles, the most effective extant, and abundant ammunition; but the absolute lack of commissary, their cotton uniform and canvas shoes with hemp soles, the ignorance of the officers, and lack of drill, made the vast army so hurriedly mobilized, useless for extensive operations. It was effective, however, for Weyler's purpose of devastation, and the disintegrated duty in the thousands of small wooden block-houses that surrounded the towns and guarded all the railways in the island, with the aid of barbed-wire barricades built from fort to fort. Weyler soon had 200,000 so-called regulars in Cuba; 25,000 guerillas

Weyler's Policy

were also raised, chiefly from negroes and half-breed scum in the cities, and freed criminals with previous military experience from Spain. The Spanish volunteer organization throughout the island was 60,000 strong. This gave a command of at least 285,000 men.

It has been easy for writers to criticise Weyler as a brutal plunderer, who cared for nothing but blood and corruption. Brute he was, corrupt and absolutely unscrupulous, but he was by no means the sensual monster represented. His orders were explicit; to crush out the rebellion at any cost and regardless of human sacrifice, and he accomplished wonders. His policy was extermination, and he neither denied nor cloaked it. His administrative ability was stupendous. With inadequate means at his disposal, he cut up the island in fortified sections, scattered part of his vast army as "beaters in," while with the remainder he attempted to kill off the hedged-in coveys in succession. He filled his own pockets, and those of his officers; yet gave his vast army enough food to keep them alive, subservient, and in some semblance of health, when food itself was terribly scarce. He planned and effectively carried out his extermination, murdering hundreds of insurgents and their sympathizers in cold blood, and starving to death thousands of innocents, whose nature and dearest associations had made rebels at heart. But for the marked steadfastness of the Cubans, their resolution to accomplish or die, and the influence of some of their leaders, Weyler could have crushed the revolution by force. Eventually he would assuredly have crushed it by extermination if Spain's finances could have sustained him.

In October of '96 all plans of campaign were formulated, and on the 21st the following order was issued from the Governor's Palace, Havana, and spread broadcast throughout the country: —

I, Don Valeriano Weyler Nicolau, Marquis of Teneriffe, Governor-General, Captain-General of this Island, Commander-in-Chief of the Army, hereby order and command: —

1. That all the inhabitants of the country districts, or those who reside outside the lines of fortifications of the towns, shall within eight days enter such towns occupied by the troops. Any individual found beyond the lines at the expiration of this period shall be considered a rebel, and dealt with as such.

2. The transport of food from the towns, and the carrying of food from place to place by sea or land, without a signed permit of the authorities, is positively forbidden. All who infringe this order will be tried as aiders and abettors of the rebellion.

3. The owners of cattle must drive their herds to the towns, or their immediate vicinity, where guard is provided.

4. The period of eight days will be reckoned in each district, from the day of publication of this proclamation in the chief town in that district. At its expiration all insurgents who present themselves to me will be placed under my orders as to residence. If they furnish me with news that can be used to advantage against the enemy, it

Weyler's Policy

will serve as a recommendation — also the desertion to our lines with firearms, and more especially when insurgents present themselves in numbers.

VALERIANO WEYLER.

HAVANA, October 21st, 1896.

This was the initiation of his policy. Article 1 stamped the bando as worse than Valmaseda's proclamation of '69. The latter stipulated that men only should be treated as rebels, i.e., shot at sight; and the United States loudly protested. In '96 Weyler brazenly applied the same order universally; but the Washington Administration allowed such enforcement within seventy-eight miles of America's coasts without protest until too late.

The execution of Weyler's order commenced in Pinar del Rio. Immense columns of troops poured into the province, and operated in sections, driving the people from their homes, and looting and burning the houses of high and lowly. When the eight days of grace expired, all excesses were tolerated. Stock was seized, crops were torn up and destroyed, cattle that could not be eaten or conveniently driven off were wantonly slaughtered; even the long grass was burned to make the country uninhabitable for the rebels.

Weyler had drawn lines which prevented the easy mobilization of the scattered insurgent commands. Gomez had returned to Santa Clara, cartridges were scarce, and against so large an army Maceo and his small force could now only harass the enemy, and were powerless to prevent the great devastation. On the approach of the soldiers, many of the people fled in terror to the woods. Here the guerillas distinguished themselves by routing out the fugitives, hunting them like wild beasts with dogs (this I have personally witnessed), and frequently forcing into their camps such comely women as they could capture. If towns were handy, the terrified pacificos were bundled in unceremoniously; if not, the machete terribly and effectively cleared the country, though better fate a thousand times to be butchered in cold blood, and devoured by vultures and wild dogs, than to be slowly starved to death in the reconcentration quarter of the towns, and the younger women forced into degradation.

When Weyler's fiat was rigidly enforced near the Mariel Trocha, consternation fell on the inhabitants of the other sections of the West. In anticipation of a similar visitation, the panic-stricken people hurriedly made their decision. The men foresaw compulsory service with the Spaniards in the cities, and though until then they had no thought of joining the rebels, it was now the only alternative. The women, children, and old men, carrying their portable possessions, wended their way to the nearest township before the soldiers arrived to loot. The men gathered their livestock, took what food they could, and marched off to the hills to join their insurgent brothers. The order had the same effect in Havana, Matanzas, and Santa Clara provinces.

Pacification

Within three months it had driven the male strength of the island and an abundance of food to the insurgent ranks.

By Christmas of '96 Pinar del Rio was burned up completely, Havana Province was undergoing the same drastic treatment, and Captain-General Weyler cabled to Madrid that the West was thoroughly pacified. The rebels had only withdrawn to the mountains; and when the Spaniards evacuated one district, the Cubans moved in, leaving their base of supplies in the hills. Dumped by thousands in small towns, with the surrounding country a waste, the herded reconcentrados abjectly starved from the first. Weyler had destroyed their homes and crops, knowing full well the inevitable result.

"This is war," was his naïve reply to either question or remonstrance on the subject.

CHAPTER II

THROUGH THE SPANISH LINES. — THE RECONCENTRADOS. — SANTA CLARA. — THE INSURGENT ARMY. — CAPTURED AND RELEASED.

FEBRUARY of '97 was not an eventful month in western Cuba, and after witnessing several unimportant skirmishes in which the Cubans invariably retreated doggedly, being very short of ammunition and overwhelmed by numbers, I decided to try to reach Gomez in Santa Clara, where Weyler had mobilized his forces for an attempted pacification of that province. I hoped to cross the western Trocha, not a very formidable obstacle, but at that time strongly invested. An arrangement for me to pass it through the swamp at Majana failed, and realizing that to go eastward I should also have to cross the strongly fortified railroad passing from Batabano to Havana, I determined rather to secretly enter the Spanish lines.

When camped near Cayajabos, José was wounded in the shoulder, and stayed behind for several days in a field hospital there. The surgeon in charge was a young Havana medical student, killed a few weeks later by the guerillas. With him Señora Valdez, a Cuban lady of repute, was sharing all the hardships

A Narrow Escape

of life in the manigua to be near her son, then in Havana Province. Entirely without drugs, and in imminent risk of capture, the hospital was kept up; and many were the inventions prompted by necessity, as remedies for the sick. José's arm was treated antiseptically with plain cigar ash, and he rejoined me nearly well.

Pending arrangements to enter some town on the Western Railroad, we were riding along the highway to Candelaria, keeping a sharp watch for the enemy, when we were suddenly halted from a side road, and discovered a detachment of guardia civil, resting by the way. Their horses were tethered near, and, but for stories of their never-failing machetes, I should not have attempted to escape. We turned and urged our jaded horses back; three of them sent a volley after us, the others mounted and galloped in pursuit. The horses of these men, the élite corps of Spain, are the best animals in the island, and even with our start the race was unequal. Their hoofs thundered on the camino close behind us, the thick bush and prickly wild pine on either side prevented our following the favorite ruse of plunging headlong into the thick vegetation and creeping to a place of shelter. As I spurred my gallant little beast forward, I could feel his sides heaving, and knew he was on his last legs. Shots whistled by; so, dragging out my revolver, I replied, but without effect. Then a bullet crashed through my bridle arm; I reeled in the saddle, and the end seemed near, when loud yells and vivas greeted us. Some of Ducasse's men were camped in the chaparral, and taking in the situation at a glance, they seized their rifles and sent a few shots after the now retreating guards.

One young officer I met in this camp was Lieut. William Molina, a young American Cuban from Florida, who had recently arrived on an expedition. He was subsequently captured, and when I next saw him he was proudly facing the firing squad, as he died for Cuba libre.

General Rius Rivera was then expected in this district; but two days before he arrived, I squirmed through the Spanish lines at sunrise, and boarded a slow freight-train with the connivance of the Cuban engineer. Concealed in a car, I passed into the town of San Cristobal. A few weeks later came the disastrous battle of March 27 at Rio Hondo, between the sadly depleted forces of Rivera and a large column under General Hernandez de Velasco. Hemmed in by the Spaniards, and almost without ammunition, the Cubans were routed. General Rivera and Colonel Baccallo were both captured, seriously wounded, the latter while bravely trying to save his leader. Contrary to usual custom, they were taken alive and sent to Havana. General Weyler upbraided the humane Velasco for not killing these prisoners on the field, to save the complications which ensued. Velasco in his previous campaign in Sagua la Grande, and in every subsequent action, proved himself a brave officer and a gentleman. His duty to Spain

In the Spanish Lines

made him war on her enemies, but he warred nobly and openly, ever remembering that the people had grievances that should be remedied. With a man of his calibre as Captain-General, the island of Cuba might have retained the sobriquet "Ever faithful" to this day.

I found that I could move through the small cities of western Cuba with a greater degree of freedom than I had anticipated. Spies dogged one's footsteps on every side, and the advent of a stranger aroused the suspicion of the petty police inspectors, shabby, down at the heel men, of sneaking appearance; but their attention amounted to little. To photograph a fort meant certain imprisonment; but if I wished to take a portion of the Trocha, or any military position, two words to the commandante sufficed. The Spanish heart is susceptible to flattery. One had but to request the pleasure of photographing the brave officer and his men; out they would all tumble. Line them as you pleased. You not only took the coveted position in face of the smiling sleuth, but you had life in the picture, and had won the friendship of the military. Through my camera alone, I obtained introduction to most of the garrisons, and was a frequent guest at various Casinos Españoles, the exclusive Spanish clubs that exist in most towns. Courteous, hospitable, and good fellows in their way, were most of the officers, and ready to heap attentions on the stranger; but beneath the polished veneer they were mostly brutes at heart, though I remember many exceptions, — fine young subalterns who had come to Cuba as patriots to fight for Spain, and were horrified with the policy they were forced to uphold.

The state of the reconcentrados was pitiful in the extreme. In every town from one to six thousand were herded indiscriminately. They built crazy bohios, or huts of stakes and palm-leaf on any waste ground available; frequently several families crowded into one shelter. Stone walls and barbed fences compassed the town completely, and forts were intersected at intervals, from which sentries watched to see that no one attempted to pass the barrier. Within this pen the town existed in isolation, save for the advent of the few heavily guarded trains that passed between Havana and Pinar del Rio. The condition of these people was hopeless from the first, and in March of '97 the unavoidable horrors of India's famine were being enforced upon a civilized people, with worse effect, and without effort to alleviate the suffering.

The pen fails to describe the scenes in any one of these reconcentration settlements, — some thousands of women and children, and a few old men, hedged in by barbed wire, beyond which none may pass on pain of death. Huddled on the bare ground, or at the best with a heap of rags for a bed, the delicate wives and children of once wealthy farmers and planters were herded with negroes who once were slaves on their now ruined estates.

There was an absolute silence in the camps, — a

The Reconcentrados

silence bred of cruel despair, and broken occasionally by the pitiful wails of children, the frenzied shrieks of crazed victims, raving in delirium, or the heartbroken sobs of grief-stricken groups mourning over the body of some dear one whom kind death had released from suffering. Skin-clothed skeletons crouched helpless on the bare ground; babies, hideous mockeries of childhood, lay dying on the breast from which all sustenance had dried, their tiny bodies covered with the loathsome skin eruption that attacked all alike. Girls, still retaining traces of beauty, moaning with the pangs of hunger and without the clothing demanded by decency, begged piteously for relief from the passing stranger, or struggled and fought around the swill tubs for refuse that pigs would have rejected. They had the alternative of another fate; for an abominable traffic was carried on openly in mere children, who were taken, some through misrepresentation, others accepting the fate as inevitable, into houses of ill-fame in the large cities, many passing on from Havana to Mexico and points in South America.

Abductions by Spanish officers were not unknown, while in Artemisa, but a few days before my arrival, several orphan girls aged from thirteen to fifteen were sold by public auction to the highest bidders.

All these settlements were in a terrible sanitary condition. Absolutely no hygienic measures were enforced by the authorities, the starving people lived

Under Three Flags in Cuba

in a horrible state of defilement, and even the bodies were frequently left in the sun for days before the dead-cart arrived on its rounds to dump the corpses in a common grave. Under such conditions disease naturally appeared, yellow fever and small-pox adding to the frightful horrors of starvation. If Epaminondas to-day would fail to recognize Thebes, and Cicero have little sympathy with modern Rome, we can imagine the feelings of Columbus, could he have viewed the ruins of his glorious discovery.

By May, Weyler had extended his "pacification" to the great Trocha. The provinces of Pinar del Rio, Havana, Matanzas, Santa Clara, and a portion of Puerto Principe were completely devastated, and considerably over half a million people rendered homeless and starving.

As I went by rail through these districts, stepping off at various places en route for Santa Clara, where I was again to join the insurgents, the shocking reality of the situation was revealed. The feeling of powerlessness in face of such human suffering which could not be alleviated, made one's heart ache, and I shuddered for the future. But as a ray of hope to gladden the souls of the perishing innocents, came the stories of growing sympathy in the United States. It dawned on the stricken people that the great country from which they had drawn their ideals of liberty might now prove their savior. In the darkest hour of their distress they looked to America. Dr. Shaw, realizing the imperative necessity of

The Need of Intervention

action if these people were to be saved, opened his columns in setting forth their case. Mr. Bonsal, having personally visited the scenes of horror, returned to use his gifted pen in their behalf. The whole Country was aroused.

The Administration was just changing, but after the avowals upon the Cuban question made by the Republican platform, some expected the President, upon assuming office, to take instant measures to combat the stupendous evil that was only threatening when his party pledges were made toward Cuba. After the inauguration, however, the tariff question had to be settled first. Cuba was shelved, and the people starved on, close to the land of plenty. We may exclaim that we are not our brother's keeper, but had the people of the United States realized one-half of the horrors of starvation in Cuba, I am assured that they would have enforced their ideals of liberty, equality, and fraternity at any cost in the unhappy island. During the official procrastination at Washington the Cuban rural population was being exterminated, and the last residue disappeared as the late peace negotiations were being enacted. As I stood amid the appalling scenes of suffering, I must admit there seemed no excuse for the doubts of Cuba's need that existed in the United States. It was hard to understand why the Administration could not ignore both the clamoring jingoes and the selfish financiers, and after investigating the conditions, make a dignified demand of Spain to war only

Under Three Flags in Cuba

against the rebels and cease the extermination of the innocent. It was not a question of favoring either Cuban or Spaniard, but of the relief of starving women and children, whose condition was a disgrace to the boasted civilization of the era. An appeal to England, and possibly other powers, to co-operate in mitigating the horrors of Cuba, might have achieved more at the outset than the subsequent armed intervention.

Certain elements of the American people became convulsed over the condition of the Cretans, whom St. Paul characterized doubtfully. The half-civilized Christians of Crete were oppressed by semi-civilized Mohammedans. The powers of Europe stood by to see that they had a semblance of justice. Press and pulpit in the United States raved at the impotence of those powers, but within seventy-eight miles of America's coasts half a million Christian Cubans were being starved through the policy of Christian and most Catholic Spain. Truly, it is easier to see the mote in a brother's eye than the beam in our own.

I arrived in Santa Clara soon after Weyler had started to pacify that province. By columns of smoke by day and of fire by night, the constant coming and going of soldiers, the desultory firing, and the numbers of pinioned prisoners dragged in, I could tell that pacification, so called, was in progress, with its incumbent horrors. I crossed the Spanish lines safely by night under the nose of the forts at

The Olayita Massacre

Isabella de Sagua, and swimming the Sagua River, struck out southeast through one of the worst districts in Cuba.

Until a few weeks previous, the district east of the fortified railroad running from Sagua to Cienfuegos had been practically free Cuba, the people living on their farms as in times of peace. Now all was changed, and the Imperial columns could be traced by the trail of smouldering homesteads, rotting carcasses of cattle, and frequently the bodies of pacificos shot down when trying to escape.

In this district the famous Olayita massacre had taken place some months before. Banderas had camped on the Olayita sugar-estate, and was driven out by two Spanish columns. The Spaniards then accused the planter, a Frenchman, M. Duarte, of assisting the rebels, and by order of Colonel Arc he was cut to pieces by machetes. The cavalry slaughtered the inhabitants of the estate, — men, women, and children. The young daughter of the overseer threw herself on the prostrate body of her father to protect him from the cruel blades, and was cut to pieces with him, thus escaping a worse fate. Then all the bodies were placed in the engine-house, and the factory was set on fire. The ingenio was built partly of stone; the bodies were thus baked and preserved, and though probably the Spaniards have now destroyed the traces of their handiwork, the remains were intact a few months ago, — a speaking tribute to Spanish rule.

Camped near Sito Grande, I took to the trees one

Under Three Flags in Cuba

morning to hide from some approaching cavalry who proved to be guerillas. Trembling with fear and horror, I managed to secure first a distant photograph of the two mutilated bodies bound on horseback, and later of a young woman, and two boys tied between mounted cut-throats. As they passed in the brilliant sunlight, they were silhouetted through a break in the trees, and the sharp Zeiss lens of my binocular magazine camera snapped two excellent pictures subsequently seized by the Spaniards. The chief of guerilla at Sagua, Colonel Benito Carrera, was a Spanish officer of bloodiest repute. His assistants, Clavarrietta and Lazo, were second only to him. It was their practice to intimidate the Cubans by exposing the mutilated remains of so-called rebels, — almost invariably pacificos, frequently those living by permission on outlying sugar-estates. These bodies were exhibited to color lying stories of fierce battles with the insurgents. Colonel Barker, late United States Consul at Sagua, has undeniable proofs of these atrocities. I found the district terrorized by Carrera's cruel raids, murders were committed daily, while the Spanish comandante of the city allowed him full sway in running Cuban sympathizers to earth. In my final capture I lost my notes, papers, and pictures, from this and other parts of Cuba; but as I write, two of my photographs of this colonel's crimes are before me, — one of these, the body of a negro shockingly mutilated, is unfit for publication; the other, a young Cuban chained to a tree and used as

Carrera's Brutality

a target until shot in a vital spot, was reproduced in the London "Graphic."

Carrera one day accused a woman of being the wife of a rebel. Her son, a bright boy of twelve, a cripple, answered him sharply, and was cut nearly in two by the Spaniard, who shouted "You rebel whelp, like father, like son!" Later, to force confession, he tore off with pliers the nails from seven fingers of an aged Cuban, charged with corresponding with rebels. Consul Barker reported these cases to the State Department.

It took little time to clear the pacificos from the Sagua district, and the distress among the reconcentrados was appalling, though the edict was only enforced there at the close of the spring campaign of '97.

Gomez was in the neighborhood of Sancti Spiritus. Weyler with immense columns had hemmed him in, and daily sent confident reports of the impending capture of the old chief. It was easy now to understand the necessity for the insurgent tactics. Gomez had split his army into small commands. Robau, the Cuban-born son of a wealthy Spaniard, commanded the Sagua district, Miguel Gomez had a brigade in Las Villas; Carrillo led the forces near Santa Clara City, and in the Cienfuegos zone several small bands eked out a perilous existence. Maximo Gomez, with only his staff and escort of picked troops, about three hundred in all, constantly eluded Weyler, though always camping near him, while

Under Three Flags in Cuba

laborantes in the cities carefully spread stories of his mobilization of an immense Cuban army, in preparation for a rush west to Havana. The reports misled Weyler, whose columns were fired into night and day by invisible bands of rebels, frequently only five or six men, who would ride through the woods, marching and countermarching until the Spaniards greatly overestimated the force that they could neither locate nor engage in open battle. The Cubans often had but two cartridges apiece, and despite the bushwhacking character of such tactics, Gomez must be credited with outgeneralling Weyler at every move.

I was amazed at the stoical endurance of the Cubans, who carried on the war without food or resting-place and at such odds. Sneer who may at Gomez for not fighting pitched battles, his was positively the only warfare possible under the circumstances; and Weyler returned to Havana with an army decimated by disease and bullets, having accomplished nothing save the devastation of the province, and the starvation rather of the homeless pacificos than the insurgents. Outnumbered twenty to one, the rebel tactics inflicted a maximum amount of loss upon the enemy with a minimum expenditure of force. Even brilliant victories would in the end have proved disastrous to the rebels; the ability to endure until Spain's vast resources were exhausted could alone prove the factor for lasting success.

Gomez has the qualities and the failings of a great man, not least of which is a quick temper. He was

Story of Maceo's Death

the terror of evil-doers, and tolerated no laxity of discipline. Toward those who served Cuba well and faithfully, he was rather a brother than commander.

The loss of his son Frank, who was killed with Maceo, was a terrible blow to the old chief, and his younger son told me that since the first-born's death, his father, like the English king of old, had never been seen to smile.

The story of Maceo's betrayal was false. It was evoked by Dr. Zertucha's conflicting stories after his ignominious surrender. The insurgents in the field told me but a few days after the occurrence, that he was killed in a regular ambush by the San Quintin battalion under Major Cirujeda. Maceo, Frank Gomez, and others were shot down trying to cut through the line; Maceo fell dead, young Gomez was badly wounded. Unable to move, he wrote to his father, "I die, but I did not abandon my general."

Then the soldiers swarmed over the field, despatching the wounded and stripping the bodies. A machete blow clave young Gomez's head in two. Hearing the firing, Pedrico Diaz hurried forward with his force, and the enemy retired, the Cubans securing the bodies. Not until the Spaniards divided their loot that night, did they discover the identity of two of the dead, — Maceo by papers in his clothing, Gomez by the F. G. on his linen, and the scrawled note to his father found by his side. This account does not differ materially from the Spanish official

Under Three Flags in Cuba

story. They admitted that they stripped the bodies, they even produced the farewell note of young Gomez, but never attempted to explain how or why they despatched him after he had written it.

Captain, now Colonel, Perez Staple, who carried the tidings to General Gomez, told me that it broke the old soldier's heart. Staple rode over to the general upon Miro's arrival, and at first could not control himself to speak. But Gomez' eagle eye divined bad news. "Why do you wait? Am I a woman that you fear to tell me ill-tidings?" he demanded. The captain in a faltering voice then told all he knew.

"Dios mio! My first-born and my dearest friend both! Oh, my poor boy! What will your mother say?" exclaimed the old man. He buried his face in his hands, his body was convulsed with sobs, and he turned in his hammock crying like a child. That night he paraded his men, and in broken tones said: "My grief is unmanly. I thought I was strong, but I am weak as a child. General Antonio and my dear boy have only died as any of us may die, doing their duty to Cuba; and before you all I thank God that they died bravely. My loss is doubly severe, but it is mitigated by that knowledge." Then the tears welled from under the gold-rimmed spectacles, and ran down the furrowed, weather-beaten cheeks, and he turned to his tent, heartbroken. Did space permit, I could add many stories that show the soft heart that beats under the rugged exterior of the old warrior.

Santa Clara

Food rapidly grew scarce in Santa Clara, especially in the North. When the reconcentration was enforced, much stock was driven to the rebels, and with care might have been sustained by breeding. Unfortunately "ventre affamé n'a point d'oreilles." Reason gave way to hunger, cows and calves were slaughtered indiscriminately, and meat soon became scarce. Numbers of women and children had elected rather to be near husbands and brothers than to obey Weyler's ukase. Their homes were burnt, and they existed miserably in huts in the woods, in mortal terror of guerillas.

One prefect's family I knew in Santa Clara, once owners of a large estate, lost two daughters. They were pretty girls of thirteen and sixteen, and ventured early one morning in search of vegetables. Prolonged absence caused anxiety, and finally their dead bodies were discovered. I saw the remains before they were touched. They lay in a field on the outskirts of a wood, not a hundred yards from the highroad, their basket of vegetables beside them. Evidently they were surprised by a passing band, and were shot down from the road when trying to escape to the woods. This would justify their murder from a Spanish point of view. The stricken parents and the few neighbors who eked out an existence in the manigua divined a worse outrage, however, and as such it was reported to General Robau.

The war was indeed horrible in all its aspects, much of it too gruesome to write of. The passive

Under Three Flags in Cuba

and active cruelties of the Spaniards toward the people were indescribable.

Prefecturas in Las Villas were not always available, and guides were scarce. My visit there afforded me enough adventure to fill a book, and sufficient privations and fever to reduce me to a skeleton and make it even chance if I escaped alive. There was little real fighting, but constant skirmishing, though fierce battles were daily reported by the Spaniards which misled credulous correspondents in Havana as to true conditions. During February, March, and April the insurgent army was greatly disintegrated in western and central Cuba, and so continued to the end. The eastern veterans of Maceo's invasion had been decimated in the severe campaign of '96, but hundreds of recruits flocked to the cause in each district. Rivera's capture, as he was reorganizing his shattered brigades, proved the futility of attempting organized aggression. There were less than two thousand armed Cubans in the Pinar del Rio division, about the same number in Havana Province.

General Rodriguez, who commanded the Sixth Army Corps, extended his forces, making small mobilizations when necessary. Alejandro Rodriguez, Diaz, the Ducasse brothers, Lorente, Torres, Delgado, Comacho, Varona, Perez, Vidal, Lopez, Campbell, Castillo, Acosta, Aranguren, and Arango operated with varying forces throughout the divisions of Pinar del Rio and Havana. Given food, arms, and ammunition, a force of ten thousand men could have been

Conditions in the West

mobilized in the West within a week, but the armed strength of these brigades has been greatly exaggerated. The above leaders usually had a mere handful of men in their immediate commands. With these they skirmished or conducted daring raids, as the capture of the Regla train by Aranguren, and frequent incursions to the fortified suburbs of Havana.

Matanzas being flat and narrow, Weyler had swept the province with an unbroken line. The Cubans there suffered terrible privations from fire and sword, numbers were killed; and after Lacret went east, the revolution almost died out. Dr. Betencourt, a prominent physician, now civil Governor of the province, assumed command during the height of Weyler's devastation. By supreme effort he reorganized the depleted forces, and to the end sustained a small but effective division in the most difficult district in Cuba. In Santa Clara the commands in the cultivated sections were precariously maintained, larger forces operating in Sancti Spiritus. There were about 2500 armados in all. The conditions in the East were better; I shall deal with them in a subsequent chapter. In each province there were hundreds of men existing in the field, collecting food for the army, or supporting their families in the woods. Armed, this impedimenta would have increased the effective strength of the rebels threefold. Unarmed, they were still virtually part of the revolution. For actual fighting strength a certain percentage must be

Under Three Flags in Cuba

deducted from the rolls of any army, as detailed for duties created by the exigencies of the situation.

Those writers who have so greatly overestimated the armed strength of the Cubans by counting as insurgents all men made rebels officially under Weyler's decree by remaining in the field, have not fallen into unqualified error. The assertion that fifty thousand armed Cubans were in the field is ridiculous. I estimate that less than sixteen thousand true fighting men were opposing Weyler's hordes in '97; of these less than seven thousand were in the four western provinces. Only fourteen thousand rifles were safely landed in Cuba by filibusters before '98. But all the men, armed or unarmed, were equally opposed to Spain. The greatest honor to the unarmed asistente was promotion to soldier when death provided a spare gun; reversion from soldier to servant was the severest punishment in the army. Ere the cause of Cuba libre would have been relinquished every asistente and pacifico would have passed into armed rank and to death; all were inspired by an equal patriotism.

The western half of Santa Clara was covered with small towns and centrals, joined by a network of fortified railroads, and proved a dangerous zone of operations. Each town boasted its local guerilla. Armed with Remington carbines, they used brass-capped bullets that inflicted wounds which invariably proved fatal, gangrene supervening through lack of antiseptics in the field. The use of this bullet was a

Santa Clara

distinct violation of the rules of the Geneva Congress, to which Spain subscribed; but since the Cubans were not recognized belligerents, the laws of war did not apply, she argued. The guerilla and heavy columns of soldiers marched from place to place continuously, and we frequently found the enemy simultaneously passing in four directions. In case of a skirmish they would all advance toward the firing, making our retreat difficult when our ammunition was gone.

The province contained many sugar estates. The factories owned by obstinate planters were blackened ruins; other ingenios were surrounded by forts, but had their cane destroyed by Cubans. Flaming houses and huts, ashes of homesteads, rotting bodies of pacificos, and carcasses of cattle, marked the sweep of Weyler's columns southward. The rebels preserved the estates of planters who neither attempted to grind, nor paid Spanish garrisons for protection, and they levied taxes on wealthy property owners. Any planter, however, who attempted to obey rebel orders was soon marked by the Spaniards, and his estate burned secretly. I know of one instance in Sagua where two young Scotch planters rather favored the Cubans. Again and again their cane or other property was destroyed, ostensibly by the insurgents, and they complained bitterly of this ingratitude to General Robau. He soon convinced them that the Spaniards alone were responsible, as his orders prohibiting cane burning had been strictly enforced, and on an adjoining estate owned by a

Under Three Flags in Cuba

notorious Spaniard the cane was left intact. A few nights later the rebels equalized matters by giving the Spaniard a candela, and his crop went up in smoke.

My sojourn in Santa Clara was soon brought to a close. Passing too near the forts on the Sagua Railroad with a small cavalry escort, we were fired on ineffectively. We started to detour, leaving the road for open country to pass forts below, when a volley was poured in right behind us. A patrol, examining the line for dynamite, had waited our approach from cover. We turned hastily to gallop to shelter, and four more volleys broke out as the soldiers emptied their magazines. The bullets passed overhead, mewing like angry kittens, some unpleasantly close. Hastily dismounting, and tying our horses in a thicket, we crept back to a sheltering bank and returned the fire. The Spaniards were barely two hundred yards distant, but they held to cover and we could see nothing. There were probably twenty of them, and we were thirteen all told.

Perez, the tall mulatto lieutenant, suggested that we should mount and give the gringos "al machete;" but we had eaten little for a week, and our men were not so brave. We could not break cover and retreat without becoming exposed, and the enemy was in the same predicament. To make matters worse, the rumble of an approaching train told us of new foes. It drew up cautiously a short distance away, and the armored cars spat fire; but the shots sang high, and not even a horse was killed. I admit feeling

A Skirmish with the Gringols

apprehensive of the issue; not so the Cubans. The practico crept through the long grass and fired shots from two directions, crawling back as the enemy aimed at the smoke. Then to our front, the light blue forms of the patrol could be seen, stooping as they made for the shelter of the train. Bang! bang! went our last cartridges; the young lieutenant stood up for a moment as he ran, then fell on his face. His men retreated to the train, taking the body of the poor fellow with them. His death I have ever lamented, though he had first opened fire upon us.

A muttered exclamation from Perez sent us scurrying for our horses, regardless of the volleys from the cars. Riding toward us on our flank came the cavalry from Esperanza, summoned by signal from the forts. When they saw our small party, they spread fan-shape as if to overwhelm us. Following the guide, we clattered down a narrow trail, rounded a hill, and headed for the woods. We had a good start, our horses were fresh, and we felt safe as we forded a stream and crossed the valley leading to cover; but the soldiers had swarmed upon the cars to watch our flight, and as we rode into clear view below them, pah! pah! pah! rang their Mausers, and the bullets spattered round with an angry psit! As we neared the woods, the practico fell over his pommel dead, a hot iron ran into my leg, and my horse, galloping wildly, staggered, and came down on me with a crash. Dazed and stunned, I lay dimly conscious of the clatter of hoofs and cries of the enemy as they charged down upon us. Then a Cuban trooper, hurriedly dismounting, lifted me in front of a comrade, cut the girth of my dead horse with his machete, and carried my saddle and effects into the trees. Others lifted the practico's body over his saddle, and we were soon in the woods safe from pursuit. The Cubans gave a derisive yell as the Spaniards drew up on the edge of the thicket, fearful of an ambuscade. Dodging from tree to tree, Perez emptied my revolver and a Mauser carbine into their ranks, and they soon wheeled about, and rode off balked of their prey.

With my feet stuck out and my spurs pressed home, a bullet had struck my shin, gone through my calf, and killed my horse, beside passing through the front and side of my heavy riding-boot and a thick saddle flap. But with all its penetrative powers, the nickel bullet makes a merciful wound; treated with cigar ash, and with only a shirt cuff tied round it with grass, mine soon healed save for a fester where the tibia was nicked.

Fever followed the wound, and I found it absolutely necessary to make an attempt to reach a town and obtain food and rest. Three weeks later I crawled through the long grass toward the barricade at Cruces, waiting by the wires until the Havana train arrived at 6 P. M., that the advent of a stranger in the town might be attributed to the railway. In the manigua I always carried a cloth coat, white

In the Enemy's Hands

collar, cravat, and cap in my saddle pack. By donning these I was de rigueur for the city. Still I was unshaven, my hair long, my face cadaverous and sunburnt, and Nemesis was following. The grass was long near the forts. I crept between them successfully, and squirmed painfully under the barbed wire barricade. To escape observation I was forced to drag myself along the ground under the lowest strands; the spikes, lacerating my back, inflicted deep gashes whose scars will long remain. Only the dread of discovery held back my cry of agony, but finally I passed the entanglement, creeping on through the weeds until I reached the zona. A woman, a ragged reconcentrada whom I did not fear, was searching for boniatos as I crossed the field. She eyed me curiously, and I suppose notified the guards.

I walked erect toward the freight depot, and sauntered down the railed path to the main street. "Safe at last" was the thought that lightened my step. Fata obstant! Two guardia civil came clattering down the street behind me; they eyed me a moment, then said their officer wished to confer with me. A supreme effort for self-control failed obviously. In execrable Spanish I muttered that I had not the honor of his acquaintance. Then a celador came up on foot, panting with exertion. "Señorito, where have you come from?" Ere I could frame a reply three footguards arrived. I was taken down the railroad track, and tumbled unceremoniously into the little stone fort guarding the level crossing which

Under Three Flags in Cuba

here goes over a deep ditch. I struggled and protested at first, but a blow in the ribs quieted me. I was thoroughly searched, my British passport scrutinized and returned. Luckily I had nothing incriminating but a tiny rebel pass, which I surreptitiously swallowed, and I was soon left in peace.

A grating admitted air and light, and some large-eyed Cuban children stared at the prisoner within. Two pretty señoritas happened along, strolling in the cool of the day. They gazed up curiously yet sympathetically; one said, "Pobre joven." The sentry, grinning jocosely, remarked, "Americano! Mañana es muerto!"[1]

Cheering news, indeed, but I by no means believed they would kill me. Captured in the field, death was sure; but in the towns people may talk, and irregularities with a foreigner cause complications. However, the girls believed it; their eyes filled with tears as they passed on; evidently they had a rebel brother or lover who might one day share the fate. It grew dark; the guards were gambling round a fire at the back of the fort and cooking their rancho; I stood disconsolate, peering into the gathering darkness, and shaking at the strongly wrought bars for a chance of escape, when some one approached.

"Hush, Señor, for the love of God! You looked hungry! Here is food and wine." I then recognized one of the sympathetic girls of the afternoon. She handed me tiny loaves and a piece of meat.

---

[1] "An American! To-morrow he is dead!"

A Fair Samaritan

Some luscious plantains were next pushed through the grating; the bottle of wine would not pass.

"Leave it; they will catch you!" I cried apprehensively.

"Drink!" she replied, as she pushed the neck through the bars, tilting the bottle so the liquid poured down my parched throat. When I pressed the little hand with effusive thanks, she whispered, "Todo por Cuba," and was gone. Perhaps it was Dutch courage; but the wine infused new life into my trembling limbs, the food also proved delicious after my menu of roots and unripe fruit in the manigua. I have never been able to trace my little Samaritan. God bless her! If my plight were not so ill as she feared, her ministration cheered me none the less. I lay on the dirty floor, and forgetting my dangers and smarting back, slept soundly.

The sweet notes of "Diana" from the bugles awoke me at daybreak, and a band played before the tumbledown Casino as a bedraggled column, that had stayed the night in town, re-formed and marched wearily on its way. Then the officer of the day arrived to see the rebel.

I fear I gave but a surly nod to his courteous "Buenos dias!" but ignoring my rudeness, he began to chat affably enough. He spoke in broken English, and we later became good friends. The young Spaniard talked wistfully of his home; then we found mutual acquaintances, for he was from the Canary Islands, and I even remembered his father's place, —

a large dry-goods store near the Cathedral in Las Palmas. Not once did he question me, nor even refer to my plight; and we parted as comrades.

"Deme las llaves," said my lieutenant's voice, half an hour later. Throwing open the door, he added perfunctorily: "Aquí tengo un prisionero de guerra!" and ushered in the portly comandante. By the latter's cordial greeting, I divined that my friend had interceded for me. "You are not a Yankee; you are English, I see!" said the major, as he glanced at my passport. "Now, sir, I ought to keep you till my colonel arrives, but there is nothing against you. Next time do not take country walks without a permit. It is not allowed. There is a train for Cienfuegos in ten minutes." I took the train.

I was thankful for my escape a few days later, when the local sheet printed a story of a negro who had either deserted or been captured at Esperanza. To save himself he made a full confession of all that had occurred, and much that had never occurred, in the field; but I was the central figure of his fiction, being made responsible also for the death of the unfortunate officer in the skirmish. My entry into Cruces he duly reported, but knew nothing of my capture and release. Furthermore the paper added that this miscreant was El Inglesito who had recently been defaming Spain and her brave army. Certain articles of mine that would have passed notice in New York had created interest in London, where the Cuban situation was less known. Some de-

A Fortunate Escape

spatches also had been intercepted en route, and Weyler, ever anxious to stifle news direct from the field, had ordered a watch to be set for the writer. Fortunately my name was not known, but Cienfuegos was not a desirable residence just then; the comandante at Cruces might think better of his laxity. I needed rest also; so returned to the United States to recuperate.

Feeling secure from recognition, with the loss of my hirsute appendages and a change from ragged clothes, I entered Havana openly by steamer three weeks later, to rest in that city, and witness the situation from the Spanish lines.

CHAPTER III

HAVANA. — THE VOLUNTEERS. — THE EXECUTION OF MOLINA. — GENERAL WEYLER. — THE RAID OF MARIANO.

"HE that has not seen Seville has seen no marvel," says an Andalusian proverb that certainly may be applied to Havana. The Antillian capital is a cosmopolitan city, in which a striking reproduction of a dozen latitudes are merged into a harmonious whole. From the approaching vessel a distant view suggests an entirely eastern city, but nearer the shore, on the west, the white stone and general structure of the one modern church, and the rows of buildings backing San Lazaro beach, resemble Cadiz viewed from the sea. Upon entering the harbor, Casa Blanca and Regla, nestling upon palm-capped ridges on the eastern side of the bay, transport one mentally to Las Palmas of Grand Canary. Once ashore, the narrow streets and multicolored houses around Teniente Rey seem a bit of old Seville transplanted. Cross to the Prado, the theatres and row of palatial cafés in the Central Park, with their orthodox marble tables on the sidewalks, and the lounging crowd, are truly Parisian. Within a stone's throw, behind the Villanueva terminus, the great markets and streets of clothes-dealers represent East London. The Indian

Havana City

Park district resembles Madrid; but just across the railroad, the Chinese quarter, with hordes of pigtails, the native theatre and pagoda, opium dens and "chop" houses, is truly Celestial, though the African consorts of the Mongolians, and the naked Chino-Negro offspring, swarming the gutters, are hardly congruent thereto.

Given strong olfactory nerves, penetrate the fœtid negro quarter, at the head of the bay and near the Recogidas. With the slovenly termagants, squalling brats, and the languid squalor, it could be mistaken for Sierra Leone or Liberia. The occasional black swells and their gorgeous "ladies," who arrogantly sweep through their fellow "trash," en route for cheap ball or promenade, resemble their church-going prototypes in civilized Africa. The nightly racket, with obscene Congo songs and dances, or the occasional outrages by the nanigos, both relics of ante-slave days in the Dark Continent, could only be equalled in Darkest Africa with its fetish dancers, Porros, human leopards, or other blood gangs of the Imperri country, or Ashanti.

The city was ever gay, despite the hideousness of the struggle for human existence of the oppressed lower classes. The three distinct races of Cuba are more strongly marked in the capital than elsewhere. First, the Cuban proper, wealthy or once wealthy planters, and the professional class — descendants of the old, blue-blooded Castilian stock, in whom noblesse oblige is by no means dead. They are refined and highly educated, a number are graduates of American colleges; and with them the hope of free Cuba lies.

The Spaniard in Cuba is not even typical of his race. As in days of yore, Cuba to the poor Spaniard at home has been El Dorado. Dazzled with the prospect, he emigrated to Cuba by his thousands, at an early age. He was soon employed, at a small pittance and board, in one of the innumerable bodegas, small groceries that stand in each corner, or in the cafés or stores. At seventeen he must serve his country; and to escape conscription, he enlisted in the Volunteers of Cuba, a body in which no Cuban is eligible for service.

The one thought of the Spaniard was to make money and retire to Spain; he worked hard for sixteen hours per day, was frugal, and slept in the cellar or under the counter. He could seldom write or read, and was more or less an ignorant brute from his earliest days. Thus the hard-working and commercial class in the large cities, shop assistants, police, waiters, janitors, carters, laborers, boatmen, messengers, and stevedores, were all Spaniards. Banded together in the Instituto de Voluntarios, they formed a strong and armed body politic, — an intransigeant party, ignorant and rabid, to whom even the Captain-General was subservient. As an absolute political factor, these volunteers have been the great curse to Cuba. There were thirty thousand in Havana, sixty thousand in the island.

Spain's Proscriptive Policy

What cared the Spaniard for the future of Cuba? To secure all the riches possible, and to return to Spain, was his aim in life; and to this end the Spanish party, from Captain-General down, strenuously upheld the proscriptive policy that meant dollars for the moment, but disaster eventually.

One instance: just before the war, London speculators were negotiating for the construction of a railway across Puerto Principe, with great additional projections to join Santa Clara and Santiago. An immense wave of prosperity to eastern Cuba would have followed, but the road would take time to build, and the officials then in power might not have remained to benefit by its completion. They commenced extortion at once. First an utterly ridiculous valuation was clapped on the land over and above the price first asked by the owners, an almost prohibitive tariff was imposed on all imported materials, taxation on every pretext was in course of evolution, and the promoters threw up the scheme in disgust. Thus for the sake of a few paltry thousands for the pockets of rapacious officials, the great eastern provinces of Cuba are undeveloped to this day, and millions of capital shut out. These sections instead yield the few dollars squeezed annually from the miserable squatters who alone occupy the glorious valleys. The immense mining resources of Santiago are undeveloped for a similar reason.

By a simple system of political jugglery the Spanish party retained absolute control of the government, internal and municipal. In large cities Peninsulars owned much property, and might have been expected to control the franchise; but in the typically Cuban town of Guines, only 500 Spanish-born residents are registered, out of 12,580 Cuban inhabitants. Yet the electoral list contained the names of 415 Spaniards and but 32 Cubans, and even on the Municipal Board there was not a single Cuban member. Guines examples the whole.

During the past twenty years the province of Matanzas has had twenty governors; eighteen of these were born in Spain, two only were Cubans, — one, General Acosta, had served all his life in the Spanish army, and fought against his own people; the other, Señor Munoz, was educated in Spain, and a rabid conservative. In the Spanish Cortes, usually three, never more than six, deputies represented Cuba out of the four hundred and thirty members. Their representation in the Senate was even more easily restricted. A crown minister, bishop, grandee of Spain, a general, vice-admiral, ambassador, counsellor of state, judge, or attorney-general was eligible. There are but three Cuban grandees, and no Cuban had a chance to fill the other positions, so the above qualifications were practically prohibitive. This restricted their senatorial representation to professors of over four years' presidency in a university, those who paid over $800 annually in taxes, or mayors of cities of over 20,000 population. No one else was eligible. It was therefore possible, rather than

Official Defalcations

probable, for a true Cuban to enter the Upper House.

Obnoxious tariffs were permanent, for the Custom House proved an easy means for corrupt officials to rob the government of millions by fraudulent entry. In Cuba compromise was always possible. All officials had to purchase appointments that paid a meagre salary but with unlimited perquisites.

Fraud was incumbent on the whole political system. Its existence was known and tolerated in Madrid. Señor Robledo, speaking of defalcations in certain accounts in Havana, asked the government what had been done to recover one proven deficit of $32,811,516. General Pando, speaking in the Cortes in March 22, 1890, said: "This liquidation of estates confiscated in Cuba during the war shows a deficit of $14,000,000, the defalcations of the Board of Debt are over $12,000,000, and in addition to the Oteiza frauds and other items, we have a grand total of $40,000,000 shortage." Pando complained of the wrongful diversion of money from the Spanish treasury; but these vast sums are only a part of the amount drawn from Cuba by corrupt officials, who have spared no effort to extort sufficient to satisfy themselves and their superiors in Madrid. All the frauds were but part of the huge political game, and were perpetrated without risk of punishment.

The deferential duties also forced the colonists to pay an exorbitant price for goods from Spain, or submit to 100 per cent ad valorem duty on imports from other countries. During the depression in the sugar market after the '68 war, many wealthy planters closed down their ingenios, being unable to replenish their grinding plant by reason of the tariff on the machinery which Spain herself could not furnish and had no reason to protect. Needless to add, under such proscriptive policy even the riches of Cuba had dwindled, and were speedily becoming exhausted. During the twelve years prior to the late war the exports of both sugar and tobacco, staple products, decreased to less than one-half their former value. Spain and Spain's alike suffered from national decadence, that moral debility and social corruption, called by Aristotle oliganthropy, that has destroyed great ancient powers, and which is slowly but surely menacing the very national existence of the Latin today as a factor in the world's development.

Many of the Spanish emigrants rose to become property owners, and obtained official positions in spite of illiteracy. They were distinctly ambitious, and some of the social functions of the wealthy were ridiculous, the pompous but ignorant "Four Hundred" aping a patronizing air of superiority which could not cloak the blatant vulgarity exuding from every pore.

Everything Spanish centred around the loyal Instituto, the members of which have placed themselves beyond the pale of civilization by certain acts, which probably culminated in the "Maine" outrage. In May of 1870 the volunteers raided the Villanueva

Murder of the Students

theatre, where an exclusive Cuban opera was in progress, and poured volleys indiscriminately into the audience, killing many women and children. Captain-General Dulce, who had the temerity to attempt to arrest the culprits, was driven to a warship by a tipsy mob and forced to retire to Spain.

Two years later, scratches were discovered on the tomb of Colonel Castenon, a volunteer killed in a duel with Orasco, the Cuban writer. Suspicion fell on some medical students of the Havana college, a Cuban institution; the whole medical class was arrested by General Clavyjo, and released when their innocence was proven. Enraged at the acquittal, the volunteers seized the innocent lads; they were tried by illegal drum-head court-martial, and since none would confess the crime, all were sentenced to death. One-fourth of their number was selected for instant execution; these were shot down on the Prado in cold blood by the citizen soldiers. Among the dead were four lads of fifteen. Sentences on the remainder were magnanimously commuted to imprisonment for life. Later Castenon's son arrived from Spain and testified that the scratches were made by masons in fixing the tomb; the students were innocent. A magnificent monument to-day marks the grave of the young Cuban martyrs. Built of pure Carrara marble, weeping Justice stands above with broken sword and distorted scales. History, at her side, points to the open doors of corruption through which an exquisitely chiselled figure of Innocence is emerging with Truth.

Under Three Flags in Cuba

On the anniversary, November 27, '97, despite the threats of the volunteers to destroy the tomb, the families of the boys went to lay flowers on the grave. Their grief had been assuaged by time, but mothers and sisters still wept silently, and I could not fail to notice only old men in the party paying tribute to the martyrs of Spanish infamy. The younger male relatives of these, the most prominent Havana families, were away, fighting to free their country from the grip of their brothers' murderers.

Early in the war an aged planter, sitting under the portals of the Tacon café, talked earnestly to a friend. The waiter, a volunteer, overhearing the words "Cuba libre," denounced him as a rebel, and armed loyalists shot him in the back as he rose, astounded at the accusation. General Campos in '95 refused to execute insurgent prisoners and estranged the Instituto. After his failure to check Gomez, instead of the volunteers offering their services to help the hardly pressed troops, they paraded round the palace, swearing to hang Campos, and at daybreak he resigned and retired. Weyler was a man after their own heart.

One beautiful morning early in June, I was aroused by an unusual excitement on the Prado where the volunteers were assembling for early parade. It was barely 6.30, but already crowds of uniformed men had gathered in excited groups near my hotel, and I soon learned that one of their number, Fernandez,

The Execution of Molina

who had killed his captain in an unseemly quarrel over a woman, had been sentenced to be shot next day. Greatly enraged were the redoubtable patriots that one of the loyal Instituto should be forced to pay the penalty of his crime, and wild talk was indulged in; but after recording a protest, they went to duty quietly and waited for the morrow.

"La Lucha," Weyler's official organ, that afternoon announced the execution without comment, and added that William Molina, a rebel lieutenant of Pinar del Rio, would also be shot for the crime of incendiarism. A few weeks previously General Weyler had received instructions from Madrid to withhold the extreme penalty for rebellion. The incessant executions were arousing notice in Europe, and I learned also, on excellent authority, that the Queen of Spain had for once been able to influence her iron-willed mentor, Canovas, whose brutal procedure was by no means her Majesty's. The Captain General was ordered to follow a conciliatory policy in the "conquered" West, with the view of inspiring the "defeated" insurgents with confidence and inducing their surrender. Weyler, who knew the absolute falsity of his successive reports, realized the futility of conciliation, but from that day forth, every insurgent who surrendered or was captured, unless it were expedient to execute him secretly, was court-martialled for rebellion and incendiarism, formally acquitted on the former charge, and sentenced to death on the latter. Thus Molina was to die for incendiarism.

Under Three Flags in Cuba

It is obvious that he was selected to die as a mere stage effect to offset the execution of the volunteer. When I met Molina in Pinar del Rio in February, he had but recently landed; he was captured soon afterwards, sick and travel-worn, by the humane General Velasco. His leader, General Rivera, and a dozen other high Cuban officers were confined at the time; but he was the least known, if the least guilty, and could be killed without foreign comment. There was no attempt made to specify charges; as in all cases, the court-martial was a farce, lasting as many seconds as it took the officers of the court to affix their signatures to the charge sheet. There was no true charge against Molina beyond his presence in the field, and he was entirely unprepared for his fate when he was told to prepare for the chapel where the condemned spend their last hours on earth. He was completely dazed, but wrote a short farewell to his widowed mother and sisters in Florida, in which he deplored that they would now have no protector, but that they must remember he died for Cuba. The kind-hearted officer of the death guard promised to, and did forward the letter, and a few trinkets, including the silken scapular that he wore to the last, the handiwork of his sister before he left for the war.

At daybreak next morning I crossed the fœtid cesspool from Havana to La Cabana, and without molestation passed with a group of officers down the slope to the death-ditch, Los Laureles.

It was a glorious morning, and below the heights

Scene at La Cabana

of the fortress lay the city, white and glistening in the sunlight. The bells of the churches called to early mass; their discordant tones, softened by distance, mingling with the resonant swells of the organ and voices of the choir that were wafted across the bay from the cathedral. Beyond the ramparts a vast crowd had gathered, jostling and cursing in their attempt to gain a point of vantage where they could look over the heads of the guard. On several occasions I have stood with barely half-a-dozen people at the bi-weekly executions; the shooting of a "rebel dog" was far too common to attract or interest. But the death of a Spanish volunteer was a different matter. Some hundreds of his comrades had their arms, and were muttering ominously in the Fosso; the general crowd also were volunteers in mufti or their friends, and trouble seemed imminent. The hour had passed, and the mob yelled for the mambi; but not until another battalion had been marched from El Morro to reinforce the guard did the tragedy begin.

The preliminary thump of the drum was the signal for absolute silence, the silence of excessive anticipation. Then the band joyously blared the inspiring strains of "El Tambor Mayor," and the regiment of Cazadores marched blithely across the parade and formed three sides of a square, facing the musty wall of the fortress. The comandante and staff of the fort, smoking cigarettes and chatting gaily, sauntered into the centre; the band stopped suddenly. Putting into his instrument the pathos possible only to an emotional Latin, the trumpeter sounded a pitiful silencio, and the postern was thrown back.

First came the lay brothers, negroes in black gowns, capouches, and dirty lace capes, bearing cracked lanterns, and a cross rusty with age and use; then the guard, with fixed bayonets, and the tightly pinioned prisoner supported by the shambling prison priest in a faded robe.

Closely and with sad heart I watched the face of the condemned, worn and emaciated from long confinement in a dark dungeon; the sunlight blinded him, and it was painfully apparent that all hope had been crushed from the young officer by his captivity; that he was meeting death as one for whom life had long ceased to be of pleasure or value. Then came the frightful awakening. The open air, the sunlight, the birds singing in the laurel trees; the sight of the glorious country; the sparkling bay below, in which he had bathed as a boy, before political oppression drove his family to exile; the tolling bell of the cathedral in which he had worshipped; the hum of the busy city awakening for the day, — all this caused a sudden revulsion, awakened a desire to live, to taste freedom once again and breathe God's pure air. The change was apparent to all; the listless attitude was gone in an instant. Life is precious at nineteen, and the poor fellow suddenly realized what he was losing.

While the priests were chanting, the fanatical crowd held their peace, for the Spaniard is igno-

The Death Scene

rantly superstitious of the Church. But when Molina, awakening to his position, faltered, reeled back, and stopped undecided, "Cuban dog!" "Nanigo!" "Death to the mothers that bear such offspring!" "Life to Weyler and Spain!" rang from all sides, and some of these noble Spaniards mingled "Coward!" with other vile epithets. A few humane persons expostulated; an aged Cuban near me had the temerity to pray audibly; but the effect of the uproar was electrical upon the prisoner.

He straightened up. His mother and his country were insulted; his pride of race was touched. With shoulders back and head erect, he stepped firmly into the square, his eyes blazing with indignation. He glanced contemptuously at the crowd. He listened to the priest, a little impatiently I thought, and as he was roughly dragged forward, he shook himself free and knelt on the ready sanded strip. A sergeant and four men formed three feet behind him. They levelled their rifles; the triggers clicked ominously. Molina braced himself for the shock, and waited in suspense. Then in refined and unintentional cruelty the crisis was delayed while a negro lay brother came leisurely across the parade with the cross for the condemned to kiss. Perfunctorily he applied his lips to the sacred emblem; again he prepared for the volley. But a further delay followed, during which his tried fortitude almost forsook him; the young body was shaking with convulsive trembling. But at last the sergeant held his sword in the air; the squad were taking aim. With a flash the sword fell; the volley rattled out. The young martyr was dead.

The band burst into the Cadiz march, but stopped after a few bars, and the renewed execrations died away when the mangled body was dragged off, and fresh sand spread over the bloody tracks; the great event was yet to come. Again the postern opened, and the death procession hove in sight. Trembling in every limb, the murderer Fernandez was led forth, held up by two priests. As he reached the square there were shouts of recognition from all sides, which the homicide was too frightened to heed. Loud murmurs and protests arose, and dispensing with all preliminaries, I supposed to get the execution over before a riot arose, the comandante jerked Fernandez into position, and the firing squad stepped out. A loud chorus of "No! No!" arose from all sides; the volunteers shouted, howled, and gesticulated; a rescue seemed imminent. I saw the officers suppress a smile with difficulty. Then the postern swung back again, an aide dashed into the square, shouting, "Alto!" and waving a blue paper.

The squad fell back promptly; if the farce had not had previous rehearsal, at least the actors were perfect in their parts. The comandante then announced that in view of the loyal services rendered by the volunteers in the past, General Weyler had craved and received the Queen's pardon for Fernandez, that no slur might rest upon the honorable name

The Death of Hchevarri

of the loyal Instituto. A roar of exultation went heavenward in reply. Fernandez arose dazed, and with yells of "Viva Weyler!" "Vivan los Voluntarios!" "Viva España!" the volunteers danced in their delirious joy.

"Thank God that first poor boy died so bravely!" said a voice in my ear, and turning, I found a young lieutenant of artillery who had read my feelings in my face. Then with an angry "Get to your pigsties before you grunt, swine!" he flung some gesticulating soldiers aside, and strode away: one Spaniard ashamed of his race.

Executions were frequent throughout Weyler's régime, and every week if there were no shooting there was the garotte, and the local verdugo reaped a rich harvest. Two weeks after Molina's death, the aged patriot Hchevarri was shot in the back like a dog. The execution was soon over, and I stood on the steps at La Punta as the body was brought across the bay for burial. A gray-haired Cuban lady knelt with her daughters over the rough box, the wife dry-eyed and silent, the sweet-faced girls weeping bitterly; but they were refused permission even to possess the remains after death. Soon the lumbering deadcart drew up. "Come, Widow, ' vende listas ' to a loyal man next time!" shouted the brutal sergeant; the soldiers pulled the coffin from the recumbent women, and tilting it roughly, pushed it over the stone balustrade. This caused the blood to rush to one end, and pour through the badly fitting joints, splashing over the kneeling forms on the steps, and making a pool on the ground that the brave man had given his life to free. The soldiers drew their machetes and dipped the points in gore; "to warm the soul," as the guerillas say.

Mrs. Hchevarri died broken-hearted a few weeks later; the fate of her unfortunate daughters, who were left penniless, I have never heard.

Beside the public executions, secret official murders frequently took place. Prominent Cubans of revolutionary sympathies were taken outside the lines at night and shot. Their bodies were then brought in and buried without recognition, as insurgents killed in battle.

Colonel La Barerra, the infamous chief of police in Havana, had a complete system of espionage, and swayed his power rather to blackmail than to stamp out the revolution. I could fill pages with revolting details of cases that came under my personal notice, of murder and outrage perpetrated by this blackguard and his assistants Escalante, Pratts, Prinn, and other satellites. They blackmailed with impunity under threat of exile, and to intimidate others they deported many innocent people, who were finally pardoned by General Blanco. Their dupes were forced to play the spy, and, as in the case of Beato, who betrayed Mrs. Sctolongo, were hung when their usefulness was over and their knowledge dangerous.

A young Cuban friend of mine named Arisa and his companion Posada came under Barerra's ban, and

An Official Murder

were murdered in cold blood on the night of August 13, '97. Arisa was the son of a sugar-exporter; Posada, the son of the Consul-General of Portugal. During the summer they visited friends, expatriated Cubans, in Mexico. On their return they were arrested, but released. We sat that night in the annex of the Inglaterra hotel, joking at their experience, and discussing the coming fiesta at the Vedado. We broke up at a late hour, and next day I learned that Arisa and Posada had disappeared. Their friends feared the worst, and while aiding in the search, my assistant Garcia learned that they had been arrested as they left the hotel, thrust into a coach in Central Park, and driven rapidly away.

Señor Diego, a stock-broker in the Casa Nueva, had told me that day of cries for help, and shots near his house in Tulipan during the night, and of a waiting deadcart in El Cerro driving rapidly away. "El Diario" also mentioned the arrival in the Colon morgue of two bodies of rebels shot crossing the lines. The coincidence seemed suspicious, and since the municipal doctor was an acquaintance of mine, I drove over and asked for a permit to view the dead insurgents. "They are interred already," he stated, "buried at daybreak by order," adding, sotto voce, "The rebels are wearing patent boots, silk vests, and white shirts, it seems; at least, these were. They were no insurgents!" He would say no more, for "still tongue, safe neck" was a good Havana maxim; but our suspicions were fully confirmed when the cemetery morgue-keeper openly sold the clothes of the missing men as his perquisite.

The relatives obtained no redress until General Blanco's arrival, when the bodies were exhumed and recognized. The miscreant police-officers had then sailed for Spain, save Colonel Escalante, who was suspended from office. Angered at my share in this and other exposures, Escalante and some of his gang swore to kill me. Twice I was waylaid at their instigation, but escaped scatheless. Following the discovery of a huge dynamite bomb at the American Consulate on November 26th, a small bomb in a sugar-cane sample case was delivered with my newspapers. I threw the package to the janitor to open for me. He carelessly split the lid instead of withdrawing it, thereby disarranging a clever fuse attachment that otherwise would have ignited and blown us to atoms. Escalante was implicated in these outrages, and finally dismissed by General Blanco.

Hatred to Spain seemed to be imbibed in the air of Cuba, and Cuban-born sons of Spaniards proved invariably rebels, especially when born of Cuban mothers. "Take a Cuban wife for a rebel son," was a pertinent Spanish aphorism, and the revolution caused houses to be divided, son against father, the mother and daughters usually siding with the son. The colonials were persecuted terribly under Weyler's reign of terror, since they all had some relative with the insurgents, and in consequence were rated

The Cuban Inquisition

as "suspects" against whom any outrage would be tolerated.

Famous desperadoes, as Alcade Maury and Colonel Fonsdeviela, who murdered many people in Havana suburbs, including the American Dr. Ruiz, had their prototypes all over the island, — Spanish ruffians by no means typical of their race, but who had the official backing of Spain in her effort to crush the rebellion at all costs.

The prisons in Cuba were filled to overflowing with political prisoners charged with most trivial offences. General suspects were herded like animals in filthy pounds and given scanty sustenance, though their friends could send in food and comforts by sufficiently bribing the jailer; prominent prisoners were more closely guarded. Inquisitorial tortures were frequently used to extract confession. The methods used in Montjuich by Narcisso Portas and others — the terrible componte, the mordaza for the mouth, and the lash were also employed.[1]

Every week a ship loaded with deportados and invalid soldiers left Havana; the Cubans, political suspects, gazing wistfully on their fatherland for the last time, were bound for the African penal hells, Chaferinas or Cueta, or the pestilential isle of Fernando

---

[1] Among instances of tortures I investigated, at San Severino Fortress, Matanzas, Fidel Fundora, a planter, was for weeks subjected to infamous barbarities, including the thumb-screw, suspension head downwards, the lash, and a mock execution, to extort the names of the local patriotic Junta in that city. Fundora was released by General Blanco, a shattered wreck, crippled for life.

Under Three Flags in Cuba

Po in the Gulf of Guinea. Their sobs were drowned by the exultant cheers of the inutile soldiers, who looked back at the fading coasts and realized that they were exchanging hardships and the tyranny of compulsory service for home in their beloved Spain. The deportados, sent to exile, had less hope than their more active brothers captured in the field, whose torture sooner or later would be ended by the firing squad.

The insurgents in Havana Province were very aggressive during the summer of '97, which was extremely dry. During June and July great efforts were made by the Spaniards to entrap the young leader, Nestor Aranguren and his dashing cavalrymen recruited from the best families in the island. I applied for permission from the Marquis Ahumada to join the Spanish columns, but received a courteous refusal, since "the rebels might capture and murder" me. It was not politic to explain that I should fall among friends, so I had to view the operations from the railroad and interior towns. General Molina led three columns into the Guira Melena district, which is shut in by a triangular barrier formed by the railway lines running from Havana to Batabano, and the Guines and Matanzas roads, joining at Aguacate.

For days the troops operated in this zone, but the tireless Cubans, hemmed in but never caught, skirmished with the Spanish hordes with impunity until the operations were abandoned. To follow Molina's discomfiture, Weyler took the field again in person,

Weyler's Meat Trust

and bravely rounded up a vast quantity of cattle, corralled by permission under the forts on the outskirts of the towns. He had placed an embargo on the importation of livestock from abroad; so hundreds of head were driven into Havana and sold at an exorbitant price. I could name a dozen reconcentrados who thus lost their only means of subsistence. They did not get a cent for the stolen stock, and starved to death. If, as Weyler affirms, starvation was unavoidable, why did he loot cattle and sell them for his own benefit? The beasts could have been taken, and the meat issued to the perishing reconcentrados; but I saw in Santiago de las Vegas and Guines droves of milch cows seized and sent to Havana to be sold, while in both places the blood from the beasts killed for the soldiers was lapped from the ground by famished people, and the discarded entrails fought over and devoured raw. It was a sight I shall never forget.

A meat trust was formed; the Spanish Fernandez de Castro, and Weyler's secretary, Colonel Escribano, had sole rights as middle men in issuing the captured beef, controlling the price at will.

On his return from this campaign I first met Weyler. He rode into Guanabacoa with a large force, harassed all the way by bushwhacking Cubans, who tried in vain to get through the flanks for one shot at him. When the general arrived, Alcaide Maury provided a luncheon, at the close of which I was presented. To describe this man or brute, to whom human life was as nothing, is a difficult task. He greeted me cordially enough, and apologized for his travel-stained condition due to the campaign. He was a dapper little man, decidedly under the medium build, with bushy eyebrows and side whiskers, a determined face, with thin cruel lips over a sensuous double chin. He wore the regulation light blue and white cotton uniform, rough riding-boots, and a large straw sombrero. He looked hot, tired, and dirty; given a black patch and cutlass, he was the orthodox pirate of fiction. He talked simply, in a thick voice, and exhibited a trying, nervous twitching of eyebrows and hands with every sentence. His keen, blasé eyes pierced one through; their glance was absolutely distrustful, and showed that he would suspect his own brother. We talked of the reconcentrados, of war, and chiefly of the United States. He seemed suspicious at my knowledge, and asked me sharply: "How long have you been here?" I equivocated, replying I had been in Havana but a few weeks.

The Americans, he thought, were encouraging the Cubans with the ultimate hope of seizing the island. As to the insurrection he declared that there were not five hundred rebels in the west, — a statement I knew to be false, — and said he would soon pass eastward and destroy Garcia and the rebels there. He believed Gomez dead, or a fugitive.

"In that case these poor reconcentrados can go back to their homes soon?" I remarked interrogatively.

Weyler lifted his eyebrows. "Ah, but these Cuban

COLONEL CARRERA'S GUERILLAS AT SAGUA.
With bloodhound used for tracking fugitives.

I Meet Weyler

women have borne rebel sons and will encourage them," was his significant reply.

"Then, General, what of their future? Must all starve?"

"These people are but eating the fruit of the tree they sowed," he said. "I am here to crush the rebels, others must see to the resettlement of Cuba. This is war. I meet war with war. I have done as Sherman did. The distress is bad, but the measure necessary. The rebels will not fight us openly, and as it is difficult to quell them by bullets, we must starve them out. It is their own doing. They could surrender and end the war, and save their wives and children, but they persist in combating Spain, and this is the result. What of the families of our soldiers killed in the war?"

That was the only excuse I ever heard the general make for holding as hostages and starving 500,000 innocent women and children.

A Cuban lady in deep black approached, and was received with deference, though Weyler frequently shook his head and frowned ominously, for his visitor was imploring him to grant something. "Madam, I kiss your feet. May God guard you many years!" he said as he dismissed her. Then I saw the true Weyler. He was in a boiling rage and cursed his officers. The mask of affability was off. His quick eyes snapped viciously, and his features were distorted with passion, but for no apparent reason. He was not Beauty before, he was decidedly the Beast now. It is impossible to picture an expression so completely changed. His heart was as adamant, but I believe that man's life was a hell, that, in re-echo of Cleomenes of old, "scenes of blood lay dreadful on his soul." Hence his varying moods and frequent outbursts. He did not entirely regain his equanimity; but he invited me to ride into Havana with him, and failed to hide his relief when I declined the honor. That afternoon, as he rode in triumph through the capital at the head of his men, I was surprised at the coolness of his reception. His bodyguard, his Celeres, — picked men recruited from the negro Bomberos, or firemen, — commanded by a seven-foot black of ogrish aspect, marched first, then the Captain-General and a guard of dragoons; but even in Obisbo Street only the gamins yelled "Viva Weyler!" the volunteers saluted, and cried "Viva España!" The general public received the hero with contemptuous silence.

"There can be slain no sacrifice to God more acceptable than an unjust and wicked king;" but, in a wide application of Seneca, but one attempt was made on Weyler's life, — a bomb thrown in the palace. Yet he walked nightly down the Prado with only an aide and three secret police sauntering behind. Some Cubans often debated with me the feasibility of seizing him there one night, dragging him down the steps to the Punta beach and shipping him down the coast to Gomez, to be held as a hostage for all Cuban prisoners. This would have been easy

Weyler's Capture Planned

in the darkness with a launch, and a tug in the offing that could race the obsolete boats in the harbor. We worked persistently in planning this. The guards were to be overpowered by sudden onslaught from the rear; the general seized, pinioned, and embarked. Lack of funds delayed the attempt. Finally we chartered a tug in Key West; but the owner drew back at the last, and just as another boat was offered, Weyler was recalled. It would have been a master stroke, and one I regret that was not carried out. "It is good for one to taste the meal he cooks for others," as the Spaniards say.

The general was absolutely implacable. When the devoted young American lady Miss Someillian begged on bended knees for her father's liberation from imprisonment on a groundless charge, she reminded him that he too had a daughter. "Yes," was the prompt reply, as he roughly threw off the pleading girl, "and if her father were a filibuster she would loyally disown him."

Colonel Laborde, who had served Spain faithfully at home in the past, and whose Cuban-born sons became rebels, pleaded in vain with Weyler for the life of his son Edward, captured on the filibuster "Competitor." "We have been soldiers of Spain together," said the old officer, "and you, General, have also a son you love." "Yes," was the reply, "and if my own son were disloyal and rebelled to-day against Spain, with my own hand would I sign his death decree."

Under Three Flags in Cuba

These incidents throw side lights on Weyler's character, and he is one of the few men of whom it seems impossible to relate anything really redounding to his credit.

If Premier Canovas had replaced Weylerism with true clemency at an early date, the history of Cuba to-day would have been different. The dead statesman supported him to his last day, and after six months of the brutal régime the loss of Cuba to Spain was obvious to all but the blinded ministers in Madrid. Using turf and scriptural metaphors, Spain backed the wrong horse; and when reason prevailed and Blanco arrived with the autonomy that two years earlier would have saved the situation, like the doom of the foolish virgins, "Too late, too late, ye cannot enter now!" was the cry that greeted him.

At the end of July the insurgent fires burned nightly on the hills behind Havana; the cane of Fernandez de Castro and on other fortified estates nearer the city blazed repeatedly. The rebels were at the gates of the capital at that time, and I had secret information that General Castillo, a young professor of languages then with the rebels, and Delgado and Hernandez, would simultaneously attack the fortified barricade guarding Havana, Castillo, at the suburb of Jesus del Monte, and the two latter at Mariano, a pretty little watering-place on the western side. Thinking the latter would be the more interesting fight, I drove to Mariano on the evening be-

The Raid of Mariano

fore the date, and registered at the dirty and only hotel Santa Clara.

A heavy thunderstorm had cleared the air, and it was a glorious night for the rainy season. As I sat on the piazza, the soft throbbing of the organ from the little iglesia blended with the rippling of the sea on the sandy shore; the moon shone clearly, making a flow of silvery sheen on the water, the pure radiance lighting up the distant spires and domes of Havana city and softening the squalor of the reconcentrados' hovels. Campfires flickered from the Vedado and the forts along the Almanares River. The great Santa Clara and Vedado batteries loomed grimly in the distance; the moon's pale effulgence rested on their massive guns, making them gleam like polished silver. Too far away to heed the racket of the gay city, the suburb seemed sleeping.

The silence was broken only by the bugles of the outposts sounding the nightly retreat, and the faraway baying of dogs. From a fort in the valley a few conscripts, thinking of Spain, were singing the constitutional hymn as they lay round the campfire. I looked almost sadly on this peaceful scene, as I thought of the horrors the morrow would bring forth, the bloodshed and strife that was inevitable.

Up the main street some troops now approached. A passing column I thought, as a party of horsemen rode along, followed by some shambling infantry. As they marched under the shadow of the piazza, I could not see them closely.

Under Three Flags in Cuba

"Alto! Quién vive?" challenged the sentinel at the Cuartel.

"Viva Cuba libre!" shouted a dozen voices, and the warning shot of the sentinel was drowned in the volley that followed. At the same time mine host, also an officer in the volunteers, dashing up with a cry of "Los Mambis," dragged me inside and commenced to barricade the door and windows. The Cubans had rushed the forts, and entered the very outskirts of Havana unchecked. The firing now became general, the insurgents trying to storm the Cuartel from which the soldiers blazed incessantly. Finding the door resisted their efforts, they placed a guard over the building and commenced to search for clothes. They were terribly ragged and emaciated, several clad only in sugar-sacks, and they went from house to house demanding food and apparel, giving a receipt for the same to be redeemed later.

"Open that door!" demanded a stern voice at the hotel; "open or we will burst it in." The proprietor and his assistants lay on the floor still as death.

"This house belongs to a bad Spaniard; let us burn him out," suggested one; and then a woman beside me began to whine, and call on the Virgin for protection.

"Oh, there are only women there!" growled another. "If you want to find a black-hearted Spaniard, there is one!" and at this they trooped over to the opposite corner, a large bodega owned by a notorious volunteer, Colonel Echezaretta. Here they were

The Raid of Mariano

met with a volley; for the owner and his assistants, all volunteers, had formed a barricade of rum-barrels and were intrenched. Amid the lurid flashes the Cubans could be seen tearing down the iron bars of the windows, the shutters were demolished, and then they poured in. The brutal face of the colonel loomed above the crowd; he felled the first man with the butt of his gun, then a machete flashed, and with a sickening gurgle he in turn sank back dead; the others fled from the rear. The insurgents cleaned out the place, blowing open the safe and obtaining a rich haul, for this man's goods were as the spoils of war.

By this time the garrisons from the forts were formed, and led down against the Cubans by one brave young officer. As usual, every one of his superiors had deserted their posts and gone into the city for pleasure, and when the rebels suddenly dashed up to the barricade, the leaderless soldiers had not attempted to stay their passage. This lieutenant now formed his troops behind garden walls and on the azoteas of houses where they could sweep the town. The rebels likewise entrenched themselves, one shouting to the people to lie flat on the floor to escape shots. From house to house the fight raged; the bullets crashed through our shutters, ricocheted on the roof and pavement. The young lieutenant was wounded, and then the Spaniards retired. Delgado next posted guards at the head of every street to hold the approaches.

Under Three Flags in Cuba

I tried to get outside when the firing ceased, but the hotel-keeper dared me to unbar the door. "You must be crazy," he said, "or are you a rebel trying to betray me to your comrades?" and the rascal got so excited I thought he would shoot me in my tracks. Still both from front and back I could see all that I wanted. The Cubans did not come to the house again, but visited a large café opposite. Two young Spanish waiters, half dead with fear, had concealed themselves, one in a barrel, the other in the refrigerator. Several rebel officers came in and opened wine; a piano stood near, and some played and sang. Suddenly, like Jack from the box, a terrified head and shoulders popped from the ice-chest, and begged not to be killed. Nearly frozen, the Spaniard had been forced to come out. How the Cubans laughed! They rubbed his hands, gave him wine, and quite reassured, he played while they sang.

Foraging parties went from house to house and searched for food and clothes. Several invaded the residence of an English shipper, Mr. Hall, taking the clothes from his wardrobe with apologies, stating that he could buy others and their needs were great. Some English ladies staying in the house were terrified, but two lieutenants assured them they need fear nothing, and no one else spoke to them. Though told one door led to a lady's bedroom, some soldiers pushed in and opened the wardrobe. Delgado, seeing this, gave them several strokes with his sheathed machete. "Are we fiends that we war on women,

The Raid of Mariano

or do you want corsets to improve your ugly figures?" he demanded; and then the party withdrew. Some of the men afterwards returned demanding money, and obtained several dollars, though they begged that they should not be reported, as they would be shot if discovered. Houses of Spaniard and Cuban were treated alike unless the owner was known as a volunteer. Then they took everything he had.

After the fighting, parties carried the dead and wounded off through the lines to the woods. All the clothing was collected, and the men came up in batches, obtaining such garments as they most needed, and according to fit. Behind the church in the Plaza Domingo, Hernandez had a clandestine meeting with his fiancée, Leona Calvé, sister of a dentist of Philadelphia then staying with them. It was a terrible risk for the girl, though she were an American born in New Orleans; but these Southern beauties will go through fire and water for the man they love. With little addition, a novelist in Cuba could write romances of life by the tome, far stranger than fiction's fairy flights, but with unhappy and thus unorthodox sequels. The brave Spaniards were all in hiding, and only friends saw her; but the little tête-à-tête was rudely broken by the advent of the cavalry from Havana, who suddenly charged down on the Cuban guards.

"Venga Mambi! Viva España!" they yelled; their sabres flashed in the moonlight, and my heart froze as I saw the weak outposts turn to withstand their furious onslaught. A line of Cubans was thrown across the road, two sharp volleys rang out, and the cavalry drew up, wheeled, and retreated in confusion leaving their dead on the street. But they were only the advance guard. The Cubans had entered at nine and it was now one A. M., and the troops from the immense Havana garrisons were at length en route. The outposts galloped in, announcing the approach of a Spanish column, and having completely outfitted their men and obtained supplies, Delgado and Hernandez marched out on one side as the Spanish regulars poured in on the other. Instead of pursuing the Cubans, the Spaniards wasted several hours drinking and investing the town.

When all danger was past the hotel-keeper came to me and presented his bill, explaining that he wanted money badly. Demurring at its exorbitance for such wretched accommodation, I paid the mercenary wretch. Then he sneaked off to the Cuartel and informed the soldiers that a Yankee at his house had tried to communicate with the rebels, and I was hauled off and lodged in the Cuartel of the Bomberos. Dr. Calvé was also arrested, mainly because he talked English, and probably twenty Cubans were brought in during the night. I was rather annoyed than alarmed, and could sleep but little on the filthy floor, swarming with scorpions and other unclean beasts. A Spanish prison is never desirable under any circumstances. Fortunately, and by the merest

Arrested and Released

chance, I had among my papers the card of Mr. McLean, managing director of the Mariano Railroad, owned by a British company. The military comandante knew him well; my passport was in order, and next morning, after a short examination, my papers were returned and I was liberated with apologies. Calvé also was freed next day. Castillo's raid on Jesus del Monte did not take place as arranged. For some reason General Acosta had sent Delgado to attack Mariano the night before the date fixed for the combined assault. Acosta was severely censured by Gomez for disobedience of orders.

CHAPTER IV

Evangelina Cisneros

STROLLING with Mr. George Eugene Bryson one hot June morning through the lower quarters of Havana, we visited the Real Casa de Recogidas, a prison for abandoned women of the lowest class. We chatted casually with the alcaide, Don José Quintana, in a dingy room pretentiously labelled Sala de Justicia, and after he had partaken of the universal copita at our expense, he graciously invited us to view the prison.

Even the sty of prisoners awaiting execution in Kumassi did not surpass this scene. We entered a passage by a heavy gate, and looked into a vast courtyard through an iron lattice work, like the open side of a huge menagerie cage. Penned within was the most frightful horde of women I have ever seen. Repulsive black viragos raved, swore, and scolded; gorgons, scantily clad, who had lost all sense of shame, clamored at the bars of their den, begging for money, cigars, or drink, and using filthy language when the jailor threw aside the claw-like arms they extended through the grating. Sitting on the steps leading to the cells, a negress accused of child murder was gambling with a hideous mulatto woman incarcerated for highway robbery, while from the

Evangelina Cisneros

incomunicado cell came the ravings of a frenzied wretch just arrested for attempted stabbing. There were perhaps a hundred of these repulsive creatures in all; and the filth, the fœtid stench, and loathsome surroundings turned me sick and faint. The place resembled rather a huge cage of gorillas; for in the degradation of these outcasts the evolutionistic theory was strongly borne out: they resembled beasts rather than human beings.

There suddenly appeared in their midst a white face, young, pure, and beautiful; a maiden of perhaps seventeen was crossing the yard. With her pale features surmounted by masses of dark hair, her simple white dress and dignified bearing, all accentuated by the horrible surroundings, she resembled the Madonna of an old master, inspired with life but plunged into Hades.

"There's money in that face if she were not a fool!" said the brutal little jailer, as he leered covetously through the bars with his one eye, the other having been destroyed in a fight with one of his protégées. The girl, intuitively divining that she was being discussed by strangers who sometimes lounged in the passage and taunted the prisoners, turned and looked in our direction, half defiantly, half contemptuously; but reading the pity on our faces, she averted her gaze as if ashamed of her surroundings, and hurried inside amid a chorus of jeers and insults from her fellow-prisoners. "Beautiful eyes, eh!" said the alcaide's voice behind us; "but they will be spoiled

Under Three Flags in Cuba

in there. She is a shameful little rebel and very brave," he added in a lower tone, "and will never get out, for she is too mulish, when her face would buy her liberty." — This was my introduction to Señorita Evangelina Cosio Cisneros.

Over a further libation the garrulous Don José recounted the story of the young prisoner. This old alcaide was by no means a bad man, the reverse as Spanish officials go; but orders were orders, he explained, and Evangelina might have better treatment if she were more complacent to officers who visited the prison. It is unnecessary to explain what such complacency meant, and my interest in the young Cuban lady was increased a thousandfold when I heard her full story. Quintana called her into the sala, where she received us with the well-bred grace of the salon; but her dignity was assumed. It was so long since she had been spoken to with respect or sympathy, and she soon broke down and wept. From that day forth we were firm friends. Her story reads so like a mediæval romance that many doubt its authenticity; but I have obtained the exact details by interviewing every one concerned, including Evangelina's great-uncle, the Marquis of Santa Lucia and ex-president of the Cuban republic, the priest of Gerona, and Arias Sagrera, secretary to the governor of the Isle of Pines.

Evangelina is the daughter of a well-known family in Camaguey or Puerto Principe province, where the old Castilian grandees settled, and have remained

Filial Devotion

select like the F. F.'s of Virginia. Her father was an officer in the ten years' war, and at the close was reduced to penury, in common with hundreds of other Cubans who lost their all in the insurrection. Evangelina was but a child when her mother died, and with her sisters she was brought up by Señora Nores at Sagua. Her education finished, she rejoined her father in Cienfuegos until the outbreak of the revolution of '95. Then their home became a centre of the Cuban party; and to appreciate the spirit of the Cuban ladies, it is necessary to hear Miss Cisneros relate the story herself, and see her eyes flash with the glow of patriotism as she speaks of the preparations to free Cuba.

But it was the old, old story. Her father was raising a body of cavalry when a traitor betrayed the organization, just before they were to take to the field on June 22, 1895. All the men were arrested. Evangelina's sisters were taken away by friends, but she patiently waited by the prison until the court-martial sentenced her father to death. General Campos was in Santa Clara, and to him Evangelina journeyed. Despite the insults of the soldiers, she waited round the palace for days, and finally met Captain Campos, and through him reached his father. The old soldier was touched by her filial devotion, and commuted the sentence to banishment for life.

Broken in health, the prisoner was removed to the Isle of Pines, where a system similar to the old Australian convict days was in vogue. Escape from the island being almost impossible, the prisoners were engaged in cultivation, and lived in separate huts. Evangelina voluntarily followed her father into exile, and, contented by the reunion, they enjoyed comparative happiness in their seclusion. The military governor, Colonel Menendez, was a quiet man, who troubled his prisoners little; but he was of the Campos' day, and upon Weyler's arrival was recalled. Colonel Berriz, a nephew of General Azcarraga, the Minister of War in Madrid, afterwards Premier, was eligible for any post of fat perquisites and little risk; so he received the appointment. Though married, he had been involved in a notorious scandal in Havana, and altogether was a regular type of blasé Spanish officer and gentleman.

In Gerona, the port of the penal colony, he missed the society of the gay capital. There were but a few wives of exiles, and some indifferent female prisoners there, and the striking beauty of Evangelina soon attracted his notice. He was governor, she a rebel's daughter; he marked the innocent girl as an easy prey, and was exceedingly surprised to find his attentions met with no response. His vanity was hurt, and he at once tried other means.

Without warning, her father was seized, and shut in the protectorado. Half divining the reason of the persecution, Evangelina went to Berriz and begged for her father's release. The governor, gallantly assuring her that he could refuse her nothing, ordered his liberation. Trembling with joy, the

Colonel Berriz

frail girl poured out effusive thanks, but her heart sank when the roué continued: "Thanks are easy, but later I will judge your gratitude;" and he then made violent protestation of love. From that day Evangelina remained closely indoors, and her father, realizing her danger, seldom left her.

After the inspection of prisoners on July 24, he was again placed under arrest; but his daughter, realizing what the persecution implied, did not venture into the brutal officer's presence. Two nights later she had retired, when a knock came at the door. In hope for her father, in fear of her tormentor, she slipped on a dressing-gown, when the door opened and Berriz in full uniform entered. Trembling with fear, she asked her visitor to be seated, and he inquired why she spurned him when she knew her parent's fate was in his hands.

She pitifully begged him to cease molesting her, and prayed him to release her father; but he swore he was devoted to her, threatened and cajoled alternately, and became so persistent in his attentions that she dashed for the door. The colonel seized her by the shoulders, and stifling her screams, forced her back to the inner room. But her cry for help had been heard. In the hotel, near by, some men were gathered, and rushed to the rescue. One, a young Cuban named Betencourt, was an ardent admirer of Evangelina; and with him were Vargas, a clerk, and a young French merchant named Superville. Without ceremony they rushed into the house, seized

Under Three Flags in Cuba

Berriz, and flung him to the ground. Betencourt, not unnaturally, thrashed him soundly, and then he was bound with rope to be taken to the civil judge.

At first the craven cur begged for mercy; then, seeing soldiers standing undecided in the crowd, he shouted for the guard, yelling that the Cuban prisoners were murdering him. From the Cuartel a company of troops doubled up, and the people scattered. They fired down the street killing and wounding several, and then released Berriz and seized Evangelina and her three rescuers. The governor thought it politic to hush up the matter, but unfortunately, prominent citizens had been shot, and an inquiry was imminent. That he was found in a lady's room he was powerless to deny, but he excused himself by saying Evangelina had enticed him to enter, and the men, hiding inside, were ready to kill him, free the prisoners, and seize the island. The story was ludicrous; but rebellion is always scented in Cuba, and Weyler ordered the prisoners brought to Havana for trial for attempted murder and rebellion.

Having locked up Evangelina in the Recogidas, he shut up not only the male participators, but Arias, the secretary of Berriz, and every one likely to have damaging evidence against the governor. Then he coolly allowed the matter to drop, for the screening of Azcarraga's name and honor was far more important than the personal liberty of a dozen Cubans. Miss Cisneros languished ten months in that foul prison without news of her father, and in suspense

The Recogidas

as to her fate. At first the wretched inmates had beaten her, but eventually they left her alone. Few girls of her age could have lived through her experiences; but the hope of reunion with her father sustained her, though her health was greatly impaired. I promised to try and smuggle a note to her parent in the Cabana fortress, and when, by bribing a soldier, the note was delivered and I took her the reply, she cried for joy.

By judicious presents to the venal warden, we soon had the entrée to the prison at all times, and at least were able to cheer her in her loneliness. At this time also Señora Agremonte, Miss Aguilar, Mrs. Sotolongo, and the unfortunate wives of Generals Recio and Rodriguez were held in the Recogidas on political charges. General Lee visited the prison, and protested to Weyler against the herding of these ladies with criminals. Orders were then given to have a separate sleeping-place partitioned off. Mrs. Fitzhugh Lee, the general's noble wife, and her daughter, also called and cheered these ladies greatly. Then the political prisoners were freed and expelled from Cuba, and only Mrs. Sotolongo and Evangelina remained. Mrs. Sotolongo was soon moved to the prison hospital, and Evangelina was again alone.

Meantime Bryson, who had considerable influence in Havana, was working hard to secure the girl's release. The publication of her story in the press we sedulously avoided, realizing that it would stir up further resentment against the helpless prisoner.

Under Three Flags in Cuba

Money is the key to all Spanish jails, and Bryson soon located the military judge in whose charge the case was pigeonholed. He demanded $2000 gold to secure her acquittal, $500 paid in advance as earnest money. He made threats when the cash was not promptly forthcoming; and Bryson, without committing himself, advanced a certain sum to stay action. With a view to extortion, and by the judicial jugglery prevalent in Cuba, the judge strove to force Bryson's hand by fixing a court-martial for the prisoners, and asking a heavy sentence for Evangelina. I doubt if the sentence would have been sustained; it was simply blackmail, and we at once formulated plans to frustrate the scheme by rescuing the girl. The judge, thinking she would induce Bryson to pay the bribe, notified her of impending exile to Africa, but she entered into our plans of rescue with avidity. No risk seemed too great for her to undertake, and finally we had arranged to reach the window of her dormitory by a plank from a house opposite, and were only awaiting the chance to secure her escape from the city, when a new complication arose.

Bryson was ignominiously expelled by General Weyler as an insurgent sympathizer, and at this juncture also the "Official Gazette" contained a notice of impending trial of the Isle of Pines case in furtherance of the game of blackmail. American papers printed garbled accounts from Spanish sources, and it became necessary to publish the true story in New York. I next planned, with the assistance of

Copyright, by the Continental Publishing Co.

Evangelina Cosio Cisneros

First Plans for Rescue

a friend, to visit the prison one evening, and having sent the sentinel from the main gate to purchase cigars as usual, to seize and gag the alcaide when he brought the prisoner out into the sala, which was beyond the inner gates of the prison. The key of the outer postern lay on the official's desk, so Miss Cisneros could then have easily left the building with us; but the supreme difficulty was to secure her escape from Havana. It was arranged with a patriotic engine-driver on the Matanzas Railroad to carry us out in disguise in a freight-car, and deposit us beyond Regla, where the young general Aranguren had promised to meet us by the barrier and cut a way through. Once with the insurgent army she would be comparatively safe, until her passage from the island could be arranged.

This plan we should have carried into effect had not the almost friendless girl suddenly found her name on the lips of the civilized world, and it seemed her release would come pacifically. Mr. Hearst of the "Journal" sent for her history, and I was able to send him the statement of the prison doctor that consumption was inevitable if she suffered further imprisonment, and also two pictures, one taken before her imprisonment and one eight months later. The story made a great sensation on August 27, when published, though unfortunately my full signature was placed above it, and from thenceforth I was under close surveillance and my movements hampered. The press in all parts of the globe took up the case. The ladies of America, and later of Great Britain, started petitions for the girl's release. In a few days over 20,000 signatures had been affixed in the United States. Mrs. Jefferson Davis, Mrs. Julia Ward Howe, Mrs. Logan, Mrs. Grant, Mrs. Sherman, Mrs. McKinley, Mrs. Hodgson Burnett, and many others worked energetically on the case. Mrs. Ormiston Chant took up the petition in England, Lady Henry Somerset and Miss Marie Corelli both actively participating.

The Hon. Hannis Taylor, United States minister to Madrid, presented the petitions to the Queen Regent, and was assured that Evangelina would be sent immediately to a convent, pending investigations; but the unfortunate lady of Spain was powerless to act against Weyler backed by Canovas.

The Spanish press of Havana was furious at the prominence given to the case, and the damage caused thereby to Spain; and "El Comercio" and an even worse production, "La Union Constitucional," were filled with filthy insults and suggestions against Americans in general, and myself in particular. Señor De Lome, the Spanish minister to Washington, did not hesitate to defame the character of the defenceless girl. General Lee had gone to the States for vacation, and he was freely quoted or misquoted in the circular issued by the Spanish legation, and which tried to prove Miss Cisneros of "humble birth." "Nobilitatis virtus non stemma character." It mattered little if she were niece to a marquis or to a

Karl Decker Arrives

laborer,— she was at least a woman in dire need; but the interest, nevertheless, was somewhat lessened. Eventually in eastern Cuba, I obtained signed verification of the relationship from the aged marquis himself, to reassure the excellent people who feared they had been unwittingly interested in the case of a plebeian.

Not only was the Queen Regent's promise that Evangelina should go to a convent never fulfilled, but upon my visiting the prison three days after I heard of the agitation in her favor, Don José met me with a long face, begging me to leave at once, as the prisoner was shut up incomunicado, and a guard had been placed with orders to arrest any one attempting to see her. Luckily Mr. Rockwell of the United States consular service, a friend of the Marquis de Palmerola, had obtained a permit to visit the Recogidas. That permit proved the only means of communicating with the prisoner.

Her rescue by force was now far more difficult, and at this juncture Mr. Karl Decker arrived in Havana. He is a Viking by nature and appearance, and had previously proved his courage during an adventurous trip to Gomez. We spent the first afternoon together at a Regla bull-fight, during which our conversation frequently reverted to Miss Cisneros, and the frustrated plans for her liberation. "She shall be rescued," said Decker, simply, but in a tone that carried conviction with it. Our past plans were reviewed, and setting aside the house I had first selected,

Under Three Flags in Cuba

Decker picked out an empty residence in the Calle O'Farrill, from the roof of which a ladder could be stretched to the parapet of the Recogidas with less risk of discovery by the sentinels of the adjacent arsenal, and the cuartels of artillery and Orden Publico.

The details of the rescue have been fully published by Decker himself in the "Story of Evangelina Cisneros;" so I need not recapitulate fully, how, on the night of October 5, the first attempt to cut the bars was unsuccessful, but on the following night the prison was broken and the prisoner freed. Also how Miss Cisneros was hidden in Havana until Saturday, while the police started a house-to-house search, but dressed as a boy, she escaped on board the steamship "Seneca," having in the gathering darkness presented a regular passport as Juan Soldado to police-inspector Perez at the gangway, without discovery. When she was safely at sea, we invited every friend on sight to a birthday dinner; and a convivial party gathered, though but three of us knew what that birthday really was.

On Sunday Decker[1] sailed under an assumed name on the Spanish steamer "Panama," just as the police obtained warrants for his arrest; for the full story was printed in New York and the Spanish consul

---

[1] Mr. Decker during the winter formulated a plan to rescue Captain Dreyfus which Mr. Hearst wished to effect without causing international complications. We should have probably started from the Cuban coast; but the Maine disaster and war diverted this unprecedented journalistic enterprise.

The Rescuers Revealed

notified the authorities. My rooms in the Plaza Cristo were raided at 3 A. M. on Monday, but I had anticipated this and departed to the country. The police tore my things to pieces, but though two hard steel saws, used on the bars, lay in a strop case on the dressing-table, and letters from Gomez to his wife, which I had been asked to forward, were concealed in the false fly-leaf of Webster's Dictionary, the astute detectives found nothing.

The entire American nation arose to welcome the sweet-faced Cuban girl, whose case is without parallel in modern history. When enthusiastic thousands greeted her and her praises were on every lip, she did not forget her bleeding country, and one of her first acts was to privately visit President McKinley to plead the cause of the despairing womanhood of Cuba, writhing under the iron heel of the relentless Weyler.

This is a well-known story, though for obvious reasons fictitious names were used at the time, that the identity of the rescuers remaining in Havana might be hidden. No one knew, then, that the one man, who, by reason of his determined pluck and thorough knowledge of the situation, made the rescue a success by superintending local details, procuring tools and disguises, cutting the bars, and arranging for the dangerous embarkation of the fugitive, was William McDonald, well known in shipping circles in Cuba, and that the mysterious house of refuge that the police hunted for in vain was the residence of Señor Carbonelle of the Casa Hidalgo. Both these gentlemen willingly ran the risk of breaking prison and sheltering Miss Cisneros, absolutely without personal interest. They had never seen the prisoner, but joined in the enterprise with avidity, McDonald for the spice of adventure he so dearly loved, and Carlos Carbonelle because Miss Cisneros was suffering for the Cuban cause. Little did this noble Cuban expect the sequel when he took such risk for a compatriot. "The brave deserve the fair," and who shall say the age of chivalry is passed? He carefully guarded his protégée through the three terrible days in Havana. When war was declared in the following April, he left Cuba to accept a captaincy on General Lee's staff. Hitherto his part in the rescue was necessarily secret. When he visited the general in his old Virginia home, he was formally introduced to another visitor, Miss Cisneros. With great surprise did host and hostess learn of the previous romantic meeting of these two guests. Need I add the finale to this chance reunion? Dressed in his simple American uniform, with only Mrs. Logan and a few friends as witnesses, Captain Carbonelle led his bride privately to the altar in Baltimore, thus escaping the vulgar notoriety that the climax of such a romance would have brought them at a public wedding. He went to the front with General Lee immediately after. Now they are living happily in Havana near the scene where manifest destiny first brought them together; there is

The Quinta of Aldecoa

also a wee Evangelina, but, as Kipling would say, "that is another story."

Several weeks after his daughter's rescue, Colonel Cosio y Cisneros was removed to Aldecoa prison hospital, where I surreptitiously gained entrance and visited him. He was terribly emaciated, but overjoyed at his daughter's release, and quoted the famous words "La Libertad" from "Don Quixote," gladly accepting the increased severity of his lot, as the penalty of his daughter's liberation.

In this Quinta, shut in cages round the wall like wild beasts, were insane creatures, chiefly Cubans driven mad through confinement or starvation. Many were violent, but no attempt was made to pad the cell or restrain patients with strait-jackets. In one cage was a cousin of General Menocal, a medical student suffering from acute melancholia, following imprisonment for aiding rebellion. Next door a blear-eyed captain of guerillas foamed and raged, "deeds of blood rising dreadful in his soul." On one side were the women. One girl, crazed by want, had torn off her clothes, and danced naked constantly, dropping occasionally from exhaustion, but renewing her orgies when she had regained her breath. A negress screamed constantly for Free Cuba and cursed Weyler; her husband had been shot. A mild-eyed little woman sat silently nursing an imaginary child, only to spring up like a tigress as one approached, swearing they had murdered her babe. Aldecoa was but another picture of the frightful effects of the

Under Three Flags in Cuba

war, by cruelty, oppression, and starvation, — far less merciful weapons than the naked swords of the guerillas. Colonel Cosio was liberated by General Blanco a few months later, a mental and physical wreck.

CHAPTER V

THE DOWNFALL OF WEYLER. — FAILURE OF AUTONOMY OBVIOUS. — GENERAL BLANCO. — THE DE LOME LETTER. — SPAIN'S FINANCIAL DISABILITIES.

"EL Gran Español" is dead. The rumor travelled from mouth to mouth in Havana on August 6th, despite the attempted suppression of the news of the assassination of the Spanish Premier. Little did the anarchist who dealt the fatal blow realize that he was striking away the main pillar of Weylerism, and bringing down the whole fabric with a crash.

Azcarraga's futile attempt to hold the reins passed, and the Liberal Party assumed power. Then, though no paper dare print the story, it was generally known that Weyler was to be recalled, and either Campos or Blanco would reign in his stead. The recall came on October 6, 1897. Every one rejoiced but the volunteers; the loyal Instituto was furious when the complete reversal of the Cuban policy was determined by Sagasta, who had long foreseen that American intervention could be prevented only by drastic measures. When autonomy was talked of, they swore to prevent it by force of arms. Indignant manifestos were posted through the city, calling all loyal Spaniards to employ pacific and active force to combat such humiliation of Spain by a weak ministry. Weyler made paraleipsical speeches of self-glorification to foster these sentiments, hoping the determined attitude of the volunteers, by established precedent, would coerce the Madrid government to retain him as Captain-General.

It seemed that October would innovate a reign of terror in Cuban cities; but Sagasta promptly cabled a threat to disarm the volunteers in case of disaffection, holding Weyler responsible for all disorder. Unused to such firm opposition, the egregious loyalists wavered, and Weyler, realizing that in playing with fire, he had nearly kindled a flame against the government that he could not control, quieted the turbulent spirits, and retired to the steamship "Montserrate," three days before General Blanco's arrival. Thus a rising of Spaniards in Cuba against Spain was narrowly averted. Any disturbances then would have precipitated a general massacre of Cubans in the city. The volunteers had long threatened a sort of St. Bartholomew's Eve, and for three weeks noted colonials who had taken no part in the rebellion dared not venture on the streets.

Weyler and his party took to Spain the spoils of the campaign, and the president of the Spanish Bank in Havana committed suicide to evade the crisis which he was left to face.

Don Ramon Blanco landed on Sunday, October 31st, and was received in ominous silence. He little realized the bitterness of the Cubans against Spain that Weyler had fostered, and optimistically spoke of

The Autonomist Cabinet

an early end of the reconcentration, and the disintegration of the insurgent forces, when they found a liberal home rule was instituted. He soon discovered his to be a thankless task. The Spaniards were opposed to him. The Cubans had fought for nearly three years for an ideal, they had previously been bitterly tricked by the Zanjon treaty, and had no further faith left in Spanish promises. They promptly rejected the new measures. The handful of autonomists in Havana assumed office, but they were either exaltados (extreme liberals), or Cubans who favored Independence, but were eager to accept half measures peaceably. Marcus Garcia, appointed Civil Governor of Santa Clara, was a rebel general in the last war. Señor Galvez and Dr. Bruson had no love for Spanish control, and the latter had been a powerful enemy to Weyler. Señores Giberga and Govin had brothers in the insurrection, and had both been forced to leave Cuba through political persecution. These men formed the Cabinet under the autonomical régime.

The chief official positions were given to Cubans, and Blanco instituted radical changes, despite the opposition of the Peninsulars. The entire change of officials in Havana made it again possible for me to move freely in the city. The English wife of one of the officials arranged for me to meet the prominent members of the new Cabinet, and I was thus able to obtain exceedingly clear ideas of the reforms. On November 6th, I had long interviews with General Pando and President Galvez. The former evidently knew the absolute impossibility of pacification, the latter thought the insurgents would accept the measures, when they found them genuine. Other officials were not so optimistic. We, who knew the attitude of the Cubans in the field, realized the impotence of autonomy either in checking the rebellion or aiding the reconcentrados.

The starving patriots never wavered, and only two brothers named Cuervo, unimportant leaders, surrendered with a handful of war-worn sans culottes, though money and position were offered to all who came in. The Cubans knew Spain's perfidy too well, and while they trusted Blanco's good faith, they could not trust the government behind him.

With a view of inducing further surrenders, envoys were despatched to offer bribes to various unimportant leaders to desert their generals and accept autonomy. Gomez published a general order that such envoys captured inciting desertion would be treated as spies and shot. If his followers wished to desert their flag, there was little to prevent their presenting themselves at the nearest town. Undeterred by this order, a Spanish engineer named Ruiz, colonel of the Fire Brigade, and a general favorite, offered to induce his former chum, Nestor Aranguren, to come in with his command. As a member of the Union Club I knew and esteemed Ruiz, and as General Rodriguez had sent me a copy of the proclamation of Gomez respecting such envoys, I showed him this, which I gave to Congressman King when he was investigat-

The Execution of Colonel Ruiz

ing the conditions of Cuba. Ruiz laughed, saying, "Nestor will never shoot an old friend." Two days later he rode into the insurgent camp near Jaruco, and was welcomed by Aranguren, who had no suspicion of the purport of his visit. Then, in the presence of the whole command, Ruiz urgently pressed the Cubans to accept the generous autonomy of Spain, adding that in exchange for their terrible privations, comforts and employment awaited all who would come in with him to Havana and surrender.

"You will come, my friend?" he said, turning to Aranguren. The young Cuban replied sadly: "You were my friend, but you tempted us to betray our country and to desert our general. You are now my prisoner." A court-martial was formed; and though Aranguren advocated mercy, the other officers stated that it was necessary to show that their orders must be respected and Spain taught a salutary lesson. Despite the prohibition, Ruiz, presuming on his friendship, had attempted to induce desertion and must pay the penalty. The poor fellow was shot at sundown. The sentence was terribly harsh, but just.

General Lee, at the instance of Señor Truffaine, acting consul of Russia, sent Señores Tosca and Chacon to try to save the unfortunate envoy, but they were too late. Ruiz went with his eyes open, and he had no more right in the Cuban lines than André in Washington's.

Only a few weeks before, a doctor had wished to take out medicine to a hospital de sangre near

Under Three Flags in Cuba

Havana. Dodging the sentries, we managed to drop over the barricade at Las Vegas, and reached Castillo's camp in safety. I had an interesting interview with this ex-professor. He foretold the absolute rejection of autonomy, and was opposed to American Intervention in Cuba. "Let us win our own fight," he said, "for not only shall we then more highly prize our independence, but we shall have earned respect abroad for its achievement."

I recrossed the lines next day with great difficulty, and Castillo moved to Managua. Three days later, he was betrayed by a traitor, a Frenchman, who, on the plea of showing him some horses, led him and a few staff officers into an ambush commanded by Captain Ruano of the Artillery. He fell, shot through the heart, and two others perished also. Young Delgado spurred his horse through the civil guards, hacking one down, and escaping with a cut from the other that nearly severed his arm. I soon saw my poor friend's body carted through Havana, exposed to the gibes of the Spanish mob. A bribe secured me a closer inspection in the Morgue. The fatal shot had been fired so close that the charge had blown gaps in the flesh, and charred the wound. With machetes the Spanish assassins had then hacked the head to a jelly. Castillo was only twenty-six.

Several chiefs of the Havana district followed him. Colonel Urra, a brave but not a highly educated young officer, was betrayed and killed in a hospital

Death of Aranguren

six miles from the capital. The following week Colonel Piterra was killed in battle, and some weeks later a negro deserter led a Spanish column to a rebel prefect's house in the woods where Aranguren was visiting that morning, to write and receive despatches. A file of men could easily have surprised and captured the young officer alive; but two battalions of soldiers commanded by Colonel Benidicto, fired volleys through the palmleaf walls of the house, killing the prefect, his aged mother, and baby, and dangerously wounding his wife and eldest daughter. Aranguren also fell wounded, and was prodded to death by the bayonets of the valorous soldiery. Thus perished the "Marion of Cuba," at the age of twenty-three, under the humane rule that was to conciliate the Cubans. And Spain protested against the Cuban brutality that tried and shot Ruiz for a crime that is death in any army.

General Blanco did try to institute a more humane policy; the fault lay with his officers. He liberated numbers of political prisoners, the "Competitor" crew included; capital punishment for rebels was abolished, and even the leader, Rius Rivera, was offered liberty, on condition that he would advocate autonomy. He and Colonel Bacallo refused absolutely to do this. Other charges were then formulated against the colonel, but General Pando visited Rivera in prison, and begged him in a friendly way to accept Blanco's simple conditions. "Patria cara, carior libertas." But Rivera, reversing the order, said, "My liberty is

Under Three Flags in Cuba

dear, but my country is dearer; I will never betray it." Finding him obdurate, he was shipped to Spain. Dr. Congosto in person told me that he would be given provisional liberty in the Peninsula; but he was incarcerated in the terrible Montjuich, and suffered severely until released with other prisoners of war when peace was declared.

Señor Canalejas visited Cuba in the late autumn on a diplomatic mission, and in the interests of his newspaper "El Heraldo." He accompanied a column under General Bernal that attacked Ducasse in the Cuzco Hills, and visited the reconcentrado settlements. He came optimistic, was soon doubtful, and left with pessimistic views of the situation. As a humane and intelligent Spaniard, he expressed his views openly to me, in three interviews that appeared simultaneously in the "London Chronicle" and "New York Journal."

I had just taken a long tour through the island, visiting every settlement of consequence; and a report of these horrible conditions in Cuba caused much indignation in England. A meeting was held in London, protesting against the horrors of Spanish rule. This, together with the frank utterances of Canalejas, roused the ire of Señor De Lome, the Spanish Minister in Washington, who had previously been greatly disturbed by an editorial in the "Sun" of July 29 regarding my investigations. He wrote a letter to Señor Canalejas, from which I extract freely: —

The De Lome Letter

"The situation here remains unchanged. The prologue of this second method of warfare will end the day that the Colonial Cabinet is appointed, and it relieves us in the eyes of this country of a part of the responsibility of what happens, and places it upon the heads of the Cubans they believe immaculate. . . . The Message has undeceived the insurgents, who expected something else; it has paralyzed the action of Congress, but I consider it bad. Beside the natural and inevitable coarseness with which he repeats all the press said of Weyler, it shows McKinley is weak, and catering to the rabble, and beside, a *politicastro* (pot-house politician), who desires to stand in well with me and also the Jingoes of his party * * *

"I do not believe you pay enough attention to the rôle of England. That English newspaper "canaille" swarming at your hotel, corresponds not only with the Journal, but also with the best newspapers and reviews of London * * *

"It is most important that you should agitate the question of commercial relations, even though it is only for effect, and you should send a man here that I might use to make a propaganda among senators and others in opposition to the Junta and to win over exiles * * *

"Always your attentive friend and servant who kisses your hand"

Enrique Dupuy de Lome

Señor Canalejas had accorded me full permission to publish his views both in New York and London, and stated that he hoped thereby to remove misun-

Under Three Flags in Cuba

derstandings in both places. Such frankness did not accord with De Lome's dissemblance.

Unfortunately for the minister, the letter was afterwards dropped in Havana, found by a Cuban, and forwarded to New York. Its publication led to his retirement in disgrace, for having insulted the president elect. He subsequently charged me with stealing the letter from the Hôtel Inglaterra, though I was not in Havana at the time. Previously, being unable to disprove certain statements, he had cast puerile aspersions on my character, first representing me as a deserter from the British army, and later as a cashiered lieutenant. Since I had an honorable discharge for injuries sustained in the Queen's service, and being neither politician nor public character, his reflections were immaterial.

On December 6, I started through the island by rail, and shall never forget the sights I witnessed, moving from town to town. Settlements I had visited in June containing five thousand reconcentrados had now but five hundred emaciated wretches on the last verge of starvation. In Matanzas City twenty-five dead bodies, many of them women and girls, were collected in the streets in a single morning, and flung into a common grave. The photograph I took of the scene was too indecent for publication. On the "centrals," in the towns and villages, on the railroads, it was the same story, — oppression, starvation, disease, and death. The uncertainty of life, the preponderance of pain over pleasure, and the malig-

The December Message

nity of human existence in this great age of progress, were truisms forcibly thrust on one in Cuba.

The President's December message, advising further delay, that the efficacy of autonomy in restoring peace and prosperity to Cuba could be tested before intervention took place, was plainly the death-knell to the dying residue of the half-million people dispossessed by Weyler. General Blanco solicited aid to relieve the distress. His army was nine months in arrears, the officials were long unpaid, and the meagre subscriptions collected were sequestered long before reaching the reconcentrados. He provided large zones for cultivation, — the people were too weak to till the ground, and then weeks must have elapsed even for the growth of the succulent tubers so easily raised in Cuba. It was impossible for the people to return to their devastated farms; their houses were destroyed, crops and stock gone. Spain's impotence was obvious. With her exhausted treasury, the insurgents saw the futility of her promises and refused to surrender.

Some brutal Spaniards still ill-treated the hapless reconcentrados.[1] The day before I arrived in Santa

[1] Shameful atrocities continued in the field when Sagasta was loudly proclaiming his policy of peace and good-will toward the rebels. Among many I can vouch for, the murder of Señor Sardovar, the Insurgent Civil Governor of Havana, and his wife, and the abduction of his daughter, by guerillas at Juraco on December 8, '97, were the worst. The eldest girl, Corinne, seventeen years old, has never been traced; the mutilated body of Eloise, aged fifteen, was found at the foot of a cliff by a newly arrived and humane Spanish officer of the Tapaste garrison, Captain José Nestares. Searching further, he discovered the youngest girl, Celina, aged five, lying

Under Three Flags in Cuba

Domingo, an aged pacifico passed the lines to the zona in search of food, and failing to return by sunset, slept outside. At five A. M. he was found sleeping not one hundred yards from the forts by guerillas, and dragged in. At the railroad crossing the leader, in the presence of the military commandante and the old man's daughter and her two children, swore that he would teach these dogs to stay outside and talk to rebels, and with a vicious lunge, drove his sword through the old man's body. I saw that corpse just before it was buried. I returned from Santa Clara with Mr. Madrigal, United States Consul to Columbia, and he and his assistant can vouch for the unburied bodies being torn to pieces by vultures, and of women and children dying by the railroad track.

The countryside was inhabited with spectres. The real-life scenes were as pages torn from the "Inferno." The shame of it, that under the shadow of Free America the despairing cry of these innocent people should have passed unheeded until too late! The insurgents were soldiers, — they had invited their fate. The women and children were innocent, helpless, and starving. We may now hurrah over the glories of the past campaign, and wave the Stars and

stunned and bruised in the bushes. He sent the child to the Paula hospital, the body to the morgue. The little one soon recovered consciousness, and told a revolting story of the murder of her parents, and the treatment of her sisters which culminated in the death of Eloise. The child had clung screaming to her sister's corpse, so was struck on the head and thrown over the cliff with it. The bushes had miraculously broken the descent. Celina is now in the Cuban Home in Key West.

Reconcentration Figures

Stripes on high; but what has been accomplished at the cost of many brave lives is too late for the achievement of the true object, — an object that might have been peaceably attained had a firm policy been followed two years ago, by an appeal to Great Britain and perhaps another power for combined intervention. The starving reconcentrados are no more; they are already exterminated, — a statement verified by General Blanco and Secretary Congosto when peace was declared. In the light of present knowledge, one sees many reasons for a conciliatory policy in dealing with Spain, that peace might be maintained; yet, with the cries of the stricken ringing in our ears, it seemed that the Washington Administration was like a strong man watching the life beaten out of a child, intervening when the child was dying, and the bully exhausted by his efforts. The monster is now dragged off and given his quietus — but lo! his victim also is dead.

Between Weyler's band of '96 and Christmas of '97, twenty-two months, the parish priest of Artemisa registered 5123 deaths. More people died in that small but overcrowded town, in that short period, than the old register recorded from 1806, i. e., ninety years. In Santa Clara district alone 71,847 burial permits were issued during Weyler's régime, and such figures are representative of the island, during the extermination of the Cuban population. The Spanish conscripts were also in dire plight, and of the army that Weyler mobilized, the following rough reports were published for deduction after he left: —

Died in hospital	32,534
Killed and missing	10,000
Invalided to Spain	25,000
Under treatment	14,413
	81,947

Thus one-third of the force had gone, and to close observers the day when Spanish honor could no longer sustain such sacrifice was rapidly approaching. It was a question of endurance, and, despite their straits, the insurgents promised well to be victors in the trial. Many intelligent Spaniards, seeing the abandonment of the island to the Cubans imminent, advocated its loss by war with the United States, as an honorable solution of the difficulty.

The acts of officers emulously Weyleric, the rioting of the volunteers, and continued rebel successes, might have intimidated an officer less resolute than General Blanco. Though he bravely held to his post, he was also facing a dire financial crisis, which could not long be tided over.

Despite legal enactments, the colonial paper money sank lower and lower, until it was finally worth only the value of the actual cash deposit covering this wretched currency, in the Banco Español. The soldiers and army contractors would no longer receive the paper money at face value, more especially since their accounts were many months in arrears.

Spain's Financial Condition

To consolidate her debts, including notes raised during the ten years' war on the Spanish bank in Havana, and to convert the remainder of the six per cent Cuban bonds raised in 1886, Spain in 1890 created thirty-five millions sterling nominal of Cuban five per cent redeemable bonds. Both these issues, Cuban bonds so called, were not raised for use in the colony, but for the benefit of the Imperial treasury, though they were guaranteed by the proceeds of the Cuban customs and by all the revenues of the Cuban treasury,— Imperial liabilities coolly saddled upon the colony. But the conditions were so unfavorable that the government succeeded only in consolidating the floating debt and war notes with seven millions sterling of the new bonds; and the conversion of the '86 bonds could not be carried out. I have shown in a previous chapter, how the insurrection had been precipitated by the introduction of the sham Abarzuza reforms, to satisfy certain capitalists, who had refused to accept Spain's mortgage of Cuba unless self-government were instituted to insure peace, and thus the value of their security. When the insurrection broke out in February, 1895, one million sterling of the '86 bonds and the unused twenty-seven million sterling of the '90 issue lay unused in reserve. The Cortes authorized the government to use these bonds, and from March, 1895, to July, '96, $64,625,300 was realized from sale of bonds, and cash advances made by Spanish and foreign banks, covered only by a deposit of the bonds to an equivalent of the amount. As the revolution spread, and an extension of the advances was asked, a lien on Imperial sources of revenue was demanded and given to the banks. The '86 bonds sold at 101.70 in August, '95; in February, '96, they realized 94. The five per cent bonds of '90 opened at 89.50 and dropped to 86 in December, '95. The Spanish Transatlantic Steamship Company accepted bonds at 80.23 for transporting troops to Cuba. The Hispano Colonial Bank of Barcelona accepted the '90 bonds at 71.95 to cover their advances to the Imperial treasury. The Banco Español and other banks also accepted these securities with varying limitations. By September, '96, all the bonds were sold or pledged; their proceeds were almost exhausted, and the government found they would experience stupendous difficulty in raising fresh funds.

 The Bank of Spain then demanded a lien on the Spanish Custom House as a guarantee for their advances. The Banque de Paris et Pays Bas refused to renew the bonds it had received. Not only was war in Cuba increasing, but the Philippine insurrection was also raging. An interior loan at 5 per cent guaranteed by the Peninsular customs was authorized by the Cortes to meet the crisis. It realized 372,000,000 pesetas ($72,019,200). This loan was quickly absorbed in reimbursements and current expenses, but the bonds given as guarantees to the banks were released.

 The year 1897 opened with a paltry balance of

Spain's Financial Condition

$1,576,721.96 from the loan, and the surplus Cuban bonds were then quoted at low and still sinking prices. By the summer all was gone. The expenditure of the Cuban war alone was costing $10,500,000 per month; and, only by heroic effort, non-payment of pensions and wages of civil servants and soldiers at home and abroad, and by deferring the payment of army contractors, the Imperial treasury managed to just sustain the struggle: the crisis was rapidly approaching, when General Blanco arrived in Cuba. The financial condition was unsupportable. Even had the government in Madrid authorized unlimited taxation in the Peninsula, the expenses of past loans and the meeting of liabilities would have swallowed up any amount that could have been raised from the overburdened people.

War with the United States delayed the crash. It stirred the patriotism of the burdened Spaniards to make fresh effort, and stilled the claims of long-suffering creditors. Spain is still deeply involved, and even with the repudiation of the Cuban debt can hardly be solvent. Had the United States not intervened in Cuba, the financial crisis [1] would have be-

---

[1] The Spanish Minister of Finance has now accepted the Cuban and Philippine debts, thus raising the national debt to 380,000,000 sterling. He reduces the interest on the debts, however, by forty and thirty-five per cent, respectively. Even this leaves a permanent deficit of eight millions sterling per annum in the Revenue. Reduction of interest on national bonds held in Spain may aid this deficit a little. By a revised income tax, a succession duty, and surtaxes on existing imposts, he hopes to cover the residue; but

come acute long ere this; and even if the island were not relinquished to the Cubans, the army could not have been sustained there, and active operations against the rebels must have ceased. Thoughtful Spaniards may well sigh, "Pobre España;" but the unfortunate country is but reaping as she sowed.

Spain's solvency cannot be possible until the cessation of the colonial drain of the past four years has proved reactive.

CHAPTER VI

A TRIP ACROSS CUBA. — REJECTION OF AUTONOMY. — CROSSING THE SPANISH LINES. — A DEVASTATING COLUMN. — A NIGHT OF HORROR. — THE ATTACK ON ESPERANZA.

THE President in his December Message asked Congress to allow Spain time to test the efficacy of autonomy in restoring peace to Cuba. Many friends of the islanders realized that the reforms were futile. In '95 autonomy might have been applied as a national prophylactic for rebellion; Weylerism had made the disease chronic, and ultimate death to Spanish sovereignty inevitable. It was evident, from the attitude of the Cuban leaders, that compromise was too late. Despite the blows dealt their cause, the robust energy of their faith, and hope, which Voltaire says is God's greatest gift to man, had sustained them through the past, and would sustain them until their penultimate object — the withdrawal of Spain — was accomplished.

The situation was anomalous, — the Spanish legions could not subdue the colonials, neither could the latter expel the legions by force of arms. But endurance in the end would win the day; fever, food, and finance presented problems that must sooner or later overwhelm the Spanish army. But from Spanish sources roseate reports of impending disintegration, colored by the surrender of a few war-worn patriots, led many in authority to believe the end of Cuba's struggle by the general acceptance of autonomy, was approaching.

Senators and congressmen were discussing the matter in Washington. Upon the success or failure of autonomy, the whole question of intervention and almost certain war with Spain rested. It was suggested to a certain journalist that he should visit the Cuban leaders and ascertain their exact attitude. He declined, and then my name was suggested for the mission. Far more competent men would have been glad to go, but previous knowledge of the country was essential for success. Mr. Henry Norman in London, and Mr. Hearst in New York were keenly interested in the issue, and warmly commended the mission to determine if the insurgents would or would not accept autonomy, and if there were any disposition of the under leaders and men to surrender.

Upon receipt of a cipher message in Havana in December, I first applied for a pass from the Spanish authorities, pointing out that as they were unable to send envoys to the field, the actual attitude of the rebels, of extreme moment to them, might be obtained by issuing me a permit to cross their lines. Knowing full well the firm attitude of the rebels, and not unnaturally wishing to hide the truth from the United States, that permission was refused, but without comment. I had anticipated this, and two

Rejection of Autonomy

days later I started on my mission in Pinar del Rio.

I will not enter into details of my journey through the West, as I wish to deal more fully with my trip through less known districts across the Trocha. Sufficient to say that all leaders were absolutely against compromise, and after some trials and adventures, I obtained, both by courier and personal interview, the signed statements of all Cubans of note in Las Villas and Occidente, rejecting in every detail the autonomy offered by Spain. In the division of the West, Pinar del Rio and Havana, General Rodriguez, the respective chiefs of his brigades, General Betencourt and his commanders in Matanzas, General Maximo Gomez, Miguel Gomez, Carrillo and Robau in Santa Clara, and all subordinate officers in their respective commands, attested their solemn determination to continue the fight until Spain relinquished the island. "Independence or Death" was the universal motto, and in Havana and Matanzas divisions it seemed that death was more likely to claim the rebel force before victory was theirs. They were in a pitiful condition, ragged and absolutely starving. December was an exceptionally cold month, and pneumonia made sad ravages among the emaciated patriots. But recruits constantly slipped out through the barriers, and when General Rodriguez read to his assembled command his rejection of autonomy, loud "Vivas!" were raised, and it was evident that the leaders and men of superior intelligence were not alone in the determination to fight on to the bitter end. I had finished the first half of my journey on January 1st, in Las Villas.

To reach eastern Cuba from Santa Clara, the great Trocha had to be crossed. Finding the trip by land fraught with difficulty, I took the more devious route, passing round it by sea. On January 3, 1898, I safely entered Nuevitas to take the train for Puerto Principe City. My boatman smuggled saddle and riding outfit ashore that night. I had registered at the Hotel Telegrafo under an assumed name. The proprietor, a Cuban Spaniard born in New York, was a lieutenant in the Spanish service, but an ardent patriot at heart. I soon learned that the authorities in Havana had cabled the commanders of various ports to frustrate my mission, and a celador of police visited the hotel that night after I had retired, to make inquiry into my identity; but mine host assured him that I was the engineer of a Minas sugar-estate, and he retired satisfied.

There was an American prisoner under guard in the hotel, who was to leave in the morning. My curiosity was aroused, and I soon learned that it was Colonel Funston, commander of Garcia's Artillery, who had been captured at Minas a few days previous. He was fortunately without arms; thin and emaciated by a long campaign, he did not seem an important prisoner. The officers searched him carefully, and finding nothing upon him, concluded that he was a deserter, and sent him to General Latorre in

Colonel Funston

Nuevitas. Had they known that the man in their hands was the redoubtable American artillerist, who had virtually shelled Spain from the interior of Santiago, he would have fared badly; but he was sent to the consul at Caibarien on the following day, on condition that he should leave Cuba. He was under close surveillance, and I did not attempt to communicate with him, since it might have compromised us both. He weighed but ninety-five pounds then, and I feared he was going home to die. We met again at Tampa in the following June. He then wore the uniform of Colonel of United States Volunteers. "I do not believe in giving commissions to such small men; they do not inspire the respect of their troops," remarked an officer one day as Funston passed. His opinion may have been altered since by the continued dash and bravery of that officer at the head of his Kansas regiment in the Philippines, and his promotion on the field to Brigadier-General for his gallant services.

The insurgents were strong in Puerto Principe. Consequently but one train per week ran from Nuevitas to the inland capital, Puerto Principe City, though that railroad furnished sole means of communication with the outside world. General Pando was in the town, holding a conference with Generals Castellanos and Latorre, and evidently important operations were pending. The hotel was crowded with officers, and I had to keep close in a fusty little chamber to escape their demand for cedula and passports. I was relieved to hear that a train left on the second morning.

Punctually at six A. M. we pulled out. The American cars were moving forts, each cased in loopholed sheets of iron. A company of soldiers marched beyond the engine, prodding the track with long poles for dynamite. Other companies were posted in fortified freight-cars, and a rough dining-car was fixed in the centre of the corridor, as the journey of seventy miles might take that number of hours.

On the trip I met a young captain of commissary, a Cuban of Irish descent, named O'Reilly, who had entered the military supply service before the war, and continued to hold his position, since it entailed no hostile act against Cuba, and his resignation or desertion to the insurgents would have led to reprisals against his family, living on an estate at Minas.

The railway runs for forty miles through dense woods and swamp, after which the country becomes clearer, and Principe City stands in the centre of a vast savannah. We were keeping a sharp lookout for insurgents; the train fairly crawling through the woods, as frequent attempts were made to blow up the troop cars. This seems reprehensible warfare, though either the engine or troop cars were always the objective, and passenger cars were spared. By thus attacking the line of communications, the Spaniards were forced to employ thousands of men to guard the tracks and trains, and consequently had

Our Train Attacked

less strength to employ in the field. Singularly the largest stockholders in this particular railway were Cubans then in the manigua, and they were constantly destroying their own property, to prevent the enemy's use of the same.

Some twenty miles from Nuevitas a shot rang out. I ran to the outer platform of the car and saw our advance-guard tearing back toward the train, dragging the body of one of their number. From the dense underbrush dropping shots came thick and fast, though not a leaf stirred. The troops in the armored cars were now replying vigorously, the train pulled up with a jerk, and the guard tumbled aboard. The limp body was handed up with scant ceremony, but the poor boy was already dead.

The fire was too hot to stand exposed, and I withdrew inside. The Mausers crashed regularly, and above them rang out staccatoed detonations of the Cubans' Remingtons, while the bullets slashed angrily against the iron facings of the cars, and rang on the metal fittings, like the bull's-eye shots in a Coney Island shooting-gallery. The Cubans soon realized the futility of wasting fire on such defences, and did not shoot long after the guard had gained cover. Then we could see the glint of machetes in the trees, and the Spaniards yelled that the mambis were charging. I quietly seized my things, thinking if the Cubans rushed the train I could go back with them. A few only broke cover, yelling like fiends; the leader fell. To charge in face of such a fire was suicide, and they wheeled and disappeared in the forest.

It was evening when we reached our destination, and, thanks only to my friend the captain, did I get through the station unquestioned, for at every turn the secret police scrutinize strangers, opening their parcels and searching their clothes for insurgent papers. I was carrying several private letters to leaders in the field, and a note to a lawyer, Dr. Prada, a member of the local Junta, who had been sentenced to imprisonment for life by Weyler and reprieved by his successor. A friend gave me a trustworthy guide to carry me to the house, and in due time I reached a handsome residence, was presented to a comfortable matron, the Señora Prada, and in turn to her three vivacious daughters.

"Their house and they were at my disposition, and the señor would be in soon." With feminine inquisitiveness the good lady tried deftly to elicit the purport of my visit, the girls chatted nineteen to the dozen, and I made myself very much at home. We discussed the situation, I with great freedom. Later a young son entered. Wishing to air the only English he knew, he remarked unappropriately: "Spanish vera good, Cuban no vera good, me Spanish!" This was a revelation, and put me on my guard; I retired shortly after, promising to see the señor later, and returned to my friend for explanation.

"Bobo! Sin Verguenza!" he exclaimed angrily, "why, he took you to the house of Colonel Prada.

Doctor Prada

I congratulate you, amigo, that the colonel was out. Had you delivered the letter you would have now been in jail, and who could tell the end? The colonel is not a bad man, and his wife is muy simpatico; but then his clear duty to Spain?"
Later he guided me in person to the man I sought. I found Dr. Prada an exceedingly intelligent gentleman. Though under surveillance and but recently released from horrible imprisonment, he was still allied to the cause. His brother, a graduate of an American college, joined us later, and they formulated plans by which I could reach the field.[1]

---

[1] Of the hundreds of correspondents who have visited Cuba but few have actually passed to the field. George Eugene Bryson was with Maceo, under the Campos régime. Dr. Shaw Bowen, guided by the son of the British Consul at Santiago, interviewed Maceo on a neutral sugar-estate. Charles Michaelson visited Havana Province in 1896, and was imprisoned and expelled by Weyler. Grover Flint, I believe, was the only correspondent to cross the Trocha into Camaguey. Scovel and Rea witnessed the western invasion. Thomas Dawley spent some weeks in the field, and was ten times arrested. Crosby was killed by Gomez' side during the battle of Santa Teresa on March 9, '97. Karl Decker made a daring and difficult trip to Gomez. Frederick Somerford, one of the bravest if least pretentious, has travelled again and again through Havana Province at critical periods, and has thrice visited Gomez for the "Herald." The son of Judge Govin, late U. S. Consul at Leghorn, landed in Cuba on July 2, 1896, representing a news syndicate. He was captured on July 9 by a Spanish column under Colonel Ochoa at Correderas. The colonel tore up his American passports, the unarmed prisoner was bound and macheted in regulation form. Melton, the western writer, was captured on the "Competitor," off the Cuban coast. He was first sentenced to death, and lay two years in a Cabanas dungeon. Released in November, '97, by General Blanco, he emerged a physical wreck, prematurely aged by his terrible experience. Count Dirizia, an

Under Three Flags in Cuba

The difficulties of passing the Trocha debarred correspondents from the eastern provinces. The conditions in Camaguey and Oriente were as an unknown book, though the insurgents were better organized there than in any other part of the island.

Puerto Principe, of some 40,000 inhabitants, is a typically Cuban city. Shut in closely by forts and barricades, and practically besieged by the insurgents, small news travelled fast. I discovered that my advent had been passed in strict confidence from mouth

Italian military correspondent of note, attached to the Spanish army, sought to pass to the insurgent lines near the Trocha, and was recaptured and held for two years as a spy. He was finally deported to Spain, and I had a heartbroken letter from him last July, dated Montjuich Fortress and stating that he was still held without trial. Frederick Hughes, artist correspondent of "Black and White," visited the field, as a guest of the military commander of Pinar del Rio. Later, however, he was robbed and maltreated by guerillas, and reached Havana in a pitiful condition. Singularly, he was refused aid at the British Consulate. I had been with Hughes in Africa and Madeira, but was in hiding at the time, and without money or friends the poor fellow perished miserably of starvation in the streets of Havana. The British Representative reported to the Foreign Office that Mr. Hughes's death was certified from natural causes by the municipal doctor, and, from the fact that a dollar was found upon the body, he disposed of the starvation theory. "Hambre!" the morgue doctor had said to Señor Pichardo; hunger also had killed the other attenuated corpses on the slabs, but "Heart Disease" was entered on all such certificates. The Consul-General did not state that the dollar in Hughes's pocket was of Weyler's waste paper. Mr. Call, of the Scripps-McRae League, made a perilous trip to Camaguey in a small boat. George Reno, whose daring work in sustaining communications between the Cubans and New York is well known, may also be mentioned in the category. War correspondents who visited the rebel army received little clemency from Spain. Personally I have no cause for complaint.

A Spanish Swashbuckler

to mouth until half the town knew of it, and the authorities would assuredly get some inkling erelong. On the street also I met Captain Baccalo, who, as a swashbuckling subaltern, had been deputed to uphold the honor of the Spanish army, impugned by an article of mine in a British military paper. His insults to evoke an acceptance of his challenges to mortal combat were so tiresome that I had been forced to cool his ardor some weeks before by thrashing him in the Tacon café, in answer to his loud-voiced remarks on the cowardice of the foreign pigs who feared to duel. My companion and myself were then set upon by all the officers in the place, some drawing their swords, and only prompt intervention of a colonel of Weyler's staff had saved us from their fury. This colonel courteously apologized for his compatriots, but Baccalo swore to be revenged, and later Mr. Decker, with a chair in his stalwart arm, held off some friends of the gallant captain, who attacked us on Teniente Rey. Fearful of a scene now in Principe, I averted my face, and passed quickly onward; but the captain turned suspiciously, and I felt that he recognized me. My hotel-keeper, a rabid Spaniard, was a suspicious knave, and watched me closely, while I was also shadowed by the omnipresent sleuths. It was imperative that I should strike out at once with my papers. I walked to my room, telling the waiter not to disturb me, and bolted the door. A stealthy jump from the back window landed me into an adjoining yard, and I soon had my effects in a Cuban butcher's house. A patriotic milkman, who served the outlying forts, put everything in his panniers, crossed the barrier on his usual rounds, and dropped the stuff in a bush near the outposts. For thus risking his liberty, he refused to accept a cent.

I had that morning ridden with Captain O'Reilly beyond the defences, and with a bold face I again passed through the same embrasure, unquestioned by the guards. I lay trembling under the bush where I found my effects; the cover was scanty, and risk of capture imminent. The air was fragrant with perfume of flowers, wafted from the glorious gardens in the outskirts, and gradually a sombre veil seemed drawn over the brilliant scenery; the distant hills turned from emerald to purple, and then died away as dusk crept up stealthily. The moon ascended even as the sun disappeared. The wait had seemed eternity; but the sunset bugles now rang out, the sweet strains of the "Ave Maria" stole across from the little chapel, deep-toned chimes boomed from the cathedral, and the nocturnal buzzing of the insects heralded the approaching night.

Then I heard a bird-like whistle, and my guide crept up. True to his word, Señor Prada had arranged everything. This muscular practico, a Columbian by birth, shouldered my pack, and we crept fearfully forward toward the forts. It was then pitch dark, the campfires at the outposts gleamed fitfully; a cavalry patrol clattered noisily toward us, but we

Crossing the Lines

crouched unseen in the grass, and they passed on. Then we reached the wire barricade and patrol road, intersected with forts, passing round the city.

The silent form of a sentinel loomed up not ten yards from us, and we lay quiet until he resumed his march. On the left a group of soldiers were gambling, the pale light of the campfire playing on their swarthy faces. Another sentry approached and forced a second halt. Then again we crawled on through the long wet grass until water gleamed below. "Careful, Señor! Not a sound!" warned my guide; and we cautiously waded in, sinking deeper and deeper. We were soon swimming; the practico with my bag, fortunately waterproof, on his back. A whining "Sentinela Alerta!" rose from the opposite bank. "Alerta!" echoed another sentry nearer yet, and I fitfully imagined the volleys that would ring out if we were discovered, and the story of some heroic engagement that would be colored by our dead bodies on the morrow; but we passed the lines at last, and waded to land, some distance beyond the forts.

There was one spot now where ambushes were frequently thrown out to intercept the insurgents passing down the disused highroad toward the outposts. The Columbian reconnoitred it. Again his reassuring whistle, and we pressed hurriedly along the camino, past once beautiful estates, until a clump of royal palms was reached. A bird-like chirrup greeted us, the guide answered, and then I descried two fig-

Under Three Flags in Cuba

ures on horseback silently awaiting our approach. "Los Cubanos!" said my guide; and I soon made out the familiar jip-jap hat and white uniform of the Cuban cavalry. The rebel vedette lent me a mule, and we rode out to the chief of the zona. Our coming was unexpected, and as the loud challenge rang out, twenty forms seemed to spring from the ground. I was a little ahead, and glanced down the barrels of loaded rifles covering me, until the guards came up and explained matters.

"You are very brave, my friend, to cross those lines!" said the captain commanding the zona, agnomened Canon, as he warmly greeted me; but my trembling hand belied it, and I was more than relieved to find myself safe at last within the Cuban outposts.

Before us stretched the vast forest, in the dark vistas of which the sun never penetrated; behind lay the plain I had just crossed. The half moon was partially obscured, but a dark arcade on the edge of the woods was illuminated by a blazing log fire hissing with the night dew that dripped from branches above. Around it moved a group of rebels, their very surroundings making them brigand-like. They crowded round to hear the news, but Canon came to my relief, saying I was tired and needed rest. I had brought a hammock and canopy, which two asistentes fixed, and I turned in.

"Surely this is a land of milk and honey!" I thought, when I awoke to find a breakfast of sweet-

Insurgent Headquarters

ened coffee, plantains, a roll, and fresh beef cooked on the parilla, awaiting me. I learned, later, that the luxuries formed the greater part of a repast sent for the special delectation of the commandante, but unselfishly apportioned to me in that courtesy which is the unfailing attribute of every true Cuban I met.

At an early hour an orderly had ridden over to headquarters with the report of the previous day. I here witnessed a military organization impossible in the troop-ridden west. Round Principe and other points held by Spain, regular Cuban zonas were established that prevented the egress of any small force, and harassed large columns that marched out until warning had reached headquarters and the army prepared for the attack.

At midday the orderly returned with general orders, one of which directed Lieutenant Betencourt to provide a horse for the stranger that had entered the lines, and selecting efficient escort to bring him with every care to the "Cuartel General."

We set off without delay through a well-wooded country, intersected with large plains of magnificent grass that rose over our horses' heads. Fording several rivers, and passing delightful cocoanut groves, we rode through winding trails for twelve miles, when the picquet halted us. It was then six o'clock, and the sudden roll of horse-drums awoke the echoes, and the inspiriting strains of the Cuban national hymn rose through the trees. Victor Pacheco's band of the crack regiment of Camaguey cavalry is not

Under Three Flags in Cuba

pretentious, but on that cool tropical evening the distant music was as sweet as the siren's delusive melodies that caused Ulysses to wax his ears. As we rode toward General Recio's pavilion, the soldiers who had swarmed from their rude quarters to hear the music, threw up their hats as we passed, with loud vivas for the strange officer.

General Lopez Recio received me at once. I delivered my papers and messages, and received a cordial welcome. We sat and talked, long after silencio had sounded, and the camp sunk to sleep, and at a late hour I crawled under my own bit of canvas and turned in.

It was still dark when "El Diana" rang out, the sweet reveille admirably sounded by the trumpeters aided by cornets of the band, which then struck up a lively galop entitled "Al Machete." A heavy miasma hung over everything; the moon, trying to pierce the dampness, made one vast spot of translucent vapor in the white cloud. In wide avenues opening through the forest, campfires of the army gleamed through the mist, forms of the soldiers who had emerged from their palm-leaf huts to cook a frugal meal, being faintly discernible. The general's orderly brought me coffee and camp-made cigarettes. It was growing rapidly lighter, and finally the sun rose like a huge red fire-balloon, mounting slowly above the trees. Gaining strength, its rays effectively dispelled the mists and dried off the dripping country with incredible rapidity.

Recio and his Staff

General Recio, a wealthy planter before the war, was a brave and capable officer. His delicate wife, whom I had met in Havana prison a year before, suffering for her relationship, had just managed to reach the field to join her husband. He had secured her the safest place possible in a distant prefect's house, but he felt her risks and privations and the separation from his family keenly. The long struggle had made him taciturn, and war was eminently distasteful to him. Yet the mention of autonomy made his eyes flash. He had never looked for American intervention, and evinced no surprise when I showed him the President's message. "We have but one life to give to Cuba," he remarked sadly, "and that may be expended in vain, but this generation must give it willingly to free their country for future ages."

His staff were all men of wealth and education, most of them exceedingly young. I especially recall Doctor Clark, a surgeon of English descent, Majors Bazan and Delmonte, and Captain Arostigui, brother to the British proconsul in Havana. Singularly also the brigadier of this command, General Bernabe Sanchez, was formerly British Consul at Nuevitas. He had been badly wounded just before my arrival and sent to New York for treatment.

The sun is unbearable in the manigua from ten until two, and the camp was drowsily resting in the shade. The bright young lawyer, the chief of judiciary, whose name I have forgotten, was under my canvas, initiating me into the mysteries of Cuban law.

Under Three Flags in Cuba

Bazan came over and advised a photograph of the Escolta, and when I promised to take it on the morrow, he said significantly, "Manana sera otre dia." And at that moment a solitary horseman galloped into camp, drew up before General Recio, and saluting gravely, said, "El enemigo!" Some one echoed his words, and, as if by magic, the camp was infused with life.

"The enemy! The enemy!" shouted the troopers. The bugler of the guard sounded the alarm. "Boots and saddles" followed, and then "General assembly."

Within five minutes the cavalry had struck camp and formed up, staff officers galloped off to report the strength and disposition of the Spaniards, and the long line of ragged infantry was moving forward, laughing and chatting glibly as they marched. When the columns did move out in Camaguey, they came prepared to fight; the Cubans were too strong to permit any of the tactics employed in the west, and there were no towns for the soldiers to crawl into each night before sunset.

The chief of staff gave me a serviceable horse, and I was instructed to go with Colonel Molina, commanding the infantry. Delmonte joined us later, and then, to my chagrin, I learned that Molina was only to act as rear guard with the impedimenta, and see that supplies were pushed up to the force. His orders were to give me a practico and escort, and facilitate my journey to the insurgent government at Esperanza. As that was the object of my visit, I

Colonel Molina

could not complain, much as I regretted the lost opportunity of witnessing a fight of fair proportions. Molina [1] was an interesting companion, and we rode several miles together to a prefectura from which I was to start on my journey as soon as possible. Cuban-born, he had accepted a commission in the Chilian army, and attained the rank of major, when he resigned and returned to Cuba to fight. With a practical military training, he was speedily promoted to colonel of infantry. He used the regulation kit of Chili, which I was surprised to see equalled the most approved equipment of Europe.

I was fretting with impatience in the prefect's house, having decided to secure my guide and ride toward the combat; but not until next morning could we start, and adjudging it too late to overtake the general, we headed for the Government. After a ride of thirty-two miles, we off-saddled for the night

---

[1] Molina has a sister as fearless as himself. On several occasions she collected medicines for the sick, and travelled boldly down to Minas, where, from a sugar-estate, the insurgents could slip in and secure them. Travelling on one occasion from Nuevitas, the officer of the train-guard questioned her closely as to the contents of her trunk. Without making direct reply, the spirited young lady held out her keys, saying, "If you suspect me search it." The Spanish officer is invariably gallant, and would usually refuse to doubt such inference, but this captain took the keys and turned the lock. "You dog! you would search a lady's trunk in face of her assertion. Lock that box!" shouted a gray-haired old colonel travelling in the same car. That box contained lint, bandages, instruments, and drugs, all contrabands of war; but the trembling girl was saved, and the supplies in the Fonsecca Hospital near Najaza are the result of her achievement.

in an old cattle-shed, and made the best meal possible of plantains, and it was just after midnight when the practico's stentorian voice sent me springing from my hammock.

"Alto! Quien va?"

"Cuba!" was the prompt response from the approaching party. One advanced and gave the countersign, and then a party of scouts rode up. "Be on your guard. Castellanos with a strong column is marching to attack the Government. The force advancing south was a blind to draw off the general; they too have now wheeled, and are making a forced march to rejoin the main body," they said, as they galloped on to spread a general alarm and hurry forward all outlying divisions.

This was news indeed, welcome and unwelcome. After all, we were in the path of the fight, and were even ahead of Recio, who was not apprised of the feint until he had lost a day. We rode hard next morning, keeping to winding side-trails, and avoiding the highroad leading from Puerto Principe to Moron on the north coast, along which the Spaniards were advancing.

We camped after sunset on a loma, loosening our saddle-girths and tying our horses near. Not daring to light a fire, we went hungry. In a camp of four, and a country swarming with the enemy, the feeling of loneliness and uncertainty is depressing, and we turned in early, posting guards at an hourly relief. About seven o'clock a sudden glare in the sky about

A Night Raid

a mile distant aroused us, and the cracking of rifles and loud yells and shouts were borne over on the cool night air. The enemy at last!

We mounted and rode cautiously toward the firing. The practico led us through devious trails, the glare appearing one moment in front, then on our right or behind; but he was never at fault, and we finally came to the edge of a wood bordering a vast savannah. A stream was before us, and beyond it the Spaniards. Crouching in the underbrush, we could see everything plainly. The soldiers had halted on the highroad near two plantations. Both charming residencias were blazing fiercely, a plot of cane in rear was also alight, and the scene was thus as bright as day. The soldiers ran fiercely to and fro, waving firebrands, like imps of darkness, in the brilliant glare. Five hapless prisoners — an aged Cuban lady, a girl of perhaps seventeen, a sturdy boy, and two negro women — were brought out and taken to the rear.

The cane burned furiously, and the heat forced out a white man and two negroes hiding therein. They made a wild dash for liberty, but volleys rang out, and two dropped, while one gained the road and disappeared. But the white man, an old retainer, sprang up again and continued his flight, though wounded. The soldiers shot at him wildly, and we could scarce forbear a cheer as he sprang at the fence with an agility born of fear. The woods were close, but he missed his footing and rolled back, scrambled

Under Three Flags in Cuba

up again, and was all but over as the foremost soldiers sprang at him. Two machetes glinted in the firelight, and he fell back with a thud.

Several outhouses and homes of the farm workers were now blazing, and then we saw an example of the crass superstition of the Spaniard. Before each house in outlying districts of Cuba where churches are few, a plain wooden cross is erected. To prevent ignition, soldiers were stationed at each, to pour water over the sacred emblem. Yet before that cross they could burn homes, loot, and commit unspeakable excesses, upon the very people whose hands had fashioned it as sanctifying their residence.

We watched this pitiful scene of destruction until the flames died out, and the soldiers, selecting cows from the looted stock, prepared supper and camp for the night. Then we crept back to our horses, and pushed ahead toward the Government.

The district north of Puerto Principe is fertile; and though the lack of railroads is an insuperable drawback to the production of sugar for export, charming "centrals" abounded, and immense farms for cattle-raising occupied the glorious savannahs. The Spaniards held but two towns in the interior, and three beside Nuevitas on the coast. Consequently there had been no attempt at reconcentration except in the vicinity of those places; and shut off entirely from the west by the Trocha, the interior of the eastern provinces was Free Cuba to all intents and purposes.

Spanish Duplicity

The inhabitants dwelt on their farms or in the little Cuban villages as before the war.

The Spaniards were now laying waste the most fertile and populous district of Camaguey. General Blanco and his Government in Madrid had assured the civilized world, not two weeks before, that there should be no further destruction of property, their desire being to build up Cuba, and inspire the people with confidence that they should return to their homes. The Presidential message that asked Congress to give time to Spain was hinged on this very clause, and in treacherous duplicity here were Weyler's tactics religiously followed.

On a by-path in the Espinosa district we soon overtook fugitives warned of the enemy's approach by the blaze of burning houses. They had dashed from their homes, thinking the soldiers were upon them, and when they found we were friends, they embraced us as deliverers.

It had rained heavily the day before, and the road was a quagmire in which delicate Cuban ladies in their night-clothes waded to their knees. An old man suffering from fever fell by the roadside; a pretty girl of sixteen threw herself on his breast, weeping bitterly, and exclaiming, "Padre mio!" She was scantily dressed, having in her haste donned a tiny pair of satin shoes, relics of city balls before the war, and then been forced to fly in her undergarments. I wrapped my coat round her, and allayed their fears by assuring them that the Spaniards had halted. Some of the men returned with us to two unpretentious houses deserted near by, and we seized all the clothes and food we could, and rode back rapidly to the fugitives. Behind a bush we found one woman crazed with terror, and clasping convulsively to her breast a girl of twelve who had escaped quite nude. A young English girl, daughter of the resident engineer of the Sanchez estate, who had remained in the interior with friends, dragged one bedridden member of the family nearly a mile.

After cutting a way through the bush to a safe retreat for the refugees, and making several trips, carrying the women on our horses, we masked the gap against chance discovery, and rode on, promising to send pacificos to help them into a more comfortable haven in the morning. Later we met a scout who reported that Recio was then riding hard with the cavalry, to overtake the enemy, who had two days' start, leaving the infantry to come up as speedily as possible. We then decided to halt until daybreak where the road forks to La Rosa and Moron.

We lay in the wet grass, and I slept soundly. It seemed but ten minutes when the guide aroused me, and I found the gray dawn breaking to day. We were sore, hungry, and tired, when we remounted, and rode toward Esperanza. But the Spaniard was up betimes to escape the heat of the day, and smoke rising on our right showed that he was taking the other road toward Cubitas. The character of the country made it possible for us to keep near the

A Narrow Escape

enemy, who invariably marched on the highroad, — their canvas shoes, and the risk of ambuscade, keeping them severely to beaten tracks.

Turning our horses by a trail, discernible only to the practico, we rode toward San Jacinto and emerged on the road, ahead, but uncomfortably close to the Imperial troops. The people in the district had just been alarmed, and were hurrying out in all stages of dishabille to reach the prefectura, which stood back in the woods and could hardly be attacked. Two columns of smoke now rose barely half a mile behind us, and the fugitives from those houses came screaming down the road, fortunately all on horseback. They were preparing to dress when alarmed, and had escaped by the rear gates as the Spaniards tore down the fences and swarmed in the front.

The last family caught my attention especially. Three children were riding a stocky pony; a Cuban, evidently a planter, carried his prostrate wife in front on a tall gray mare that resented the double burden, while a girl, riding bareback, nestled a pet cat under the arm that held the halter, and with the other hand urged her parent's mount forward with a riding switch, calling "Papa corre!" She was extremely pretty, her complexion fair for a Cuban; but her brilliant eyes, classical features, and glossy hair that fell over her shoulders in glorious profusion, were typical of her race. "How like Miss Cisneros!" I thought; and some days later I learned they were first cousins.

Under Three Flags in Cuba

As we reined up, she perceived that we were strangers, and crimsoned with shame at her scanty attire, vainly trying to hide her bare feet under her petticoat. By so doing she dropped her pet cat; and puss, with no fear of Spaniards, darted for home.

There was no time for conversation. "Hurry, Señorita!" I said as we closed in behind them, for the road, flanked by woods here, soon passed over a wide savannah, which we must cross before reaching cover, and if the Spaniards came up we should make an easy target. The scout took the half-conscious woman before him, and by hard riding we gained the woods as the advance guard of the enemy broke cover across the plain. Wide cavalry flanks came through the bush and closed in, and the enemy formed into close column to cross the open.

"We must check them here!" said the practico, I supposed in joke; but I soon saw that he was in earnest, and I tried to imagine Spartans about to hold Thermopylæ, for surely the odds, three facing an army corps, were greater than Leonidas against Xerxes. But the nonchalance of the Cubans reassured me.

For some distance the road ran parallel to the fringe of the woods, with some six hundred yards of low bush intervening. Tying our horses some distance back, we crept forward through the trees, and could soon hear the Spaniards talking, the hemp soles making a curious shuffling as the tired hordes slouched along. I was trembling too much to take

The Enemy "Held"

aim, but blazed indiscriminately at the massed light uniforms that appeared a haze through the tangle. The practico and soldier fired steadily, changing their position repeatedly. Some distance down a Mauser and Remington "pahed" and banged alternately; and I afterwards learned that two of General Roloff's aides, Captain Alfredo and Lieutenant Jack, a brave young American I met later, were also "holding the enemy." The column halted on the plain, as if expecting a machete charge; our ruse was working. We could see the force stretching away for over a mile. There were six battalions of infantry, two batteries of light artillery, a regiment of cavalry, and a squad of guerillas, — 12,000 in all. It was almost as strong an army corps as one of Weyler's devastating columns, and being far less scattered, was the most formidable Spanish force I saw. Castellanos had mobilized every soldier possible to attack the insurgent Government. But a few days before, a practico named Perez, court-martialled for theft, escaped arrest, stole a horse, and rode to Puerto Principe. He offered to guide the Spaniards against his former comrades, and Castellanos had taken advantage of the offer. Luckily there have been few such traitors in Cuba, or the cause must long since have been lost.

Before us some companies formed in double line, the front rank kneeling, and firing with rifle butts on the ground. Their bullets chipped the leaves off the highest trees, while those in the rear fired regular volleys that spat angrily against the trunks well above us. Then a shell screamed overhead and burst half a mile away, but others came nearer. It was getting too hot; the Spaniards were "held," and we crept to our horses and rode off through the trees. We could hear the enemy banging away for twenty minutes to clear the woods of the fictitious enemy, and then they threw out flanks and went on again, later burning Pueblo Nuevo and the houses on the highroad to La Citia.

This was on January the 11th, I believe, though the track of days is lost in the manigua. We found General Recio had countermarched, and was already near Esperanza, so we pushed our jaded horses toward Cubitas. A cocoanut grove made our bivouac near the little Cuban capital. The pacificos had torn down the roughly made bridges and thrown barricades on the road; but at daybreak, scouts announced that the Spaniards were closing in. The Government then packed all their belongings and rode out of the town one hour before the attack began.

A popular fiction credited President Maso with holding nominal office away in the wilds of the Cubitas mountains, hunted day and night by the Spaniards. His Government, however, had occupied the little town of Esperanza, renamed Agremonte City after the first president of "Cuba libre," for eight months, dwelling in houses almost on the highroad. The enemy had never previously at-

A FLANKING PARTY OF CASTELLANOS' COLUMN ENGAGED WITH FORCES OF THE CUBAN GOVERNMENT AT ESPERANZA.

From photograph by a Spanish officer, taken during the engagement

The Attack upon Esperanza

tempted to march into the heart of Camaguey, though the route lay on one of the best roads in Cuba.

A little party of rebel infantry checked the soldiers at the last destroyed bridge, but thanks to the traitor Perez, the artillery gained a ridge near the town and opened fire. Thirty rounds I counted, and not one shell struck the place; but the handful of men were finally driven from the river crossing, and fell back with loss, while Recio with his cavalry tried vainly to hold out until his infantry should arrive. Clinging to every bit of cover, the troopers replied to the withering volleys of the enemy, and the fight raged for two hours longer. Cavalry carbines are at great disadvantage against Mauser rifles, and gradually the long line of Spaniards crept forward.

Everything portable had been carried from the houses to the woods; so Recio sent troopers with firebrands to various points, and at a given signal the torch was applied. The Cubans then fell back to a hill behind, where they took up a good position, and the enraged Spaniards rushed into the burning town, to be met by a withering fire that killed nine, and drove them back.

By Blanco's orders, placards had been posted on fences and trees as the columns marched, pointing out the advantages of autonomy, and advising every one to return to the nearest town, where work and food would be provided. The Cubans knew little of the thousands then dying of starvation in the cities, but they placed no faith in Spain, and no one followed this advice.

"Death to Spain! Death to autonomy! Long live Cuba free!" yelled the insurgents during the fight. "Long live Spain! Death to autonomy! Death to Cuba!" were the vituperative brickbats sent in reply.

"In some things we differ. In this we agree. Neither Cuban nor Spaniard wants autonomy," rhymed a New York Cuban. And both sides cried down autonomy, though they would have equally welcomed the termination of hostilities.

Dr. Clark dressed the wounded Cubans by the river, and they were either sent off through the woods to a hospital, or returned to fight. Recio's infantry arrived next day thoroughly worn out, but he posted his force to hold the road leading to the government workshops and official printing-office. Castellanos, apprised of the location by Perez, had wished to capture these talleres, and both forces took long-range shots at each other for two days, when the Spaniards started to retire. The tireless Cubans, though short of ammunition, harassed them every step of the way; their food ran out, and as they were obliged to forage in force instead of marching all day, their return to Principe became unduly prolonged.

CHAPTER VII

THE INSURGENT GOVERNMENT. — PRESIDENT MASO. — HIS VIEWS OF THE SITUATION. — MINISTERS OF THE CABINET. — AN OFFER TO SPAIN.

AFTER the burning of Esperanza, I turned off to overtake the Government, and found them ten miles away, settled in Palmarito, as if nothing had transpired. Travel-stained, unshaven, and filthy, I presented a deplorable appearance; but the officials received me warmly, and first the Vice-President, then General Lacret, and finally the President, placed their quarters at my disposal. There were but few houses in this Cuban village, but they were well-built and commodious, the residents eagerly competing for the honors of hospitality. The Vice-President, with whom I stayed, was the guest of a charming Cuban family. They had but one spare bedroom, which Dr. Capote had insisted on relinquishing to a sick officer, Dr. Betencourt, while we slung our hammocks on the spacious veranda. But a few minutes after my arrival President Maso invited me to dine with him. I accepted with alacrity, and not wishing to lose time, plunged into the object of my visit.

He at once dispelled any existent doubts as to the absolute rejection of Spain's autonomy by the Cubans in arms. The conversation was carried on entirely in English, for the general understood it perfectly, though with a limited vocabulary, and both his secretaries spoke fluently.

"Señor Presidente," I said, "I wish to know your exact position regarding the autonomy offered by Spain. There are many in Havana who say the Cubans are ready to surrender, being tired of the war."

"I am glad you are here," he replied; "we are unable to treat directly with any government, and shut off as we are from the outside world, we can now state our position through the Press. At the close of the ten years' war, I reluctantly gave up my command, accepting the terms of the Zanjon treaty in some degree of faith. My force was the last to disband, but when we surrendered to General Campos and returned home, we found we had been duped. In defiance of the amnesty many officers were seized and killed or deported, and history records the shameful repudiation of every clause of the agreement by the Madrid Government. Not one of the promised reforms was instituted. I protested to the Governor-General, and was flung into a dungeon, held for months without trial, and finally exiled. In 1881, I returned to Cuba, to find affairs had gone from bad to worse, — the same corrupt Spaniards held absolute rule, and a reign of terror had been instituted to silence all protestors by deportation without trial — always the right of the Captain-General."

"We had some hope from the Liberals and the gen-

The President of Free Cuba

uine reforms drafted by Señor Maura; but when that bill was rejected, and in January 1895, the Abarzuza law was passed by the Cortes, we saw that all promise of reform was a sham, and we must fight. On February 23 I gathered my plantation hands together and proclaimed the independence of Cuba. The Spaniards sent me envoys offering bribes, but I burned my estate and went to the field. General Gomez soon landed; recruits flocked to our flag, and though we had no arms but our machetes, the wave of revolt spread from East to West, from Cape Maisi seven hundred miles to San Antonio, until it assumed its present dimensions.

"Many wealthy Cubans devoted their whole fortunes to the cause, and arms and ammunition have been purchased at exorbitant cost and stupendous difficulty. Our army has been outnumbered ten to one, but for three years the struggle has been maintained. Our women and children have been ruthlessly starved to death, and our men hunted like wild beasts; and General Weyler was assured that his policy was Spain's policy, until the island became soaked in innocent blood and entirely laid waste. Then, when action by the United States became imminent, and not until then, was the order to kill everything Cuban — man, woman, and child — reversed. General Blanco comes to offer us autonomy; and we Cubans, who have hitherto been spoken of as bandits, without principle or reason, whose only fate was the garrote or the firing squad, are suddenly asked to surrender on the promise of self-government, posts being assured to all the leaders. Do you wonder that we are suspicious of Spanish promises?

"The reforms which were indignantly refused us before the war are now too late. We can accept nothing from Spain but absolute independence. There is no guarantee for us; Spain can repudiate her decrees; a change of ministry can sweep aside the reforms instituted by Señor Sagasta; and we should have endured all this for nothing. 'Independencia o muerte!'"

"And in its present critical condition do you not fear for the stability of your country suddenly cut loose from Spain?" I inquired.

"Our crippled condition alone is a great argument for independence. If we Cubans are capable of self-rule, as outlined by Señor Sagasta, we should certainly be better without the despotic Spanish Captain-General. Spain also is so heavily in debt, that she will not only be unable to aid the re-development of the island, but we shall be heavily burdened by sharing the war debt, much of which has gone to the pockets of Weyler and his corrupt staff. Our one hope lies in the removal of Spain's proscriptive policy, and an influx of foreign capital, which is sure to come when all obnoxious tariffs and taxes, which restrict every chance of trade or improvement, are removed.

"We realize fully that our path will be difficult; but notwithstanding our incredible commercial shackles,

An Interview with Maso

oppressive taxation, and the false political economy of our past rule, this island has produced a magnificent revenue, all of which has gone to Spain by fair means or foul, except a meagre sum voted for local repairs in the cities. Cuba has not one road worthy of the name except in Havana, and not fifteen per cent of her rich soil is under cultivation. With facilities for transport, we could hold the markets of the world for cane sugar, coffee, and tobacco. In this province you see acres of valuable land, clear and well-watered, but with nothing but bridle-paths through the woods to take produce to the cities.

"Our mineral wealth is practically undeveloped. The best iron used by the Carnegie Company for their steel comes from their mines in Santiago, and the whole province is rich in metal, but unworked. Trade must necessarily be stimulated by the removal of the preferential duties which have kept the bulk of our imports in Spanish markets and caused retaliatory tariffs on our exports to the United States. The price of bread through the duty on flour alone is a disgrace to the Spanish administration."

"There is a visible difference between Cuban and Spaniard. Despite propinquity, their characters are widely altered. How do you account for this?" I asked.

"The Cubans have been reared in different conditions. With the exceptional advantages of education in the United States, many of our children have been educated there at less cost even than in Havana colleges. Constant' intercourse between Cuba and the United States has also had a marked influence on the Cuban; but apart from that, there are many descendants of English and Scotch planters in the West Indies, who have settled there and own sugar plantations, while political troubles have sent some French refugees to Cuba. Thus a race entirely different has sprung up. The Spaniards who flock here for a few years, make money, and retire to Spain, are usually bad specimens of their race."

"And the autonomist party?" I interposed.

"Until three months ago, there were not a dozen autonomists, and they only in name. Some Cubans who had been forced to flee by Weyler, have now been glad to return, and accept office under General Blanco. They are few and weak, and lack the resolution of the Cubans in arms. Without strong moral support from Spain they cannot stand; for the ultra-Spanish party are bitterly opposed to them, while they have little sympathy from the Cubans themselves. We who have lost our all, and see fully the effects of the war, realize that the breach can never be healed by compromise. No sign has our army given of weakening, and not one man of note has broken his word to Cuba by accepting Spanish bribes."

"If Cuba gain her independence, do you fear the negro problem will cause trouble?" I said.

"Our negroes," said President Maso, "are mostly uneducated laborers, quite unfitted for holding positions. They will have the citizen rights, as given in

An Interview with Maso

the United States, and with sufficient employment will give no trouble. The population of Cuba is composed of one-third colored, either mulatto or negro. Yet some gravely predict Cuba's future as a second Hayti or Liberia, — a negro republic. The idea is manifestly absurd. Cuba is much under-populated, and one of our first measures will be to induce a restricted immigration of those likely to assist in developing our immense resources. Our negroes will work as before in the cane-fields, and I see no reason to anticipate trouble from them. We have no colored officials in this government, and very few of our officers are black, though the slaves we freed by the last war are fighting faithfully in this."

"Do you directly favor intervention of the United States?" was my final question.

The President hesitated a moment. "Yes, for the sake of humanity I do, though I do not anticipate great help from that quarter. President McKinley has many precedents in Europe to follow, — the interference of the Powers in Belgium in 1830, and in struggles in Greece, Hungary, and other points in eastern Europe; but he long allowed Weyler's régime without protest, and is hardly likely to intervene now. Our one hope is to sustain the fight until Spain's rash boast of 'last dollar and last man' has been fulfilled, or the nation realizes that it is fruitless to prolong the struggle which has cost her dear."

President Maso has spent two fortunes and the best years of his life for his country. Ruined and exiled in the last war, he returned to his estates near Manzanillo in '81, and had again acquired affluence in '95. When nearly seventy, he again relinquished all and returned to privation in the field. He has much prestige, and is known throughout the island as "Honest Maso." Before donning the Cuban cockade, he drew heavily on his invested capital, paid his debts, and taxes for a year in advance, and destroyed his plantation.

The other members of the Government were all men of education. The Vice-President, Dr. Mendez Capote, now chief adviser to General Brooke, was professor of law in Havana University before the war, and counsel for the Water Works, Electric Light and Power Company, and Regla Railroad, three vested interests of Americans in the capital.

The unrecognized republic was divided into four districts or states, — Oriente (Santiago de Cuba), Camaguey (Puerto Principe), Las Villas (from the Trocha westward to Palmas and Cochinos Bay in Matanzas), and Occidente (from Las Villas to Cape Antonio, the extreme west, thus including part of Matanzas, Havana and Pinar del Rio).

Each of these equal divisions elected six representatives for the Assembly on the basis of universal suffrage, which the exigencies of the situation made practically a military vote. Members from the West had a perilous journey across the island, but finally the twenty-four were gathered at La Yaya, one day's march from Puerto Principe.

The Cuban Cabinet

On October 29, 1897, the new constitution was adopted, the Assembly being convened for two years. President Cisneros, Marquis of Santa Lucia, retired, and the following officials were elected : General Maso, President; Dr. Capote, Vice-President; Colonel Alemen, Secretary of War; Colonel Fonts Sterling, Secretary of Treasury; Dr. Moreno de la Torre, Secretary of Foreign Affairs; Dr. Silva, Minister of the Interior; Dr. Freire, Chief of Judiciary; Colonel José Vivanco, Secretary to the Assembly. Civil governors for each state were then appointed.

Most of the above officials were elected unanimously, though a few votes were cast for Garcia as president, and Cardenas for secretary of war. There was not a single colored representative, all being men of refinement, and several graduates of American colleges. The Government then moved to Esperanza and there had held regular sessions twice a week.

I witnessed animated discussions carried on entirely in English. During one of these, Dr. Capote, on behalf of the Assembly, made a stirring speech rejecting autonomy, of which I repeat the closing sentences : —

"No reforms, no autonomy, nothing under any name that means a continuance of Spanish domination in Cuba can end our struggle. We have fought too long now for simple political measures, supposing them genuine. We will sustain this struggle until the flag that has covered so many butcheries, presided over so much injustice, protected so many iniquities, shall be hauled

Under Three Flags in Cuba

down from Cuba. Between this people and the Spanish Government there extends a bottomless ocean of tears, there surges a great sea of blood, and there is an impassable mountain of hate. Thus we wish the absolute independence of this island, where we desire to constitute a free, ordained, prosperous, and happy people on the ruins of an exhausted colony.

"The attitude of Spain in the past guides us now. The offer of autonomy is an explicit declaration of impotency, a bait to-day to sustain a situation which but yesterday was to be sustained by fire and sword, by extermination. The logical process of this we have seen before. We were once tricked to peace, and the old régime was then re-enforced. To-day their strength has failed, and they try again for peace by compromise. The Peninsular Spaniard will rule and control as before, and nothing can guarantee tranquillity but absolute separation, since Spain is Spain."

Colonel Alemen, a Cuban writer of eminence, was by far the hardest-working member of the administration. He had reports of weekly "states" of each army division in Cuba; and if, owing to broken commands, the organization were not perfect in the West, in the East the officials could tell at a glance the number of cartridges at their disposal, who was sick, and who in prison. Each regimental commander sent a daily report to divisional headquarters, and these were collectively submitted each week to the Secretary of War. This zealous officer resigned in favor of Rafael de Cardenas, soon after my visit.

Characteristics of the Ministers

Colonel Fonts Sterling is a Cuban of Scotch descent, and a graduate of a New York Military Academy. The surprise was great when this popular young member of New York society suddenly set sail for Cuba, and prognostications of speedy return to the élite environs of Fifth Avenue were general. But his friends little gauged his patriotism. He soon established a name in the West, and received rapid promotion until elected Minister of Finance. All property of the precarious republic came under his jurisdiction, — the collection of taxes from wealthy land-owners, all subscriptions to the cause, and the outlay for supplies for the army, equipment of expeditions, and purchase of arms and ammunition.

Dr. Moreno, a graduate of Havana college, is well known in Washington. As minister of foreign affairs, he was concerned chiefly in directing the extension of the cause abroad by the various juntas, notably in New York, Paris, Florida, and Mexico.

Dr. Silva, then Minister of the Interior, had charge of the administration of the civil authority, directing the civil governors of states, under whom were governors of districts, who appointed prefects and sub-prefects.

Dr. Freire, a representative of one of Cuba's oldest families, before the war was judge of the Audencia, or supreme court of Havana. After Weyler's arrival he relinquished the lucrative position that, under the new régime, would give unlimited spoils, and went to the field. The various military "judiciaries" appointed chiefly from members of the Havana University who poured out en masse to the war, came under his jurisdiction.

The civil administration of Free Cuba proved a simple but interesting institution. Prefecturas were established in every district, the prefect keeping registers of births, marriages, and deaths, and a list of all people residing under his jurisdiction. He was empowered to see that no one lived without occupation, every one being placed to labor according to his capabilities. Thus a system not unlike Bellamy's ideal arose in eastern Cuba. Every one worked for the good of the republic; the shoemaker made his shoes, the carpenter furniture, the smith arms and utensils, the farmer raised produce, — all went to the main distributing agency, the prefectura. There these necessaries of life were distributed freely according to supply, the shoemaker took in shoes and regularly drew beef and vegetables in return; each worker gave and received. With the fervid patriotism then existent in Cuba, this system, that would be an obvious failure in ordinary conditions, was a success. I saw several banns of approaching marriage posted in prefecturas, the ceremony being performed by the Governor. All horses and cattle were at the prefect's disposition, he issued meat for his district and provided horses to remount the troops when needed. He had a bugle to sound on approach of the enemy, that the people might escape and the Cuban

Marriage in Free Cuba

soldiers be warned, and he was responsible for the feeding of such forces as came into his district. In the West but few prefecturas were well maintained, but in Camaguey the system was perfect.

The "lex non scripta" of the West here gave place to the laws of the republic, neatly bound and hung in every prefectura or sub-prefectura in the province. While many of the edicts were of a military character, an admirable code for the benefit of civilians was included. Especially strict marriage laws were enforced in "Cuba libre," the age limits being eighteen for the male and fifteen for the female. Incompatibility or ill-treatment was a sufficient cause for a judicial separation, and absolute decrees were only granted for breaches of the seventh commandment.

Prefects on the coast commanded the guardia costa, who watched for the approach of enemy's vessels, fired into boats coming ashore for reconnaissance or supplies, and received filibustering expeditions.

Owing to the scarcity of grass, the Government on the 13th moved to Sabana la mar, only twenty-six miles east of Moron, the terminus of the Trocha. We had a wet and miserable ride; the streams were swollen, and the official archives, loaded on pack mules, were drenched. The river Caunao was crossed with difficulty, and it was late when we reached our destination. The Government soon adapted itself to circumstances, — tables were set up in a long drying-shed, stands of records, cases of books, and writing-desks soon giving an official air to the sorry capitol.

Provisions were scarce in Sabana la mar, and the families could not be imposed upon, though they willingly proffered all they had. But the sea was only a league away and fish were abundant. The prefect, a studious-looking man with a charming wife and two smart children, was city bred, and came out with his family at the beginning of the war. The sub-prefect, Don Alberto, was a typical guajiro of the old stock. He, his buxom wife, and three pretty daughters were the life of the country-side, and many crude but enjoyable entertainments took place under their roof.

While with the Government, I met most of the prominent men of the East, who had come to confer with the President, and had been delayed by the sudden raid. Reared in every luxury, they still made the best of the life of hardship in the field, but it was telling greatly on them. These makers of a future Cuba deserve fame; and if class distinctions count for nothing, the greater sacrifice still deserves the greater honor. They dared and died to win liberties that will be enjoyed by a future generation. They have perished on the field, in prison, and of sheer privation; but the spirit of '48, that made Europe tremble, marched on in Cuba, with that heroic enthusiasm that counted life but little, and made men ready to die in an unselfish cause. What Stead says of the patriots of '48, may be said of Cuba

Heroic Endurance of the Cubans

fifty years later. The conduct of the man who goes forth to battle at the orders of a government that would shoot him if he refused to fight, cannot be considered by the side of those who have relinquished everything they love on earth, to face the dungeon, the gallows, or other violent death, in the cause of a great ideal. To them there is something nobler than a well-filled paunch. Against the soulless materialism of this comfort-loving generation they have borne eloquent testimony. They poured out their blood that their descendants might live.

"To liken the insurgent element in Cuba to the fathers of the United States is too absurd for consideration," thunders one writer; but when I hear such statements, I think of the brave fellows I have seen lying in some crazy shelter, their festering wounds unattended; of men nurtured in luxury, who have existed on grass soup until too weak to crawl into the saddle, and have then fallen in the bush, dying but unconquered; of the heroes who faced the fatal volleys unflinchingly in la Cabana fort, and died with "Cuba libre" on their lips; of the exiles marched with pinioned arms to the wharves, while weeping mothers, wives, and children looked on for the last time but dared not speak.

The Cubans had far greater cause for revolt than the thirteen colonies in 1776, when they rose en masse against tyranny, and struck the death-blow to the old imperialism. Never were those patriots under the disabilities of the Cubans,— the sturdy Anglo-

Under Three Flags in Cuba

Saxon character had been fostered in the development of their new home; they had the aid of the French, and advantages of which the Cubans know nothing.

Spain had 285,000 soldiers and volunteers and her fleet, to shut in a narrow island a mere handful of patriots, who started the fight with but a dozen rifles. Without artillery, outnumbered fifteen to one, their guns and cartridges to be smuggled with difficulty, first from the shores of the great Republic, and then into their own island, their crops burned, their cattle seized, the Cubans sustained the unequal struggle without a waver. Because, in the cursedness of Spain's rule, the lower classes of these people are uncultured and ignorant, — because, to our superior enlightenment, these islanders seem inferior to us, — is it expedient for Americans to despise those who so heroically struggled for betterment?

I spent a few pleasant days with the Government. Brave old General Lacret arranged for my benefit a simple but, for Cuba, luxurious feast, and a dance by moonlight, many bright-eyed maidens footing it with the officers to the music of two guitars, a flute, and an accordion. The cavalry squadron was holding the road in case the enemy advanced. They gave us a sham fight, using sticks for machetes, when pates were cracked with the vehemence of Donnybrook Fair, and feats of trick riding performed. Twice we rode to the sea and fished for our dinner, keeping a lookout for gunboats which were anchored beyond the cayo. At night we had long discussions on the

The Cuban Cabinet

future of free Cuba, which the steadfast officials held a sacred ideal, and spoke of with a touching reverence and earnestness.

They had roseate hopes for the future, when a restricted emigration, the removal of tariffs, and the introduction of railroads under a government guarantee of three per cent returns on invested capital, should restore the Pearl of the Antilles to prosperity. Their idea of Cuba libre was a Utopian state of which the philosophers once dreamed.

Even these men had but one suit apiece, which was washed and dried as they lay in their hammocks. I messed with Dr. Capote, Colonel Sterling, and Dr. Freire, who bunked together in an outhouse; and often amid the stillness of the Cuban forest, I have seen them sit for hours without a word, their thoughts sadly reverting to those dear ones of whom they had heard so little for three years. Dr. Freire had sent his family to Paris; relatives of the others had found refuge in New York.

Colonel Giberga, brother of the autonomist deputy, rejoined the Government on the 18th, and later Dr. Despaigne and Colonel Alonso arrived from the South, so the rebel cabinet was complete. After a warm debate, a majority of the representatives adopted a resolution, offering, as an indemnity to Spain, a sum of money in return for the immediate independence of Cuba.

"With a view of bringing to an end the fearful sacrifice of life, Spanish and Cuban, and closing the disas-

Under Three Flags in Cuba

trous struggle that is costing both sides dearly, the elected representatives of the Cubans in arms hereby offer a sum of money as an indemnity for the immediate and absolute independence of Cuba, the amount of that indemnity to be arranged between commissioners of both parties. In making this offer, the amount we would pay to-day cannot be so great in the future, for each week the desolation of the island increases, and the colony becomes of less value to Spain.

        MORENO DE LA TORRE,
         Secretary of the Interior.
BARTOLOME MASO,
 President of the Cuban Provisional Government.

No specific sum was stated, but guarantees were forthcoming to provide $100,000,000 for the purpose. With little hope of its acceptance, the Cubans still wished to show a reasonable disposition to compromise on conditions of absolute independence. I made duplicate copies of the resolution for publication in New York and London, and sent one to Señor Canelejas in Madrid. That offer was placed before the cabinet and unofficially rejected by Sagasta and Moret, who stated that "the birthright of Spain could not be sold for a mess of pottage."

The government aides were bright fellows. I remember particularly the brave young surgeon of Matanzas, Dr. Janiz of Lacret's staff, and Major Staple, an American and assistant of the Secretary of War. The aides to the President were his son, Colo-

An Unexpected Present

nel Maso, and Captain Tirado, a New York Cuban whose writings on the insurrection are well known. Colonel Cespedes also, who had his leg bone shattered by a bullet, had just returned from New York with a dog's bone grafted in his tibia, and alien flesh joined into the wound. Before it was healed he was back fighting for Cuba, and in January led a successful attack against cavalry on the Trocha, cutting up one whole troop.

General Lacret had sent me an unexpected present, a chestnut horse with a new saddle of the McClellan pattern, a full horse kit, some coffee, and a bundle of cigars. With this and an escort, I was well prepared to continue my journey East, though loath to leave the scene of so much hospitality.

CHAPTER VIII

A MODERN DON QUIXOTE. — A FAIR PATRIOT. — GENERAL ROLOFF. — AN EFFECTIVE DEMONSTRATION. — A HORSE THIEF. — GUAIMARO. — A FRIGHTFUL INCIDENT. — COLAZZO AND HERNANDEZ. — LAS TUNAS. — THE ENEMY. — A MINE. — AMBUSHED. — GARCIA AT LAST.

PREFECT DON PEDRO, ruled by his sharp-tongued wife, was the Heap of the coast community of Camaguey; when mounted on his mule like honest Gil Blas of Santillane, he was the terror of majaces, and a valiant guajiro of great repute. The mule added to his self-respect, and rebuked not. In build a Sancho Panza, in spirit a Don Quixote, in story a Munchausen, he induced me to ride many miles to witness his capture of a Spanish gunboat, and hand down his achievement to posterity. The Bahaman Channel absorbs the royal blue of the Mexican gulf; with the silver-sand cayos, coral reefs, and palm-capped ridges, backed by a sky to match the sea, the Cuban coast is a paradise; but with mosquitoes.

The gunboat had run down from Moron between the keys. Don Pedro, the coast guards, and myself packed our clothes, rifles, and supplies into the single boat, and cautiously swam from the mainland. The key gained, the guards were to sweep the decks of

An Attack Reversed

the vessel, and hold the narrow channel leading to open sea, until the boat surrendered. We were to intrench and camp in a clump of trees on the end of the reef, the shallows on the east giving a road for our escape to land.

We cautiously swam from shore with our craft. Our trouble commenced with a shark; we were stung by acalephæ, and the betentacled devil-fish abounded; but finally we reached the key, and in the garb of Adam, dragged the boat to the burning shore. But the vessel had quietly circled round to land a party for water, and drew near so rapidly that we were forced to abandon the boat, and lie flat in the sand. Then Pedro and two others foolishly re-entered the water and headed panic-stricken for the mainland. The Dons turned their glasses, then a machine gun, against the bobbing heads; and as the swimmers hurried back, the bullets followed them sizzling to the key, driving us to a hiding in the swamp. We could not procure a stitch of clothing; shelter from the trees at the point was cut off, and we suffered fearful torture from the broiling sun.

Our thirst soon became intolerable, our tongues swelled, and it was with difficulty I refrained from emulating some of the men by lapping up the swamp water. The Spaniards could not approach the shallows, so night finally brought us relief. We crept to the beach, seized our effects, and cautiously struck out from the farther end of the cayo for the mainland. The gunboat boasted a weak searchlight, and the swim seemed eternity as we strove to elude its glare.

We crawled painfully ashore, wiser and sadder for our Lungtungpen. We lit a fire in the bush to dry our clothes, but the exultant chatter of the Cubans at our escape aroused the somnolent Dons, and three shells came crashing into the woods uncomfortably near us. I stowed my blistered body into my wet uniform, and bade adieu to the luckless braves whose prowess I shall long remember, since from the sun-bake I shed my entire epidermis, like a newt in strange water, and suffered days and nights of agony.

Riding near the northern end of the Trocha, I swung my hammock wearily where I could keep one eye on the trail that led to the Spanish position. I was dozing, the practico also, when sudden footsteps coming from that direction aroused me. To cock my Winchester and spring up was the work of an instant; but only a boy in white linen suit hove in sight. Angry at an absurd alarm, I answered his greeting sharply, "Que tal muchacho? What do you want?"

"A horse, Señor!"

"A what? Do you suppose I carry round a deposito?"

"For the love of God, sir, give me a horse. Don't send me away."

"Who are you? Where do you come from? Over there?" as the lad nodded his head toward the Trocha. "Then you are a Spaniard."

A Daughter of Cuba

His dark eyes flashed at this calumny, and he dropped on his knees, weeping, kissing my hand, and begging for a horse.

Then I saw my visitor was a girl disguised; the delicate features and heaving bosom betrayed the secret. The poor child — she was but sixteen — was worn out by fatigue and excitement, and not until we had let her rest awhile in my hammock, could we learn her story. Her name was Rosa Gonzales. Her mother had long been dead; her father had marched East with Gomez, and she feared was killed. Before the war, they owned a small plantation near San Andres; but it was destroyed, and the girl, with a brother and aunt, crossed the Rio Jatibonico, where they lived in a small hut in the hills. But lately the guerilla had infested the neighborhood; and while the aunt went to the city, Rosa in boy's clothes, and her brother, started to cross the Trocha together to find their father. But they were shot at from the forts and her brother was killed. For two days she had lain hidden; and then, during a heavy rain that drove the patrols to the forts, she clambered over the barbed barricade, waded the ditch, and finally had struck our camp. Her hands were terribly lacerated, and she was completely unnerved by her experiences, but she slept quietly for three hours, and then we marched, Rosa perched on the saddle before me. By nightfall I had my weary protégée in a pacifico's house, in a fertile potrero where there were women to care for her, and food of a sort to eat. When I next saw my little friend, I found her too ill to talk.

"Silencio! Tiene calentura!" (fever), said the motherly old nurse, as I drew aside the raw-hide door, and entered the farmhouse.

I stooped and kissed the little oval face, now burning with fever, and whispered that Cuba would soon be free, she would find her father, and they would be very happy. My words brought a hopeful light into her beautiful eyes, but destiny seemed universally cruel in Cuba. Next day I fashioned a rude cross for her grave, and wrote across it "Por Cuba."

On the 21st I joined General Roloff, who was marching across the province. His father was a Russian officer who was forced to flee for a political offence and had married an American. Their son identified himself with the Cuban cause; and both in the ten years' war and the last struggle, he has been a prominent figure, though since his term as Secretary of War has elapsed, he has not held active command.

His aides, Captain Ruiz and Lieutenant Jack, I found were the two men that had shot into and unwittingly helped us hold the Spanish column at Pueblo Nuevo the previous week.

We crossed the Rio Caunao with great difficulty on logs, losing one horse in the mud. At La Citia we found the family I had previously met flying from the Spaniards, and I was formally introduced to "Señorita Consuelo Cosio." The name attracted my attention,

A Path of Devastation

and I found she was Evangelina's first cousin. They were now ruined and homeless, but received every care from Doña Petronilla of San Jocinto, until they made a fresh home.

General Recio had held his own against the enemy for some days, but was greatly retarded by his meagre supply of ammunition. Finally the Spaniards retired slowly to the city. With General Roloff and staff we followed their trail through a wild scene of desolation, — beautiful haciendas were still smouldering, and the road was strewn with rotting carcasses of cattle wantonly slaughtered to starve out the insurgents. Pueblo Nuevo and a dozen villages were destroyed, and the whole district deserted. We experienced great difficulty in securing food, until Jack and I rode foraging, and I finally stalked a deer which lasted two days. Our route for many miles lay through dense forest; Jack and myself rode ahead with a practico to scout. The marching was heavy, and the woods were infested with bandits who gathered in cattle and sold them to the Spaniards. The districts near Spanish cities were very unsafe, and caused me many adventures at various times, though in Cuba libre travelling was secure, and plateados and guerillas unknown. We encountered one suspicious band, but they saw we were both heavily armed, and kept a respectful distance.

On the outskirts of the forest, we found traces of the enemy, and camped in a half-burned house until the general arrived. We then marched quickly and reached the trail of Recio, who was harassing the enemy into the city. We found nine Spanish bodies in one place, one an officer; and in General Rodriguez's ruined plantation, two more were discovered pitched into a well. Graves also were dotted about, and evidently the Spaniards had lost considerably.

We reached the highroad of Gerinimo, and then advanced warily toward Puerto Principe. On the Camino Real, near a ruined chapel, Maceo two years before had made one of the fiercest machete charges of the war. Three hundred Spanish soldiers were surprised and cut to pieces by one-half their number of Cubans. Their dry bones lay in the dust as we rode past.

Near the city we met several wounded men en route for the hospital. One brave lad shot in the chest was obviously dying, and though suffering intense pain, the poor fellow thought only of his mother in the Vedado in Havana. He muttered out a dying message which I promised to deliver. "Mi pobre madre! she will have no one now!" he remarked sadly, and then the blood gushed from his mouth, and he was dead. I detached the bloodstained scapular from his body before we buried him, but had no opportunity for many months to send the relic to the waiting widow in Havana, and tell her how her boy died for Cuba.

The desolation around the city was appalling, glorious "centrals" devastated, the marble palaces of the old slave days toppled into hopeless ruin, the very

A Ridiculous Assertion

grass fired by the retiring Spaniards to foil the Cuban horsemen that skirmished on their flanks night and day.

General Blanco had arrived to welcome Castellanos. Hot-headed insurgents advocated the destruction of his train, passing from Nuevitas to Principe; but if the leaders hated Spain, they could at least respect a brave Spaniard, and the general came and went in safety over the worst strip of railway in the island. Weyler would never have finished the trip alive.

Castellanos spread inflated reports of his achievement. The Government that had quietly ridden out to the next village, he claimed to have utterly routed; he said that his men had seen the bodies of fifty-seven insurgents in Esperanza, while I know every killed and wounded Cuban had been carried to the rear, and he it was who abandoned his dead on the field. The most ridiculous assertion of this officer was that he had captured and burned all the archives of the rebel Government. Surely even Spanish credulity could detect the obvious falsity of this, — that a general should burn such valuable evidences of his success if he had captured them.

Captain Arostigui, with a small rebel detachment, soon showed Blanco that the mambis were still alive, for on the following night his sharpshooters crept close to Puerto Principe and drove in the outposts. Some Cuban infantry also advanced toward the railroad station and opened on the forts, several outlying buildings were fired, and the whole garrison dashed to the barricades to repel this attack on the city.

From a small hill we viewed the scene until the wild volleys of the Spaniards made the rear more dangerous than the front, and bullets whistled around us like hail. The lurid glare lit up the outlines of the quaint old city, which seemed girdled with a ring of fire, as some five thousand Mausers belched flame from the circling barricades. Their crashing, like the ripping of a Titanic carpet, almost drowned the hoarser Remingtons of the Cubans which rang out individually like the popping of champagne corks. It was an effective demonstration for two hundred insurgents, and gave the lie direct to Castellanos' report to his commander-in-chief, that the whole province was subjugated.

Crossing a glorious grazing country toward Arroyo Blanco, I rode over to spend a day with General Recio, who was resting his war-worn troops within sight of the city. Here I obtained a guide and escort, and marched down the Santa Cruz highroad to Palma. Turning sharply to the right through an invisible opening in the palmetto hedge, we struck a secret highway that led across one of the Marquis of Santa Lucia's estates at Najaza, sequestered on paper by Spain. Riding through majestic palm-groves across a savannah in which a herd of semi-wild cattle were grazing, we mounted a hill and were abruptly halted by the rebel guard occupying a Spanish fort captured by Maceo. From them we learned that the

The Marquis of Santa Lucia

marquis was visiting his estate; and though the residencia was destroyed, we found the ex-president of the republic domiciled in a comfortable, if unpretentious, thatched house. The old gentleman welcomed me warmly in purest English; I went to pay a call and stayed a week.

The son of an old grandee family, and heir to the vast Santa Lucia estates, Salvador Cisneros was educated in Philadelphia, and in his early days imbibed the doctrines of Penn. As he happily put it, "I am still a Quaker, but with limitations." He returned to Cuba to control his property, but became a participant in the revolution of '68, though never bearing arms. "There were then plenty of fighters and few thinkers," he said; and his attitude was not unlike the Quaker of old, who loaded the guns for his friends to fire. His vast estates were confiscated, and he devoted his life to Cuba, living in the woods with his compatriots, and suffering great privations. With the peace of '78, some of his property was restored, and he was on the point of securing the most valuable estate, on which stands the town of Minas, when the '95 rebellion started.

By remaining neutral, he could have spent his declining years in comfort; but he chose the good part, electing rather to lose all, that he might serve the cause. He became first president of Cuba libre.

"I am old," he said, "but please God I shall see Cuba freed, and then I can die contented."

He was deeply interested in the welfare of his fair

relative, Evangelina, and gladly accepted photographs I had taken of her in prison. This revived old memories, for civil strife divides the most united of families, and ties are rudely snapped never to be rejoined. "Poor child!" he mused, "as queenly as her mother. We Cubans have all had sad histories."

The week passed quickly, for there were many families to visit, and much to see. It was here I met Señorita Iluminada Agremonte, one of Cuba's most devoted daughters. She is happily named for her sweet disposition, and hundreds of Camagueyan patriots invoke a blessing on her for gentle ministrations to the sick and wounded. To the old marquis she is devoted; and a union of this May with December is possible, for Don Salvador is very young for his years, and wishes to leave his estates to the girl he has known from her baby days.

Here, in the heart of Cuba libre, I realized even more that the Republic was practically an established fact. In the prefect's house near by, the children of the district were taught to read and write, and study the history of their country from school books printed in the official press. There were five papers published in the field, the best of which, "El Cubano Libre," the official organ of Camaguey, edited and produced by Captain Ortiz, boasted of tolerable woodcuts, and was unique in the annals of illustrated journalism.

Though every citizen worked for the good of the republic, there was a Cuban currency of $1,000,000

Citizens of Cuba

silver, and postage stamps of all values were issued in '96. Both dollars and stamps have been eagerly sought after by curio-hunters, and the profits accruing have purchased rifles and cartridges.

According to official statistics, Puerto Principe in '87 had 67,789 inhabitants, and Santiago de Cuba province 272,319. Allowing for an increase of population until the opening of the war, and deducting the number of residents living in the few cities in the East occupied by Spain, the statement that 240,000 people in these two provinces lived under the administration of the Insurgent Government, and contributed to the maintenance of the revolution, is justified. The Cubans there address each other as "Ciudadano" (citizen) with much gravity.

The marquis kindly guided me to all points of interest in the Najaza district, including the talleres, or government work-shops, in which the skilled artisans in the field work "por Cuba." There are several shoe-shops, for hides are plentiful; and in Najaza complete equipments were turned out, tolerable machetes from scrap iron, scabbards, cases, dispatch boxes, belts, and all paraphernalia pertaining to the soldier.

In a separate taller, saddles of the McClellan pattern were made for the cavalry, and ropes of mahagua bark were woven, and straw hats and sudaderos, or straw saddle-pads, were made by the women and children. Beef fat, saponified with wood ash, served as the soap of the community. Honey was plentiful, and the melted wax made excellent "dip" candles. Salt was obtained by refraction on the coast at Cambote, the work being performed by convicts sentenced by the insurgent courts for civil offences.

The marquis was very popular. At every house we passed, tiny children would tear out, a pack of savage curs at their heels, shouting joyously at our approach; and white or black, the old gentleman knew all by name. At Peru, where several noted families reside, a feast was given in our honor, some officers from the fight also being present. Several fair patriots rode out to meet the party, singing a patriotic eulogy, and scattering flowers on the visitors. I also attended the wedding-feast of the eldest Miss Agremonte, who married one of Don Salvador's aides. A palatial residence I visited in the district was owned by Pedro Betencourt, the massive brother-in-law of my host, and who acted as chief of commissary. His daughter was delirious with fever, so we did not make the stay we had anticipated.

Well concealed in the bush at Najaza is the famous Fonseca hospital, the finest in the field. The director, Balbino Lopez, was born in Spain, but worked day and night for the sick insurgents, and such Spaniards as had cared to desert or were abandoned on the field. The wards were airy and well fitted, and among interesting patients were Major Rodriguez, brother to the Havana commander, and M. Carbon, the French chemist, and inventor of the explosive bearing his name. He had been nearly

Captain La Rosa

blown to pieces by the premature explosion of a charge, and his life was only saved by constant attention. The one-time editor of "La Discusion" of Havana was also an inmate.

One young captain, the son of a Principe lawyer, lay dying. Hit in the hip-joint ten months before by a brass-capped bullet, he had lain helpless, without comforts or luxuries. Three operations and amputation had been unsuccessful by reason of the lack of appliances in the bush; but fearing even a tacit recognition of belligerency might be claimed, the Spaniards refused the father permission to bring his dying son to the city, or even to pass their lines to see him.

Riding two leagues farther, and entering the fertile valley of the Polvorin, we descried the figure of an old woman vigorously filling a grave. Turning from her ghoulish task, she rushed to the marquis with hands extended. "Viva la Rosa!" yelled the escort, and thus was I introduced to Captain Rosa, the Florence Nightingale or Clara Barton of Cuba.

"A poor Spaniard," she said apologetically, nodding to the grave, "and my boys are all too sick." Detailing men to finish the task, we rode to the hospital. La Rosa[1] is a creole, who in '67 inherited a

[1] La Rosa in Camaguey occupied a similar position to La Reina de Cuba of the West, Mrs. Hernandez, a refined young Cuban lady who followed her doctor husband to the field to tend sick patriots. Dr. Hernandez lay ill himself in the Managua Hospital, near Sancti Spiritus, when Colonel Orozzo captured the place. This brute deliberately blew out the young doctor's brains as he lay on his pal-

Under Three Flags in Cuba

small estate from the family she had served. When the war broke out she opened her house, and devoted all for the sick and wounded. Through the ten years' war she labored, and in '95 she had treated the first man wounded in Camaguey, and again opened up her estate for the cause, for which Gomez gazetted her captain. She had fifty-eight patients when we called, and raised, prepared, and cooked everything for them. She also distilled medicines from herbs unknown in recognized pharmaceutics, but efficacious nevertheless.

At Lomo Alto, we dined with Dr. Luaces, lieutenant-governor of the province. He is virtually an American, and left his practice in Philadelphia to aid the establishment of a civil government under the revolutionists. He did effective work in organizing the prefecturas in the East and establishing a postal service. He was then preparing to dispatch one of the sorry mail-boats that slipped through the blockading line, either to the Bahamas or Jamaica at regular intervals, and thus sustained communication with the outer world.

In this district, General Xavier Vega, an officer who had done excellent service with Gomez, was camped on parole, awaiting court-martial for neglect of duty. He was the seventh leader of Cuba, but he twice allowed the Spaniards to round up cattle with-

let with his wife's arms around him. The other patients were also murdered; the young lady alone was spared. I last saw her in Havana, a prisoner, and being taken to a penal settlement, by Weyler's order.

Security in the Manigua

out attacking them, and his efficiency in the past did not save him from disgrace and loss of command. The regulations of the peripatetic Government were rigidly enforced and respected accordingly. Colonel Ramon succeeded Vega. One of the brightest officers on his staff was Captain Enrique Martinez, the youngest son of the noted Martinez family of Havana.

That night we reached the estate of Señora Pina at Sabanilla. I was amazed to find this refined Cuban home remaining intact, close to the Camino Real, but the Spaniards had never ventured in that direction, and the señora and her three pretty daughters lived fearlessly in a district swarming with rebels. They were of course patriotic to a fault, and extended hospitality to all officers in the vicinity; but that these educated ladies could live unprotected in the country with all sorts and conditions of rebels around, is an eloquent tribute to the discipline governing the scattered bands, and the respect ever shown to women by the Cuban army. Colonel Vivanco, the young Secretary of State, who has since married one of the daughters, was visiting them, and leaving the marquis to confer with him, I pressed on to Sabanita de Vie, where General Roloff was camped. He was busily formulating a scheme to destroy part of the Trocha, by exploding two hundred and fifty bombs simultaneously on the line. He had established quite a pretentious factory, but the American invasion obviated the necessity for the demonstration.

With his leg fixed in cepo de campana, or rough

stock, a horse thief, whom I recognized as the young orderly of Colonel Alonzo, was imprisoned in camp. I was asked to take him with my escort to Brigadier Portuondo, inspector-general of the Eastern forces, whose horse he had stolen. The crime was punishable by death; and I felt a double interest in the prisoner when he asked me to detour a league that he might say farewell to the wife he had married but three months before, and had "borrowed" the horse to visit. She proved a mere girl, and begged and pleaded so hard for her young spouse, that I gave him half an hour to stay with her, hoping sincerely he would mount and bolt with his wife behind him. He came up at the appointed time, true to his word; and I was subsequently able to intercede sufficiently to gain his acquittal, on the plea that he had two days' leave, and foolishly borrowed the horse to v˙ the wife he had married, only to be parted ᶠ the change of the government headquarters.

South of Puerto Principe the country is ope., and there was an abundance of supplies. The Camagueyano is hospitable to a fault, and from every farmhouse one passed, the owner came forth to take your horse, inviting you with natural euphuism to enter "your own" house for a jicara of coffee, milk, or guaparo, for the propination of Cuba Free. To refuse these attentions is an offence only exceeded by offering payment in return; for the poorest of these honest guajiros has an untainted pride of race. Descendants of the old Castilian colonials, they have

Camaguey

virtually practised endogamy; and one Cubanita I knew, was spoken of in awed pity, for she was actually going to marry a young man from the next province. Camaguey is rightly termed the Kentucky of Cuba, and the charming people of the province have good reason to be proud as the Artibans. They are the oldest and most patriotic Cubans in the island. The countrywomen are exceedingly graceful, and when dressed for fiesta in their simple white gowns, they could take their place in any social gathering without notice. Yet the education of the middle farming class is very elementary, and numbers of these graceful creatures can neither read nor write. I met many accomplished Cuban ladies also in the manigua, some who had been educated in the Sacred Heart or other American institutions.

Cuban women marry at a tender age, and families of over twenty are common. The white pacificos have many admirable traits, and exceedingly few vices. Intoxicating liquors are unknown outside the cities, and home is the only attraction they have. Though Weylerism has exterminated the bulk of these people, the residue can yet form the foundation of a flourishing race, strengthened by immigration.

Parts of Camaguey, especially the eastern borders, and the succeeding country in the Cauto district, are very thickly wooded. The exuberance of the Cuban forest is incredible, and equals the profuse tangle of the African jungle. The ground is covered with decaying leaves and rotting trunks, around which

Under Three Flags in Cuba

brilliant lizards dart continuously, and pythons of varying size abound. The lower trees form a canopy with the adnascent creepers that circle upward from the dense undergrowth. Royal palms, with smooth columnar stems and finely pinnated leaves, usually fringe the woods, but even they are entwined with the parasitic plants and creepers that tangle the branches of the brighter trees in a vast struggle for existence and upward growth, that remind one of M. Rochegrosse's "Angoisse Humaine." Wild boars and deer are common in the inner recesses, though cartridges were not, and they were thus seldom molested. The scorpion on land and the cayman or crocodile in the rivers and brooks are alone to be avoided. Cuban snakes are generally harmless, the iguana and chameleon abound. There are birds in abundance, of beautiful plumage; parrots and humming-birds are the most common. Vultures, battened on carrion, make efficient scavengers, and nature has supplied both saprophagans and saprophytes in abundance to deal with the decaying matter of their respective kingdoms. The timber of Cuba is especially valuable, ebony, mahogany, cedar, and other cabinet woods abounding.

On February 2 I visited Guimaro, a strongly fortified little city captured by Garcia the previous year. While sighting the Hotchkiss gun during the attack on this city, Osgood, the famous athlete and son of a brave American officer afterwards at Santiago, fell fatally wounded.

An Incident of Guimaro

A terrible incident of the siege was related to me by an ex-Spanish sergeant, captured with the garrison, but who, with eighty others, elected to remain with the rebels rather than be liberated to miserable treatment in the Imperial army. Rita Salcedo, the sixteen-year-old daughter of a loyal Spanish planter, was secretly betrothed to the Cuban administrator of her father's estate near the town. When Weyler's atrocities rang through the island this young man joined his countrymen in the field. Before Guimaro was attacked, he sent unsigned letters to her, by a guard he had known in the days of peace.

The rebel artillery awoke the libidinous Spaniards of the garrison one morning, and they swore that a traitor had betrayed the fact that they had little food left to withstand a siege, the convoy being then due. The officers drank up the rum stores, and a tipsy party started a spy hunt. One Cuban pacifico was killed in the street, and then the rumor that Señorita Rita, the belle of the city, had received letters from rebels, became noised abroad. They seized the sentry who had passed the missives through the lines, and the frightened man confessed, saying that none but simple love messages were sent. Mid the roar of battle this party of ruffians dashed into Salcedo's residence. The father loudly protested that he was a loyal Spaniard, and fought like a lion when they tried to seize the horror-stricken girl who clung to him. "It was too horrible," said the ex-sergeant; "the poor father prayed and cursed. He begged them to spare his child; swore she was as innocent as the Madonna; but they tore her from his grasp and dragged her half dead with fear to the veranda; a noose was put round the beautiful throat. Mi madre! The frail girl was hauled up with a fearful jerk. The graceful form was convulsed, the beautiful bosom heaved; Dios mio! the child was dead. No, Señor! I did not care to serve longer under officers that permitted such a deed."

From Guimaro to Bayamo, the road is excellent, and passing south of the historical Zanjon, where the treaty of '78 was signed, we crossed the Rio Jobabo into Oriente on February 3.

General Enrique Colazzo was at Santa Luisa, quartered in a palatial residence furnished probably by Maple. For five days previous we had traversed a bad district and suffered many privations through prairie fires. Thanks, however, to my hospitable host, and his chief of staff, Colonel Hernandez, I was soon refreshed in body and mind by a bath, a meal, clean clothes, and sleep. Colonel Charles Hernandez, then of Colazzo's staff, is the typical American Cuban. Retaining the warm-hearted and chivalrous traits of his race, but reared in the free atmosphere of the United States, and untarnished by the environment of Spain's mediæval civilization, he is a living example of what the true Cuban may be under happier auspices.

This command led the assault against Victoria de Las Tunas, the fourth city of Santiago. It was cap-

CUBAN CAVALRY AT LAS TUNAS.

A STREET IN LAS TUNAS, SHOWING HOUSES DEMOLISHED BY COLONEL FUNSTON'S ARTILLERY.

Capture of Las Tunas

tured on September 13, '97, by Garcia, after three days' hard fighting. Weyler reported the city as impregnable, and its fall caused great chagrin in Spain. Standing in an open plain, it was defended by twenty-one blockhouses, and a heavy stone cuartel, which was alone garrisoned by two hundred men. By throwing up intrenchments at night, Garcia was able to hold his ground with small loss. His tactics might have been profitably followed by Shafter, both against San Juan and Caney, where infantry were exposed to a galling fire, and positions stormed without artillery support. Colonel Funston was in command of the artillery manned by Americans and Cubans. The guns were intrenched within four hundred yards of the city, and for three days the bombardment continued, until the outworks and forts were reduced. The stone cuartel remained standing.

The Cubans then stormed the city, the dynamite gun was rushed through a breach in the back of a house, and opened fire through a window against the cuartel just across the street, which was soon in ruins. The garrison then capitulated. The insurgent loss was sixty-three, including an Englishman, Major Chapleau, killed by Funston's side. Of the fifteen hundred defenders, forty per cent were killed or wounded. The latter were well cared for, and all the captured soldiers were liberated on the signed promise of their commander that they should be returned to Spain and no longer bear arms. This promise General Luque never kept, and many of the men, enraged at their return to duty, deserted to the Cubans. The bloody guerillas taken in Las Tunas were tried by court-martial and sixty of them executed. All conscripted Spaniards were spared. The guerilla fiends received no mercy from the Cubans, and though far more equal wars give precedents, I think greater clemency might have been exercised. Men avenging the honor and death of wives and sisters at the hands of such brutes may be excused severity, but despite their crime, an execution of sixty at once was demoralizing to the victorious force.

In Tunas I discovered dozens of shrapnel, fired by the Cubans, unexploded. Upon close examination I found the fuses were dummies, the bursting charge sand. Some rascally firm had supplied the fake projectiles at an exorbitant price in New York, knowing full well that filibusters could get no redress in Federal courts.

At the end of January, '98, General Pando from Manzanillo planned extensive operations with 35,000 men. Three columns were to march simultaneously against Garcia: General Luque from Holguin; Vara del Rey, killed later at El Caney, from Jiguani; and Linares from Santiago. Thus assailed from all sides, Garcia was to be annihilated. Early in February, Luque and Vara del Rey had joined columns at San Francisco, and though warned that I could not continue my journey, I had no stupendous difficulty in evading the enemy, and seeing the futility of their movements.

Garcia's American Officers

During one running fight that I witnessed, General Luque's son was dangerously wounded, and the whole column placed at fault by four hundred rebel cavalry, who marched and countermarched on the flanks, firing into the ranks, but never fighting a pitched battle against the 12,000 soldiers. The number of Spanish shell fired into the woods without touching this skeleton force, before Luque retired to Gibara, I cannot estimate.

When riding south to Jiguani a few days later, I went ahead, and through a faulty guide I rode into the enemy, and escaped capture only by swimming my horse across the broad and swift Cauto River that threatened every moment to sweep me down stream to be riddled by the forts at Embarcadero. I recrossed later in safety, and rejoined my escort, who had camped in the woods. As we advanced eastward, cattle grew scarcer, and we should have fared badly but for the fortunate advent of Brigadier Portuondo, who had a stock of smoked beef or pemmican.

During a brief visit to the command of Colonel Esteban, I met two American artillery officers, Major Joyce, then going to the Government, and Major Latrobe, now captain, U. S. A. I had nearly starved for a week, and Latrobe generously insisted that I should take a square meal from his very scanty store. Penny, Jones, Janey, and Divine, the other American officers with Garcia, I missed by a few hours. They were then preparing to leave Cuba after months of arduous service. At Guimaro, Las Tunas, Guisa, and a dozen hard-fought battles they did yeoman service.

On February 12, camped in a cow-shed at El Jardin, I was awakened at an early hour by a breathless guide. "Despierte usted, Señorito! For God's sake get out from here! General Vara del Rey is but a mile away; his advance guard is just coming in!" We packed up and rode out rapidly, only to be stopped by a second scout. "Halt! as you value your life, sir! The gringoes are just ahead, camped on that hill." We were between two columns. Portuondo had sent his impedimenta into the woods, and struck across country to the South; but I was anxious to reach General Garcia and complete my mission. To turn off meant days of delay, so I joined a ragged Cuban guerilla preparing to skirmish, hoping to get through during the fight.

Six Cubans held a dummy position, firing repeatedly at the advance guard. When they retired, the enemy with a loud cry of "Viva España!" dashed up to capture the trinchera. In a moment I saw the tactics — the place was mined. A young lieutenant led the useless charge, and I shuddered to think of his fate. The electrician, a French chemist, lay in the grass behind me. "Let her go, my brave!" yelled our comandante. A muffled roar followed. It was a moment too soon. The young Spaniard staggered back, blinded by fragments of earth and stone, his face streaming with blood; others were

A Narrow Escape

injured, but one only was killed. Fired a second later, the bomb would have blown to pieces the entire company.

Latin courage is curious; the ardor that after success will lead men to rush unrestrained to death or victory is damped by reverse. Cuban and Spaniard show the same characteristic. The eager Cubans who had waited impatiently to charge into the enemy under cover of the explosion, now hurriedly retired, allowing the Spaniards to camp unchecked.

The major collected fifteen of his cavalry to escort me three leagues beyond the enemy. We passed the blackened ruins of the town of Baire, the cemetery of which still remained intact, though next day the Imperial troops terribly defiled the graves of those interred by the insurgents. Over the gate, under a skull and cross-bones, the following legend was inscribed: "Sum quod eris, fui quod es." (I am what thou wilt be, I have been what thou art.)

We rode on into an open plain fringed with woods, and though two houses were smouldering, we had no thought of Spaniards there, when a volley rang from the trees. Our jaded horses intelligently responded to the spur, and we crouched in the saddle and galloped madly to cover. But the enemy's aim was execrable. The pentacapsular Mausers fire quickly, and five distinct volleys rang out before we had reached the trees. At eight hundred yards' range, and despite the flat trajectory of the rifles, no one was hit, though the bullets whistled uncomfortably about us.

Under Three Flags in Cuba

It began to rain; we had lost our trail, but we plunged forward through the calamiferous swamps and dense bush, seeking a place to camp. Seeing lights ahead we rode cautiously toward them. To my relief the friendly challenge rang out, "Alto! Quién va?" I was about to reply "Cuba!" when to my utter astonishment the guide yelled "España!" and whispering "Spaniards!" galloped madly away. The Spanish outpost, thinking to entrap us, had given the Cuban challenge, and thanks only to the "practico" who detected the Peninsular accent, were we saved. The sentry, thinking by the answer that we were a friendly party, loudly shouted to reassure us, saying they were Spaniards, not "mambis," that the challenge was a ruse, and we must come back.

At a late hour we off-saddled until daylight and then found our road. On the afternoon of the 10th, heavy firing was heard at Descanso. A company of Garcia's infantry was skirmishing with Vara del Rey's column, then erecting a heliograph tower and fort on a hill to signal between Santiago city and Jiguani.

It was nearly dark when we rode round the enemy's flank, and found General Sanchez coolly camped, with his small escort, within a mile of them. We slept that night with spent bullets sputtering around, and at daybreak I reached General Calixto Garcia's [1]

---

[1] General Garcia had one of the most picturesque records of the war. His father was a wealthy land-owner, and when the war broke out in '68 young Calixto Garcia took the field with a large

General Garcia

headquarters, a league distant, and ended the perilous ride.

contingent of his father's laborers. After considerable service, during which he captured Jiguani and Holguin, he led a small force against the Spaniards at Santa Maria on September 3, 1873. His command was surrounded and cut up almost to a man. The cavalry spurred in to capture the leader, and after firing five rounds from his revolver, he turned the sixth against himself. The ball, passing miraculously up through the chin and roof of his mouth, came out of his forehead. He lay long unconscious, and an officer riding over the field recognized the leader and ordered him to be brought in. Contrary to expectation he lived, was court-martialled, and sentenced to be shot with four other leaders. On the fatal morning he was too weak to stand, so the imposing spectacle took place without him.

Maceo led his followers against Manzanillo, determined to effect a rescue, and as the guard there was small, the wounded prisoner was rowed out to the warship " San Francisco de Borja " for safety. The Carlist rebellion had broken out, and the very next day the Spanish fleet was ordered home, and Garcia was thus taken to Spain.

After eight years in prison at Valencia, he was released and went to New York. In 1888 he was the chosen leader of the Guerra chiquita, or little war. His expedition was stopped in the United States, and he went from Jamaica in a small boat to Santiago, only to find the insurgents had heard of his frustrated trip and had dispersed. For weeks, thousands of soldiers hunted for him, and a price was placed on his head, dead or alive. Then Blanco issued an amnesty, offering free pardon and the liberty also of José Maceo, then in prison, if Garcia would surrender and leave Cuba. On these terms he came in, and by explicit orders from Madrid, both he and Maceo were shipped to Spain and sentenced to life imprisonment.

Blanco protested against such treachery, and threatened to resign; so Garcia was liberated on parole. Maceo escaped to Gibraltar, where an officious police inspector gave him up to Spain. The British Government immediately discharged their official, and demanded the return of the prisoner, arrested wrongfully on British territory. Thus Maceo also escaped his fate.

Garcia, held under surveillance, made his living by teaching

Under Three Flags in Cuba

English, and finally gained a position in the Spanish Bank. He gave his sons an excellent education, the eldest graduating at Cambridge University. Carlos and Justo, the two younger, obtained their degrees in Madrid. When Weyler went to Cuba, Calixto Garcia determined to escape and take the field against his notoriously brutal enemy of '68. With his son Carlos he escaped on horseback, successfully crossed the frontier, and eventually reached New York. There they purchased and outfitted the steamship "Hawkins," for Cuba, and secretly left harbor only to be wrecked off Sandy Hook. Several were drowned, guns, ammunition, and stores were lost, and Garcia and his staff were picked up by a steamer, and landed half dead in New York, to be arrested for filibustering. He and his son were released on their own bond for $2000 each, and after cautiously working day and night to fit out the S. S. "Bermuda," they forfeited bond and sailed for Cuba, landing safely a few days later. With Gomez in the West, the revolution had waned in Oriente, but the prestige of the new leader strengthened the cause, and he mobilized and maintained the only force in Cuba that could truly be called an army corps.

Justo Garcia, the third son, was then practising dentistry in Manila, but he left to join his father in Cuba. Embarking for London on an English liner, he landed at Port Said, where the steamer touched and was pounced upon by the Spanish consul. The British captain protested, but as the arrest took place in a treaty port, where all countries have equal rights, the prisoner was removed to Spain. The authorities had only the vaguest suspicion that he would join the rebellion, but he was the "son of his father," and that gained him a life sentence in the penal colony at Chafarinas, North Africa. Being well supplied with money, the young Cuban induced a Greek fruit-seller, who made trips from a neighboring island, to take him off. In a sorry row boat, Garcia, a fellow-patriot Plana, and the Greek, set out on the night of August 4, 1897, and after a perilous and almost unprecedented voyage for such a craft, they reached Nemours. The French authorities allowed them to leave Algiers for France, but they notified Madrid, and extradition was asked and granted for them as Anarchists. In Republican France the two men were taken from the train at Cette, to be turned over to the Spanish authorities, but the prompt action of Garcia's brother-in-law, an American physician in Paris, delayed the delivery, and finally the police modified the action by expelling them from France. A few weeks later both men had landed from the "Dauntless" and were fighting for Cuba libre.

Colonel Garcia

Colonel Carlos Garcia, the most efficient officer I met in Cuba, had made himself famous by capturing a Spanish gunboat on the Rio Cauto. He organized the forces in that difficult district, isolating Spanish posts and attacking the convoys, until the two thousand mules at Manzanillo and the vast store of bullock-carts were lost or abandoned, and communication was only possible by a flotilla on the river. With Rabbi, his forces took Guisa, and he led the attack on Guamo in person. Here eighty per cent of the Cuban forces were killed or wounded. While I was in Oriente, General Garcia was giving his younger son the chance to win his spurs by detailing him for the most difficult and dangerous commissions. At the San Francisco fight against Luque, he led the cavalry and was advanced one grade for his daring. Garcia also had two daughters. The elder is married to Dr. Whitmarsh of Paris. The younger, Mercedes, the idol of her father, was an invalid from youth. At every opportunity the sick child in New York and the father in the Cuban wilds exchanged letters, and when I left the general, I was specially intrusted with a voluminous epistle for Mercedes with some flowers from Las Tunas. The doctors said that the hope of seeing her father again, alone had sustained her. When he died on his way to join her to enjoy his well-earned rest she never rallied, and followed her father one week later.

CHAPTER IX

Pando's Failure. — Garcia's Staff. — Baracoa. — Over the Sierras. — A Frightful Storm. — A Night Attack. — Unexpected Supper. — Before Santiago. — The Guerilla. — I enter the City. — Cienfuegos. — Outrages against Britons.

AFTER my narrow escapes in passing Pando's heavy columns that were attempting to hem in Garcia, I expected to see some interesting fighting. But the enemy always seemed to pass our camp by half a league, though the Cuban flag flew in an open district, and the escort of the general was quartered in large sheds of palm-leaf, similar to the camp shelters used by the British army in west Africa. After witnessing the futility of such vast operations against this small force, only two conclusions were possible. The Spaniards either realized that their cause in Cuba was lost, and exertion beyond an aimless march of devastation to mislead the people at home was useless, or the generals were wilfully prolonging the struggle for the spoils accruing, regardless of their country's impending ruin.

I was with General Garcia for some weeks in the open and fertile district of the Cauto River, close to the Spanish towns of Jiguani and Bayamo. Extra

Spanish Operations

outposts were thrown out around camp, and from a neighboring loma we frequently watched the columns moving like light-colored snakes over the plain. We could see the heliograph on El Galletta flashing instructions to the army in the field, and thus every move was revealed to the Cubans, who knew the code. At daybreak a party of rebel cavalry would sally forth to skirmish, and the thunder of musketry would roll through the trees for hours. At night the horsemen would return, muddy and bedraggled, bringing in perhaps one man wounded, or reporting one killed. I witnessed numerous skirmishes, afterwards locating the Spanish positions by piles of cartridge cases almost uselessly expended, and invariably some Spanish graves. In these so-called battles, the bushwhackers gained the advantage, and the wretched Spanish boys wondered why their officers did not either rout the enemy, or stay safely in the cities. Naturally they had little to gain, the officers everything, in the faked Spanish victories that were daily cabled to Madrid and foisted on the ever-hopeful Spaniards. The cross of San Fernando, so liberally distributed by the Queen Regent as a reward for extraordinary bravery, was seldom if ever deserved by the recipients; not that gallantry in action was an unknown quality, but because the recommendation from the general went usually to the highest bidder.

General Garcia was a great admirer of the United States, and also of England and her colonial policy. While he did not directly favor annexation, he fully

Under Three Flags in Cuba

realized that it was eventually inevitable. Cuba, he felt, must form her own government first, and become an independent republic that could then honorably seek admission to the Union. Forcible annexation would not be tolerated by the Cubans, since they had not fought three years only to change masters.

The general had selected for his staff chiefly officers educated in the States. Colonel Collazo, brother of the General of Las Tunas, was chief of staff. Colonel Arango, a well known society man before the war, Colonel C. M. Poey, commanding the cavalry Escolta, Colonel Nicolas de Cardenas, who can boast the bluest blood of Old Castile, and Colonel Torriente, once chief aide to Gomez, were prominent officers in the Estado Mayor. The son of the late General Marti had taken up the mantle of his sire and was with the staff. Another college graduate from New York, Major Miranda, Majors Lorie and Machado, Captains Ferrera and Martinez, Lieutenants Rosado and Goodrich were other officers serving at the time. A New York lawyer named Poey was in charge of a Hotchkiss battery, and had just returned from successfully bombarding a Cauto port; his brother, afterwards surgeon, U. S. A., was with the medical force. Three brothers Portuondo held commands in the artillery, which consisted of seventeen guns, ranging from the modern Sims Dudley to an old Sevillian bronze cannon. Lieutenant Preval, brother of the American vice-consul in Santiago, was chief of the line of communications.

GENERAL GARCIA AND STAFF.

Cuban Ideals

The surgeon-in-chief of Oriente, Colonel Valiente, is known beyond Cuba by his self-registering clinical thermometer. He generously insisted that I should share his pavilion, which was also his operating and consulting room and dispensary. He was with General José Maceo when he was killed at El Gato, and among other mementos of the war, he gave me the fatal bullet, which he had extracted.

A most interesting figure in east Cuba was General Rabbi, the famous old Indian warrior. He was of magnificent proportions, and made an imposing figure when mounted. General Menocal, commanding the Guisa district, is well-known in America as an engineer, and his brother, then a brigadier in the West, painted the "Landing of Columbus" for the Columbian Exposition in Chicago.

One could but be struck with the patriotism that had led such men as these into the field. Realizing that while license abounded, liberty under Spain was as the Kalendæ Græcæ, they had, with their race, struggled against the usurpation of man over man, first peacefully, but later with armed protest. The patriots lacked material, but supreme resources come from extreme resolution, and their resolves were steadfast, though many an anonymous and forgotten hero sacrificed life itself. The Cubans gilded terrible realities with the ideal of freedom, but their sufferings were intense, and since I have seen and know, I desire to pay tribute, let those scorn who may.

Early in March, Colonel Vieta, a survivor of the

Under Three Flags in Cuba

"Tilly," landed with a smaller expedition at Puerto Padre. His advent with the news of the diplomatic tension between Washington and Madrid, caused great excitement in camp. In response to inquiries brought by this expedition from the State department, to ascertain the strength of the insurgents and their probable attitude in case of war, and since I had now procured the signed statements of every leader of note, unanimously rejecting autonomy, and the exact status of the rebels was of some moment in Washington, it was deemed expedient for me to attempt to reach the capital with reports of my visits to the various commands, and despatches from the Assembly. After visiting General Sanchez, the brave and popular commander of the Barracoa district, I marched south with General Demetrius Castillo, who was then assuming command of the distracted district of Santiago City. My trip in the East had provided incident, interesting and exciting, to record which would fill many books.

As General Linares was marching north from Sant Ana, I left General Castillo, who was preparing to oppose the Spaniards with two thousand men, and made a forced march with Captain and Lieutenant Maestre, hoping to pass round the enemy by night. A significant heliograph message, however, announced that all operations were suspended, and the column retired. Captain Castillo was sent forward with an escort to accompany me through the dangerous San Luis district, but he fell sick, and unwilling to delay,

Crossing the Sierras

I pushed forward alone with a servant and guide. Riding on the camino, we were held up by a ferocious-looking cavalry squad, apparently guerillas or bandits. Fight and flight were impossible, and we fearfully threw up our hands, to discover that our assailants were Cuban irregulars, searching for horse-thieves.

At the zona I luckily met Preval, who had just been to secure mail over the barricade at Sant Ana. Colonel Congera selected guides and a fresh escort, and Preval agreed to accompany me over the mountains. The Sierras rise like a wall, and though I had encountered many steep rides in reaching the South, we were now actually mountaineering. We rode zigzag upward the whole day, and finally reached a glorious plateau, sprinkled with abandoned coffee estates and covered with cocoa in paying quantities. Apparently the fruit had never been plucked, and the ground under the trees was covered with wasted kernels. We found food very scarce in the mountains, unripe guava alone sustaining us. It was bitterly cold also, especially at night, and the change developed latent malaria. Occasionally I shot a jutia, or small species of tree bear, yielding rank but edible meat, but the journey was a hard one. The people in the higher recesses were half-barbarous, Indio-negroes, mixed descendants of those who had fled to the hills to escape cruel taskmasters. Their patois was a curious conglomeration of Spanish, Siboney, and French, and they held a precarious existence. Once we struck the stronghold of the Benitez gang, noted brigands in the palmy days. They were in sore straits then, but gave us advice, respect, and chocolate. We rode for miles, continuously up and down, encountering no one save solitary sentinels from the zona, perched on the rocks, watching the movement of the enemy in the strongly invested Sant Ana valley. The Sierras del Cobre rise in vast ridges abruptly from the sea, piled back peak on peak, their sides clothed with impenetrable thicket, jagged with stupendous precipices of volcanic rock overhanging the gloomy ravines far below.

At times our trail led through narrow gorges, the rocks rising grimly in solid walls of basalt and ironstone, while in the clefts grew orchids of the rarest kind; veritable treasures for collectors, who can now make the ride. In many places the soil was ferruginous and my compass was useless. The ruddy hue of the ironstone formed a pleasing contrast with the rich emerald of the sparse grass and luxuriant evergreen that filled the gorges; the scenery was magnificent, but we paid little attention to the stupendous panorama at our feet. My mount went dead lame; constant clambering over sharp stones, with precipitous trails and even worse descents, had completely worn out his forehoofs. It was impossible to halt, and by this time privations and lack of food had so told upon us that we had not the strength to walk. Then his back gave out, and our trip grew protracted, as I could only spur the faithful beast a few miles each day.

A Frightful Storm

The season of las lluvias was over, but we did not escape two frightful storms, during one of which, on March 17, we nearly lost our lives. It had been a bright day, but toward three o'clock when crossing a most dangerous path high on the mountain-side, the sudden darkening of the sky, and the exhalation of fœtid miasma from the valley, foretold an approaching temporal. The sky grew black as ink; we had no place for shelter, and clung against the trail cut in the mountain-side, which rose like a wall above, and dropped in a stupendous ravine below. When the tempest burst in all its fury, we momentarily expected to be hurled into the abyss. The horses snorted in terror, and reared and plunged on the ledge as we crouched beside the rock, holding their bridles. The blackness increased, but the whole heavens became suffused in light, the jet clouds rolled in flame while the rock trembled with the frightful roar of thunder that followed. The scene was wild and magnificent, the rushing wind tore up trees by the roots, and whirled them over the peaks, great boulders crashed down, fortunately bounding over our heads, but covering us in a shower of stones.

My escort, gigantic negroes of the mountains, lay on their faces, while the white sergeant prayed to the Virgin for deliverance. Leaves, stones, branches, flew by us; thunder roared at brief intervals, bursting, crashing, and re-echoing from peak to peak with the lurid flashes of electric fluid that played around.

Under Three Flags in Cuba

We were in, not under the storm, the black clouds loomed on all sides, rolling together, wrestling and parting, and I trust I may never again witness so magnificent, yet so frightful a spectacle. Twice the earth quaked perceptibly, and a sulphurous smell almost overcame us. The old craters and volcanic peaks seemed to belch fire and smoke as electric clouds hung flaming from the summits. It was as if the seventh angel had sounded, and the thunders and lightnings and the great earthquake attending the doom of Babylon had burst forth. We lay speechless with awe, and one realized the infinite weakness and insignificance of mere man when confronted with the stupendous power of the great Unknown. The impressions made upon me during that storm will never be effaced.

The tempest died out as suddenly as it came, and then we realized our cramped position, and crept painfully onward, our faces bruised, chilled to the bone by our wet clothes. We descended next day into the San Luis Valley, a pass leading into Santiago, and strongly invested by the enemy. We fell in with a negro Cuban guerilla and obtained a late and unexpected supper. The rebels in reprisal were preparing to raid an adjoining ingenio. I was too weak to ride out to the fight, but from the camp in the foothills could see the brush. The engine-house was strongly invested and every aperture belched fire. A candela soon lit up the scene, revealing the swarthy faces of the Spaniards, and the black visages

A Nocturnal Raid

of their negro assailants, for save officers there were few white insurgents in Santiago.

Above the crash of rifles rose the rally "Viva España!" mingled with "Viva Cuba y Maceo!" from the bronze-throated orientals. It was a weird scene, the outhouses were soon blazing, while the flames raced over the cane-field like the surging of rushing water; from the villa rose the frightened screams of women. But the Cuban fire soon slackened, and the fuerza came trotting back, reporting the gringoes too strong. They proudly exhibited some prisoners of war, pacificos captured in the lodge, including the milkman of the district. His cans were soon emptied down more needy throats, and the men were liberated. Later three soldiers were brought in. The insurgents were an irregular band, and fearing for the safety of the Spaniards, I hurried down to see what could be done, but the rebels shared their supper with the prisoners, and they were finally sent to Cambote.[1]

[1] I had visited Cambote previously. Here several hundred Spaniards were living; some deserters, others, including officers, had formed the garrison captured at Guisa. Garcia had liberated the garrison of Las Tunas on the written promise of the comandante that the men should not again bear arms. General Luque violated this pledge, and when Guisa fell the garrison were given provisional liberty only by Garcia, pending the assurance of Blanco or Sagasta that the officers and men should be returned to Spain if delivered to the nearest post. These simple terms were ignored, so the prisoners remained. They all looked sick and feeble, and though they expressed their gratitude to the Cubans for considerate treatment, they were indignant against their own countrymen for scorning the proviso. Their mail went regularly by the insurgent boat to Jamaica, thence

Under Three Flags in Cuba

Finding we could not pass down the valley to the city, we again took to the hills, crossing the Sierras Maestra, rounding midway the Pico Turquino, over ten thousand feet above sea level. On the Gran Piedra we were above the clouds, and while below the day was dull, our eyes rested over an expanse of cloudland resembling snow-covered steppes, with a glorious dome of sunlit sky overhead.

Passing down the mountain through the vapor was extremely dangerous, and several times my horse jibbed, where the trail gave sharp turns against the side of the rocky precipice. A false step meant certain death, and the sure-footed Cuban mounts seemed bewildered by the mist. A trooper ahead of me had much trouble with his steed. I warned him twice not to use the spur, but his horse stopped dead and he gave it a vicious dig. The frightened beast sprang forward, missed its footing, and horse and rider made a mad plunge into space. Twice the poor fellow screamed, but his fall was unbroken, and he was doubtlessly dead before he reached the gorge below. Saddened with this disaster, sickened by hardships and difficulties, my nerve gave out, and

being sent to El Heraldo for distribution, but no replies were possible. In response to the entreaties of these unfortunate men, I obtained fresh copies of the stipulations written by General Garcia, and promised to see that they reached Madrid. The general also wrote a personal letter to Señor Pi y Margal in Madrid, asking him to exert his influence on behalf of these soldiers. I saw that these letters were delivered; but the events that followed obviated the necessity of action. One officer, Captain Ferrera, and many of the soldiers joined the insurgent army and fought against Spain at Santiago.

A Magnificent Panorama

thanks only to Preval did we continue the march that day. At length we reached the Ojo del Toro, and finally sighted La Galleta, beyond which lay Santiago City. On March 18, after another frightful climb, we reached the fringe of mountains on the coast. The sea rolled in, far below us, and from that ridge, the most extensive view in the world, save the vista of Teneriffe, can be obtained. Away to the south, shrouded in the sunlit haze of the Caribbean, lay Jamaica; on the east, toward Maysi, glistened the Windward Passage fringed by the southern Bahamas and Hayti. Westward, Santiago seemed a city of Liliput, nestling at the foot of the range. Two white gunboats, a Ward liner, and the graceful "Purisima Concepcion," resembled four toy ships in a midget harbor, while a tiny train steamed leisurely out by the head of the bay. Beyond rose the opposite spur of the Sierras that extend to Manzanillo. Exactly three months later, I viewed that same scene; but with far different emotions, for below flew "Old Glory," and the American army was advancing to battle for humanity.

It took us many hours to descend to the beach, and, in constant fear of discovery, we camped in an old coffee-mill at Las Guasimas. At daybreak we passed over the Jaragua iron district, owned by the Carnagie Co. Though the insurgents had made no attempt to invest the coast valley and foothills, everything was in ruins, and Weylerism was rampant in the only district in east Cuba where there was

Under Three Flags in Cuba

positively no excuse for it. Crossing by side trails, we passed the forts and gained the camino leading to Caney. I left the escort near the Rio Aguadores, where we met an American writer, who had just reached the manigua. Giving him my spare equipment, I rode forward to reconnoitre the Spanish lines, and attempt to pass into Santiago city.

Riding to a bank I was scanning the line of wire and forts a mile beyond, when a clatter of hoofs on the road alarmed me. I sprang into the saddle, and turned my horse toward the thicket; but the half-dead steed staggered painfully, and ere I could urge it forward, a returning party of guerilla cantered round the bend. The bewhiskered leader, who proved to be Colonel Castellvi, of Bourbon blood and bloody fame, yelled "Americano, sirrinder!" as if proud of his English. I was paralyzed with terror. A commission, with government papers, and for the Yankees, would be no mean capture; and the swarthy faces of these cut-throats, their grim smiles of satisfaction as they drew their machetes and started toward me, and my impending fate, were indelibly photographed on my mind in the brief second of indecision that seemed an hour. Thrice I dug in my cruel spurs, until my exhausted horse quivered with agony; then he stumbled painfully forward. I could feel the machetes of my pursuers uplifted above me in my fright, and flung myself from the saddle, only to realize that a barbed fence had checked the enemy. Retarded by boots and spurs, winged by fear, I raced

Almost Captured

to cover as they swarmed through the adjacent gap.

A carbine popped, then a revolver, and as I ducked instinctively, I fell headlong, my satchel of papers flying from me; but I was up and on again instantaneously, and plunged into the thicket. Crawling far into the tangle, I could hear my assailants' voices as they peered into the gaps. Fearful of shots from cover, Spaniards seldom ventured into woods. It was also past their supper-time, and soon their guttural cursing was lost in the distance. I ventured out just before sunset, and found some Cubans by the ford. They stood over the body of my servant, who had gone for water to prepare grass soup before I passed the lines. The poor youth had been captured by those guerilla, and shockingly mutilated before death. His eyes were gouged out, his teeth smashed, and the hacking of the body did not conceal the evidence of unnatural torture that had been inflicted before death. It was too late for me again to seek Preval, who died, poor fellow, from the hardships of the campaign, two weeks after Santiago had fallen, and he had rejoined his girl-wife to enjoy the freedom he had fought to achieve.

Hungry, faint-hearted, weary, and in an indescribable state of mind, I directed the Cubans to bury the body, and turned toward Santiago. Flanking San Juan, I succeeded in reaching a clump of trees near the city outposts. Sentries were lazily pacing from fort to fort, the evening gun was fired, its echoes reverberating in the hills, as Spain's banner of blood and gold descended from the flagstaff and the buglers sounded the nightly retreat. Officers came from the forts, the piquet and patrols were mustered, and then, gradually, the stillness of night settled over the community. In the Plaza, a stranded American merry-go-round wheezed out "Sweet Rosie O'Grady" continuously, and my beating heart sounded louder than the base drum accompanying the melody. Eight boomed from the cathedral, and the band of the King's Battalion in the Square burst into "El Tambor Mayor."

The suspense of waiting had been awful, but it was now time to make an attempt to cross the lines. I crawled forward and scaled the first barricade rapidly; the sentry there was chatting with the next post, and I was soon against the wires, and between two forts that loomed up fifty yards apart. The guards lounged round the campfires, cooking their "rancho," the sentinels whined out "Alerta," and continued their chat, and, after vainly trying to compose myself, I started over the barbed Trocha. The posts fortunately protruded several inches above the wires, so, scaling the first fence as a ladder, I was able to step across from strand to strand, grasping each post firmly. Hearing a patrol approaching when all but over, I dropped beneath the tangled meshes, soon to realize that in the night air of the tropics hoof-beats are discernible at a great distance. My alarm was needless, for ten minutes elapsed before the "rounds"

Into Santiago

passed. Then I crawled out, my hands and legs lacerated and bleeding; but I felt nothing of the barbs. I was over, and content. Crawling across the road, I reached a large outlying garden, and encountered a fortunately friendly watch-dog who barked tumultuously as I hurried across the beds and passed out toward the city. At the cuartel I received the usual "Alto! Quién vive?" but on my answering "España!" and explaining that I was a friend of the British consul, the soldier shouldered his rifle and resumed his march. The road to the city was clear at last.

For days, in my hunger, I had craved a good meal, but now the thought of food was nauseating; and with my system enervated by fever and hardship, the relish for it has never returned. I passed the night in a villanous hotel on the wharf. The "Purisima Concepcion" fortunately was in harbor, bound for Batabano. Señor Barbosa, the supercargo, and the pilot I knew to be "good" Cubans, and through their good offices I was smuggled on board, and without ticket or permit left the port that evening. Two days later we touched at Cienfuegos, where I met a jovial Spaniard, the ex-Supervisor of Customs at Baracoa, who was returning, wealthy, to Spain. He swore eternal if unwelcome friendship; but later, when I was taken, a prisoner, to the steamer upon which he was returning home, he reviled me in the choice language of a Spanish gentleman.

In Cienfuegos I called on Mrs. Vieta with mes-

Under Three Flags in Cuba

sages from her husband, of whom she had heard nothing for three years. The colonel's family were visiting Miss Fernandez, the principal of the Cienfuegos ladies' college. I met there an English girl, an adopted pupil — Miss Dabregon — whose father, when sleeping by his wife's side, was brutally shot as a revolutionist by Sergeant Colazzo and two soldiers, by order of General Pim, on October 14, 1397.[1]

[1] The British consul-general took no action in this matter, accepting the assurance of the Spanish general, that Mr. Dabregon had been murdered by a thief. Twice Mrs. Dabregon journeyed to the Consulate in Havana; the last time Mr. Arostogui, a brother of the rebel leader, but a writer on the staff of Weyler's organ, "La Lucha," and singularly also British proconsul, alone saw the distracted widow. Finding she could not approach the consul, Mrs. Dabregon applied directly to Weyler, who ordered an investigation. Subtle as Iago, treacherous as Iscariot, he took no action when the English lady picked out her husband's murderers and they protested that they were acting under Pim's explicit orders. The Dabregon estate was afterwards looted and destroyed by the soldiers, and the family reduced to poverty. The consul-general, Mr. Gollan, recently knighted and retired, was criticised by British subjects in Cuba for his tardy action in this and other cases. Sister Mary Wilberforce, the English Red Cross delegate, slaved for two years among the perishing conscripts in Havana. In petty spite, in October, '07, the Mother Superior of the Alfonso XIII. Hospital Sisterhood, had Miss Wilberforce shut in a cubicle, and her head forcibly shorn. The consul took no action, but advised her return to England. The sister still remained at her voluntary post, however, even through the blockade, and in June, '98, paid the authorities twelve hundred dollars for a portion of Miss Barton's sequestered supplies to distribute to the needy. Three hours after they had accepted the money the Spaniards again seized the stores, as destined to feed Spain's enemies (starving reconcentrados). Sister Mary's bedroom was entered at night by Cassal; even the private stores she had purchased against the rigors of the siege, were taken. Upon her protesting, she was placed under arrest in her room, and expelled to Jamaica on H. M. S. "Talbot," which had passed the lines

Outrages on Britons

to remove refugees. The letters from President and Congress, officially thanking Miss Wilberforce for her ministration to the injured "Maine" survivors, were seized as "effects of the enemy." This gentle English lady had been blessed by hundreds of conscripts, whose cruel lot she had lightened, and thus Spain requited her. Though in shattered health, in July she crossed over to Santiago to nurse American soldiers. Mr. Pinckney, the English engineer of the Regla Electric Company, was flung into prison as a Yankee sympathizer in June, and his effects seized. He was also expelled. The consular authorities did not extend protection in the above instances. Being in ignorance of their reasons, I am unable to state them.

CHAPTER X

THE "MAINE" DISASTER. — THE SENATORIAL COMMISSION. — TO HAVANA AGAIN. — CAPTURED AND DEPORTED TO SPAIN. — WAR DECLARED. — RECEPTION OF THE NEWS IN SPAIN.

IN Cienfuegos I first learned the particulars of the impending rupture between Spain and the United States. On May 21, '97, Congress had appropriated $50,000 for the relief of starving American citizens in Cuba, which was distributed through the consuls. On December 21 the President issued a general appeal for food and money to assist the starving Cubans. Miss Clara Barton had returned from Armenia, and immediately became interested in the appalling conditions in Cuba, which, in her own words, "Out-Turked the Turk." Julian Hawthorne, fresh from the scenes of famine in India, also visited the island, and described it as worse than the conditions he had just left. The American people were roused at last, and donations of food-stuffs poured in to the Relief Committee, and were transported free by the Ward Line. The Spaniards were greatly angered at even this merciful interference. "Peaceful intervention now, to lead to armed aggression

The "Maine"

later," they argued. So arrogant did their attitude become that the battleship "Maine" was sent to Havana in February.

The Weyler faction, headed by Eva Canel, Bresmes, and other ultras, looked upon the "Maine" as an insult to Spain's integrity. The manifesto on the following page was issued broadcast through the city.

This soul-stirring address roused the volunteers to frenzy and they indulged in much wild talk in the bodegas, but their puerile bombast was not looked upon as significant by those who knew the speakers.

It was carnival season in Havana, — a week of fiestas, bull-fights, and general jollification. What recked the Spanish officers and officials if starving thousands were dying by scores each day in the capital? On the gay Prado, any night after ten, hundreds of homeless, emaciated creatures, tiny children almost naked, grown girls and women, often clad only in a ragged petticoat, lay helpless on the sidewalks. Herded in the worst quarter of Los Fossos, where the drains open to the sea, they subsisted on what refuse they could catch in the flowing sewerage. Daughters of once affluent farmers, stood knee-deep in the moving filth, grabbing fœtid morsels of offal to assuage the gnawing hunger of their family. At night some eluded the vigilance of the police, and crawled into the streets, often to die before morning.

¡Españoles!

¡VIVA ESPAÑA CON HONRA!

¿Qué haceis que os dejais insultar de esa manera? ¿No veis lo que nos han hecho retirando á nuestro valiente y querido Weyler, que á estas horas ya hubiéramos acabado con esta indigna canalla insurrecta que pisotea nuestra bandera y nuestro honor?

Nos imponen la Autonomía para echarnos á un lado y dar los puestos de honor y mando á aquellos que iniciaron esta rebelion, estos mal nacidos autonomistas, hijos ingratos de nuestra querida patria!

Y por último, estos cochinos yankees que se mezclan en nuestros asuntos, humillándonos hasta el último grado, y para más vejámen nos mandan uno de los barcos de guerra de su podrida escuadra, despues de insultarnos en sus diarios y desde nuestra casa.

Españoles! Llegó el momento de accion, no dormiteis! Enseñemos á esos viles traidores que todavía no hemos perdido la vergüenza y que sabemos protestar con la energía que corresponde á una nacion digna y fuerte como es y siempre será nuestra España!

Mueran los americanos! Muera la Autonomía!

Viva España! Viva Weyler!

The Manifesto

Translation : —

SPANIARDS!
LONG LIVE SPAIN WITH HONOR!

What are you about that you allow yourselves to be thus insulted ? Do you not realize what they have done by withdrawing our beloved Weyler, who at this hour would have finished the unworthy and rebellious rabble who trample on our flag and honor ?

Autonomy is forced upon us, and gives positions of honor and authority to those who initiated the rebellion, low-born autonomists, ungrateful sons of our beloved country !

And finally these Yankee " cochinos," who interfere in our affairs, humiliate us to the last degree, and in greater taunt, order us a ship of war of their rotten squadron, after insulting us in their newspapers and in our own home.

Spaniards ! the moment of action has arrived. Do not go to sleep ! Let us teach those vile traitors that we are not lost to shame, and that we know how to protest with the energy befitting a dignified and strong nation, as our Spain is and ever will be.

Death to Americans ! Death to Autonomy !
Long live Spain ! Long live Weyler !

Under Three Flags in Cuba

And on Havana's gayest thoroughfares, with "jalousies" flung back and window bars uncurtained, numbers of young girls — some forced to a life of shame to save their dear ones from starvation, others degraded by Spanish officers whose power was absolute, and then abandoned to these dens of iniquity — were flaunted to the public gaze by harridans, who preyed on the defenceless womanhood of Cuba, and profited exceedingly thereby. And amid such scenes the famed matadores, Faico and Bonarillo, and afterwards Mazantini, drew thousands of dollars during fiesta, and returned with the spoils to Spain.

El Prado was illuminated, and gay masqueraders danced mid the scenes of disease, starvation, and death, and drank gaily to Spain. But a few weeks before, on the day set apart for mourning the dead, the old Cathedral was filled with sorrowing Cuban ladies draped in black, while in Spain other heart-broken widows and mothers, sisters and sweethearts, were pouring out their sorrow to Our Lady, and interceding for the dear ones who had perished in Cuba.

Not a Cuban family of prominence but mourned some one killed in battle, dead from privation in the interior, executed, or done to death in penal hells. The Spanish women in Cuba cared little for their doomed conscripts, who, dragged from the Peninsula, left their women folk at home to mourn; for they were the wives and daughters of loyal Spaniards, who helped their country in the hour of peril by

The "Maine"

shouting "Viva España," and making difficulty for the brave old general who did his best to save the day for Spain. And these people danced, fêted, and sang with the officers on the night of February 15.

The Insurgents had burnt the Havana Bull Ring, but gay crowds had flocked over the ferries to the Regla "Plaza de los Toros" that day, and pointed derisively to the American battleship, comparing it to their glorious Pelayo, Carlos V., and Viscaya. The carnival was at its height at 9.40, when a sudden column of flame shot skywards, followed by a fearful explosion and a general shattering of glass in the few buildings that required it in Havana.

"El Maine," shouted several Spanish officers with significant intuition.

The battleship had been blown up, and two officers and two hundred and sixty-four American sailors and marines perished with her.

There was a general jubilation among the rabid Spaniards, and in one notorious restaurant in Lamparilla Street, "sopa del Maine" appeared on the menu for two days, and the joke was thought exceedingly funny by the habitués. Naval Courts of Inquiry were convened both by the United States and Spain. The latter, after a few hours' sitting, and a cursory examination by divers, returned a verdict that the vessel was sunk by an interior explosion. The American Court employed a wrecking company to raise portions of the vessel; they sent down the most capable American and English divers procur-

Under Three Flags in Cuba

able, and after sifting and weighing every piece of evidence, until the type-written testimony filled over twelve thousand pages, on March 21, returned a verdict that the "Maine" was destroyed by a submarine mine, exploded either by the crime or culpable negligence of Spanish officials.[1]

I firmly believe that the Spanish officials, judging Americans from their own treacherous standpoint, and fearing that the warship might enforce some ultimatum under threat of bombardment, caused the "Maine" to be anchored over a mine in case of emergency. The mine was then exploded either by accident or by some fanatics who believed they were thus serving their country.

Bad as Spanish rule has been in Cuba, it is ridiculous to think that General Blanco or his officers would deliberately connive to hurl a vessel to destruction. Rabid Weylerites were ready to do anything to embarrass Sagasta and Blanco, and damage

---

[1] During this critical period Consul-General Lee gained universal admiration for his firm and dignified attitude in dealing with the Spaniards; but when eulogizing the brave Virginian, work done by his lieutenant, Mr. Joseph Springer, must not be overlooked. His years of consular service and knowledge of the language and people made him an invaluable servant to the nation. His experience and advice were indispensable to the Consul-General; he was the wheelhorse of diplomacy in Cuba. Yet I have seen no tribute paid to him, and the State Department has overlooked his qualifications and years of service. After the declaration of war he was retained only as a consular employee, while positions that he could have filled with great efficiency during the war were given to absolute incompetents with political backing.

The American Commission

America; and if the explosion were wilful, the blame lies with them.

Soon after the disaster, an American Commission visited Cuba to investigate reconcentration. We,[1] who had moderately described the conditions, had been disbelieved, thanks to the previous lies written by unscrupulous correspondents on Cuban affairs. Now, through the enterprise of Mr. W. R. Hearst, who placed his yacht "Anita" at their disposal, Senators Thurston, Gallinger, and Money, and Representatives Cummings and Smith, made a semi-official visit to Havana, Matanzas, and Sagua, to inspect the reconcentration settlements. There were hundreds of worse places, but these sufficed. Several ladies were in the party, including the wife of Senator Thurston and Mrs. and Miss Money. Their sympathetic nature was overcome by a glance at these horrors, and the shock from the sights and scenes proved too great for Mrs. Thurston. She was carried gently back to the yacht, but never rallied, and passed away a few hours later.

Typical of her noble countrywomen, she was ready to devote her last moments to the cause of the oppressed women and children, and penned an appeal for Cuba to the mothers of America. A few days later, crushed and broken-hearted, Dr. Thurston

---

[1] Mr. Pepper, Mr. Caldwell, Mr. McCready, and other well-known journalists in Havana at this time, had eloquently pressed Cuba's crying need. Caldwell was forced to leave for refusing to allow his pen to be moved by Señor Congosto.

Under Three Flags in Cuba

arose in the Senate and gave a message from those silent lips, in the most impassioned appeal ever heard in that assembly.

"For myself I went to Cuba firmly believing the condition of affairs there had been greatly exaggerated by the press, and my own efforts were directed in the first instance to an attempted exposure of these supposed exaggerations.

"Mr. President, there has undoubtedly been much sensationalism in the journalism of the time, but as to the condition of affairs in Cuba, there has been no exaggeration, because exaggeration has been impossible. . . . Please God I may never again see so deplorable a sight as the reconcentrados in the suburbs of Matanzas. I can never forget to my dying day the hopeless anguish in their despairing eyes. Huddled about their little bark huts, they raised no voice of appeal to us for alms, as we went among them. . . .

"I shall refer to these horrible things no further. They are there: God pity me! I have seen them; they will remain in my mind forever — and this is almost the twentieth century! Christ died nineteen hundred years ago, and Spain is a Christian nation. She has set up more crosses in more lands, beneath more skies, and under them has butchered more people, than all the other nations of the earth combined. God grant that before another Christmas morning the last vestige of Spanish tyranny and oppression will have vanished from the Western Hemisphere."

In closing, the Senator's voice was broken with emotion, which overcame him as he resumed his seat.

Arrival in Havana

There were few dry eyes in the Chamber, and many who had hitherto opposed action in Cuba were converted. The American nation was awakened as never before, and the speech cabled to London was published throughout Great Britain, stirring the apathy of people hardly aware, until then, that there was a Cuban question.

Petty politicians and financiers could no longer hold public opinion in the United States; and not only did relief pour in, but President McKinley, at the instance of a united nation, delivered his historical warning to Spain.[1]

After landing at Batabano without difficulty, on March 28, and hearing that war was declared with America, I hurried to Havana, fearing that it was too late to escape from the Island. My despatches were now dangerously compromising; so I dropped off the train at the Cerro, crossing to avoid the spies infesting the depot. The crisis was acute, and Americans were flocking from the Capital. Since Señor Congosto had placed my name on the proscribed list, a half-tone cut of myself from "El Figaro" graced the

---

[1] There had been men in power in Washington who had worked steadfastly against intervention. After the return of Senator King from Cuba in January, he and a deputation placed the true conditions of the Island before Mr. Reed. It is said that the Speaker remarked in reply: "If God Almighty allowed these people to starve, I think we in the United States can." A New York clergyman has since said that the "Maine" disaster seemed to follow as a rebuke from the Almighty, for the fatalism of the elected rulers of the nation.

Under Three Flags in Cuba

Rogues' gallery in Colonel Perez's office at the Marine Inspection wharf, and with the close surveillance of outward-bound vessels, both my plans of "buying" a false passport or swimming at night to a steamer were negatived. Colonel Decker, however, was at Key West with the despatch boat "Anita," awaiting the advent of the fleet, and by underground mail he arranged to steam at night to the San Lazaro beach to pick me up. The attempt was to be made on April 1, but on the previous afternoon I lay resting in a secluded room at El Pasage, sick, worn, and anxious to feel the security of American soil again, when heavy footsteps broke my reverie, and a rough demand was made at the door. I glanced hopelessly at the barred window, seized my revolver, to realize the madness of resistance, and hesitated, trembling, until a second thunderous demand nearly burst the door from its hinges. Colonel Trujillo and his valiant myrmidons entered as if bearding a tiger in his den when I withdrew the bar, but grew wondrous bold when they found no resistance intended.

Said the bewhiskered Trujillo, with a malicious grin of recognition, and tone and manner suave, "General Blanco, sir, wishes to hold conversation with you. To a gentleman as yourself it is needless for me to say my sergeant is prepared for resistance; but a coach is in waiting if you care to come quietly." To the coach I went, as one in a dream, forgetting that I was compounding the secrecy of my arrest by such surrender.

Captured as a Spy

I was taken to the cuartel at the Punta fortress, and within an hour was before some semblance of court martial. Colonel Pagaleri fortunately presided; he showed me much consideration during my examination. I answered all questions frankly, denial was futile, but my heart sank as charge after charge was substantiated by the seizure of the despatches I had risked so much to secure. A letter from the Government to President McKinley, a full list of the rebel forces in eastern Cuba, the official offer of their co-operation with the United States, and three maps I had myself prepared, I felt would seal my doom. A private letter from Major Poey to Mr. Bisbee of New York, regarding private financial business, caused the officers more food for thought, however. Might not this Bisbee be McKinley? they argued.

I asked, as my right, that the British consul should be notified of my arrest. "Spies have no rights but the rope," sneered the portly comandante, and I was taken out "incomunicado." My prison chamber was dirty, but the rats broke the solitude; it was at least airy, a large grated frame opening seaward. No bed was provided, but rodents and dirt were forgotten, and I sank on the floor worn in body and broken in spirit, at this sequel that meant failure of all I had tried to accomplish.

Toward morning I dropped into a troubled sleep, and woke at daybreak in a raging fever. The loneliness also grew terrible as the hours passed on, and I

Under Three Flags in Cuba

had so little spirit left, that I began to feel the sensations that lead men to dash their heads against prison walls, and wondered how many days would elapse before insanity supervened. In the afternoon, I bribed a passing soldier to bring me coffee. My dollar brought a tolerable cup with a stale roll, but the fever increased with the chill stone floor, and during the second night I wandered deliriously, and forgot my troubles. About 3 A. M. the officer of the guard came, and he very considerately ordered me a cot and rug, which induced sleep, and I awoke refreshed.

I knew nothing of my impending fate. From my window I could see La Cabana fortress, and as the bloody executions of that death ditch recurred to me, I wondered how I should face the rifles of the firing squad.

Below my grating the black waters of the bay surged against slimy rocks, and hungry sharks showed occasional fins, as they hunted for morsels expelled by the fœtid sewer at Los Fossos. My bars were loose and rusty; but escape from La Punta meant a horrible death below. After retreat sounded, the guards in the courtyard chattered noisily, and interesting snatches of the "spy's" impending fate were served up for my special delectation. I had accepted those despatches without thought, but I could not now face the penalty with fortitude. Spain could not have been blamed for dealing harshly with me. At such a crisis other countries would have

The Foreign Office Notified

shot me without compunction, and in such a war life is but of individual value.

On Wednesday morning the "Olivette" passed my bars. Scanning her decks, I saw that she was crowded down with Americans, merchants, Red Cross workers, and correspondents, leaving the Island. Before my capture, General Lee was preparing to sail, and I suddenly realized that with my secret capture no one would know of my plight, and I might rot in prison before I could communicate with the outer world. But my disappearance had been rightly attributed; Lewis, McReady, and Bryson had made inquiries, and assured themselves of my capture before they sailed. Long cable messages were sent to England, the British Foreign office was notified, and Lord Salisbury at once wired Havana for full particulars. Mr. Creelman, Mr. Norman, Mr. Massingham, Mr. McKenzie, Mr. Brodhurst, and other prominent journalists in London kindly interested themselves in my behalf. Mr. Labouchere, Mr. T. P. O'Conner, and Mr. Kelly, M.P. who tasted Spanish prison in the last war, brought my case before the House of Commons, and the authorities in Havana found they could no longer keep my incarceration there a secret.

I was not anticipating help from the British Government. When one is identified in quarrels of strange nations, the consequences must be borne. I had frequently gone beyond my province in Cuba, but, as Canini says, "Spain's history in the Island shows one that man can descend to an animal far inferior to a dog, and little better than a tiger." Neutrality is forgotten when humanity is outraged, and it had been impossible to stand by apathetically in the midst of such atrocities.

The Spanish authorities decided to avoid complications by quietly shipping me a prisoner to Puerto Rico. Sir Alexander Gollan was then informed that I had been "expelled" from Cuba; he reported it to London, and the incident was apparently closed.

Fortunately there were some friends who were not satisfied at the consul-general's terse report of my expulsion. Only two boats had left Havana — one to Key West, the other a transport bound for San Juan; and when it transpired that I was not on the American vessel, and that Colonel Perez and a guard were seen taking me toward the Spanish transport, fresh representations were made.

In the stifling lower hold of the transport[1] "Buenos Aires," with a negro murderer named Hernandez, and several hundred yellow-fever convalescents, my condition was not enviable. When we reached San Juan, thanks to the kindness of Mr. Bronson Rea, then in Puerto Rico, I obtained a change of clothes.

The British Government were demanding the release of my friend, Freeman Halstead, corre-

[1] When Decker heard of my deportation, he ordered steam up on the "Anita," and prepared to chase the Spaniard to demand my person at the point of his two small pieces. Strict harbor regulations prevented the "Anita" leaving Key West that night, and ere he could clear in the morning the transport had too long a start from Havana.

Deported to Spain

spondent of the "Herald," and also a British subject, then in Morro Castle, under sentence of nine years' imprisonment as a spy for taking photographs of San Juan harbor. Governor-General Maccias, having no wish for further complications over one of Blanco's prisoners, refused my landing. I was rushed off to the "Buenos Aires" again, and sent to Spain.

Shut below in that filthy transport were over a thousand invalid soldiers, yellow-fever convalescents. To be invalided from Spain's army was to be an invalid indeed, and the poor wretches packed in the sorry bunks were too weak to move. They vomited and defecated where they lay, and the condition between decks may be imagined, but not described. At night those who had died were carried out and dropped over the side; but the thought of repatriation in their beloved Spain buoyed up the men wonderfully, though many died directly they reached the shore. When I was first conducted below, some of these poor fellows reviled me as they lay in their misery, "Yankee pig," "mambi," and "nanigo" being among the most complimentary appellations. Seeing one young soldier, after a fit of retching, was hanging exhausted over his bunk, I gently laid the limp form back, and readjusted the blanket, thinking nothing of the incident. His comrades witnessed this simple act of common humanity. No more gibes were cast at me, and before I had divined the reason of the change, a few petty services to the stricken

Under Three Flags in Cuba

men had gained me the friendship of every soldier below decks.

A few had brought bottles of common red wine from the hospital, and they were not satisfied until I had made a pretence, at least, of partaking of the precious store. At the end of that terrible voyage I was called from berth to berth to say farewell, and was deeply touched by their manifestations of regard won by simple kindness. These poor fellows had been torn from home, and impressed into hateful service; and next to the women and children of Cuba, I think humanity called for intervention on behalf of the Spanish conscript. Ignorant he was — often a brute; but he was treated as a galley slave by the officers who robbed him, and he at least faithfully served the country that treated him so badly.

We all suffered severely from cold, and, but for the kindness of the supercargo, one of those true Spanish gentlemen that retain one's hope for the race, who permitted me to sleep on deck several nights, I believe I also should have succumbed in the stench of the frightful "Black Hole" below. But for the hostility of certain officers on board, he would have accorded me better accommodation. The chief engineer of the vessel proved a Scotchman, Mr. Cook, and he also extended me much kindness on the trip to Cadiz, which we reached on April 15. Neither General Gonzalez Muñoz nor any of his staff who were on board the vessel, visited their men's quarters in the holds on the voyage.

A Pitiful Disembarkation

The disembarkation at Cadiz was a memorable sight. On the starboard side, steam launches, gay with bunting, brought out high army officers in resplendent uniforms, diplomats, and a vast crowd, to welcome officers and officials returning rich to Spain.

The port gangway led down to large floats manned by Red Cross helpers, who lifted the emaciated forms of fever-stricken soldiers from the terrible hold, placed them temporarily in clean uniforms to save the comments of the crowd on the wharf, among whom were country people, wives and mothers and fathers, in the last extremes of poverty, waiting to see their dear ones. They had walked fifty, sixty, and seventy miles to greet the returning heroes — they waited on in suspense: they gave cries of horror at the wrecks Cuba had sent them. It was inexpressibly sad. As I watched those silent tragedies, tears blinded my eyes, and I forgot my own distress, — impending imprisonment as a spy, possible deportation to North Africa, and the anxiety of my friends to learn my fate. One group of Andalusian women questioned some of the invalids, — their friend must have died on the voyage; several uttered ear-piercing shrieks; one maiden lay writhing on the pier in violent hysteria. Mothers at first failed to recognize their boys, and then, with gurgles of pain at the change, yet joy of reunion, they clasped the saffron-hued skeletons in their arms: "My son! My son!" Two soldiers died on the pier, and a frenzied mass of relatives surged forward, impelled by a sickening dread for their individual dear ones. But the guards drove them back; the ambulances were now full, and the people were forced to endure the suspense until the next day.

The chief of police assured me that I should be sent to Africa on May 1, and there was some excitement among the crowd of sight-seers when I was taken ashore. The advent of a "Yankee spy" had been heralded, and with minds inflamed by the spectres of manhood from Cuba, their jeers and expletives aroused neither my wonder nor resentment.

The smouldering fires of Castilian anger burst into flame when Minister Woodford was given his passports ere he could present the American ultimatum. The Spaniards rejoiced over their diplomatic victory, and showed no concern as to the result of the war thus virtually declared. Popular voice had spoken never so strongly as the demand of the American people that the strife in Cuba should stop, in the name of humanity and civilization. No undue favoritism to the rebels was manifested; Spain's impotency to check the rebellion had been too long proven. On the anniversary of Concord, where the American patriots struck the primary blow to tyranny and oppression in the Western Hemisphere, both Houses adopted resolutions declaring that the people of Cuba should be free and independent, empowering the President to use the forces of the United States to that end, and explicitly disclaiming intention to

A Solemn Fiesta

exercise permanent sovereignty or control over the Island, — the government, after pacification, to be left to the Cubans.

The day before the formal declaration of war, I was released upon the demands of the British Government. Charges formulated against me for bearing arms against Spain were withdrawn when the Spaniards found that I must be sent to England for trial under the Foreign Enlistment Act, when impolitic truths of their rule in Cuba might be evolved. Being captured before declaration of war, the designation "spy" could not be sustained, and I was ordered over the frontier, with warning not to return to Cuba on pain of death. Chaperoned by two celadores of police, ordered to see me over the French boundary, but by no means adverse to enjoyment en route at my expense, I watched the gay fiesta in Seville, where the great Andalusian fair was turned into a jollification, to celebrate the impending success of Spain. As the great religious procession of the 19th wended its way from the Alcazar to the glorious Giralda, the people knelt reverently in the picturesque streets, and it seemed that the whole nation, fearful of threatening peril, sought blindly for divine protection. The incense permeated the closely packed crowd, familiar phrases of the solemn chant were re-echoed from mouth to mouth, and as the two massive set pieces, "The Last Supper" and "The Crucifixion" passed along, grandee, caballero, and peasant, squirming on the sanded sidewalks, prostrated themselves before the sacred emblem in a touching humility. Two days before, the garrison in Cadiz had tendered their vows to " Our Lady " in anticipation of the conflict, and to the stranger it seemed that the civilians also were preparing for a crisis with becoming devotion. Before the beautiful strains of the Constitutional Hymn had died in the distance, a change came over the scene.

The abject reverence of the crowd was actuated only by ignorant superstition, and with the fumes of incense thick about them, the worshippers again became a mob. Coarse jests were bandied from side to side, and mingled with the rallying cries of the bull-ring. " Mazantini ! " " C—— ! No! Bombetta ! " " Otre caballo ! " " Mas picadores." Sparkling Andalusian beauties snapped their fingers, or rattled castanets, and whirled through the intricacies of the voluptuous "fandango;" the bodegas were crowded, while the peasants, dressed in finery purchased by many days' previous hunger, drank deeply from the kid-skins of wine slung behind them. Away the crowd jostled toward Las Delicias, through the Vasco de Carruages, while from the picturesque low quarter across the Guadalquivir, a stream of unshaven bullies and cutthroats poured over the bridges and joined the throng.

The proletariat held the sidewalks, the broad highway was filled with carriages of every description and horsemen, the animals gaily caparisoned, the young ladies vivacious and beautiful in their national costume, their mammas and chaperons fat and vulgar

News of the War in Spain

in the same trappings. With a roar of acclamations and a cloud of dust, a party of picadores galloped by, and later, riding like a queen amid her subjects, came "Lolita," the lady matador, — a sweet-faced girl of seventeen, modest and lady-like in appearance, despite the gorgeous toreador costume. Yet she kills bulls calmly, though the "torro magnífico" on the programme is always a small bullock.

Horns, whistles, bells, added to the din of voices and laughter. It was a pandemonium, clad in the gayest of colors and softened by the semi-tropical background of palms and orange-trees, the blue river, and the picturesque architecture massed indescribably in the rear.

One hour later the stillness of death reigned over the city. From afar rose the distant sound of ten thousand voices merged as one: "Bravo, matador!" "Muy bien! Muy bien! Mazantini!" and I realized that no dire disaster had overtaken the gay throng, — the bull fight had started, and the first bull had fallen.

That evening a dozen men gathered outside a bookstall. In a glazed frame, ten inches square, the day's bulletin was posted, announcing the decision of the Cabinet to resist to the utmost, and that war was imminent. It was fiesta, so the issue of a special edition was out of the question. "Mañana" the twenty-five words scrawled there would be placed in type. The few who read the significant tidings smiled contemptuously, nay, pityingly. "Pobres

Under Three Flags in Cuba

Yankees," said one, in irony; others shrugged their shoulders, drew their capes in place, and swaggered off down San Fernando.

Thousands of pesetas had been spent on lavish decoration; and as night fell, and the parks and avenues were lit with millions of colored lights, the famed old city was a veritable fairyland. I stood on the balcony of the Vasadera and looked down on the gay masqueraders. Away in every direction they spread, promenading in the brilliantly illuminated avenues, showering confetti, dancing to the dozen bands in the dozen plazas, flirting, drinking, laughing. On the Guadalquivir, boats flitted from side to side, festoons of lamps were reflected in the blue waters, until the river was as a flowing stream of light, and the heavens were ablaze with fireworks.

The unsurpassed brilliance of the scene was intoxicating, but my mind was suddenly filled with other sounds and visions, — the despairing cry of the starving women and children in Cuba, perishing by thousands; the moans of Spain's conscripts, wasted by fever and hunger, and unpaid for months; the horrible shambles of the Cabanas, where those who had rebelled against a nation's oppression were shot like dogs; the rattle and crash of battle in the manigua, the screams of the wounded, and rallying cries of the patriots and Imperialists.

On the eve of a crisis, when the integrity of the nation was at stake, and a tottering ministry was striving to raise a paltry sum by public subscription,

April in Madrid

all over the country the people were wining, dining, and dancing, and expending in worthless spectacle hundreds of thousands of pesetas. And Sagasta, in an interview with a foreign correspondent, referred with pride to the vast sacrifice Spaniards were prepared to make in defence of their country.

On arrival in Madrid next day, I found nothing to indicate the war on hand, except that the great daily papers had three of their columns devoted to it. I was more amused than flattered to find one-third of a leading column devoted to my presence in Spain. To give an equal space to one who, as the papers remarked, was extremely ignorant, for he spoke execrable Spanish, and to the manifesto of President McKinley that involved two nations in war, seems an inexplicable editorial vagary. "Don Quixote" signalized the rupture by an indecent cartoon of the United States. A valiant mob of "counter-jumpers" and students paraded the "Street of Carts," tore down a shield of an American Insurance Company with impressive imprecations, and fled precipitantly when two policemen appeared on the scene. Excited crowds of Madrileños gathered at night in the Puerta del Sol and round the prime minister's headquarters in the Calle de Alcala; but Colonel Morera had proclaimed martial law, and the people satisfied themselves by yelling for the bandera nacional and Cuba Española. Weyler was at his house at San Geronimo, where he entertained his satellites with multifarious stories of his sole ability to crush the Yankees, and

Under Three Flags in Cuba

the Government's duty to act thereon. Statesmen had lost their heads; the most gifted of them were urging plans of campaign that must obviously fail, and the result of their confabulations was nil: they left all to God — and Blanco.

Before crossing the frontier, the celadores suggested that they would not seriously object to my witnessing the great patriotic bull-fight, provided I took them with me; and being interested therein, I earned their undying gratitude by buying tickets for the extraordinary function. In whispers, audible across the arena, they begged me not to open my mouth lest my accent betray me to the audience. With the Latin hate of the Anglo-Saxon at that time, in the presence of twelve thousand élite Spaniards inflamed with bloodlust and patriotism, the warning was pertinent. "Yankee spy" greeted every one who spoke English, and Britishers as well as Americans had received rough handling on the streets.

The audience was distinguished, though Sagasta and his ministers were too pressed for time to come as anticipated. Weyler, who had just reached Madrid, was greeted effusively, and the boxes were crammed with the highest in the land, the lower class audibly commenting on the absence of the unfortunate queen regent and the boy king. "Del rey ninguno abajo," a Spanish proverb, implying the equality of all below the king, is a truism at the bull-fight, if at no other time.

After a splendid bout between bull and troupe,

A Patriotic Bull Fight

Bombetta stepped out, and with a master-stroke brought the panting animal down amid frantic acclamations. The famed matador responded with a smart simile:—

"As I have triumphed over this magnificent bull, so will the glorious Spanish nation, upholding the traditions of the past handed them by their illustrious sires, triumph over that shameless animal, the Yankee pig!" Yells and filthy expletives rang from all sides, though the highest ladies in the land were present,—"Death to the Yankees!" "We will tweak their noses!" rose with cries unfit for publication. Above the din could be heard the screams of agony from a disembowelled horse, and the moans of the dying bull which had fallen under the thrust, but died slowly. After this the people wanted more excitement, and in response to the yells of "Fuego! fuego!" the next bull was decorated with explosive banderillas that burnt holes in the poor brute's sides and drove him mad with pain; he had previously killed seven horses, and blood ran in streams from the wounds inflicted by the picadores in the encounter. After six bulls and twenty-seven horses had been killed, the bloody scene closed.

Two days later I passed the frontier, spending a few hours in the Valladolid district, and in the valleys north of the Ebro, with Father Patrick Sinnot, of the Irish College, Malaga. The northern districts of Spain are the antithesis of the languorous South, and a merchant of Alicante has little in common

Under Three Flags in Cuba

with the sensuous Andalusian. The frightful ravages of the Carlist war are still apparent, and the boundary walls of the high-roads are marked by hundreds of crosses, where rebels or suspects were stood against the wall, and summarily shot by the heated Bourbonists. The homely Basques of the Pyrenees had heard little of the war, and were far more concerned over the depredations of the wolves, and the attempt to capture a party of bold brigands who were terrorizing the district, despite the advent of carabineers and guardia civil to aid the red-capped frontier guards in their suppression. The manifesto of Don Carlos that had just been issued roused the dormant enthusiasm of a few grandee supporters, but the mass of the people wisely looked on the cause as lost, and an uprising as futile.

Once over the border, French antipathy to America became strongly marked. At Bordeaux a large crowd yelled, "Viva España!" and "Death to McKinley!" and even in Paris hostility was painfully evident, and cartoons against the Yankees, coarse and disgusting. Though Rochefort bade them remember Lafayette, and denounced Spain, French sympathy, directed by the Bourse and holders of Spanish bonds, was strongly for the Spaniards. Crossing from Boulogne to Folkestone, were several American families, going to England to escape painful manifestations, and for days there had been a general exodus of Americans from Paris. The antithesis of this feeling in England was distinctly refreshing. Never were the two great

Blood Thicker than Water

English-speaking countries on more cordial terms, and with few exceptions, press and people extolled America's "holy war." The feeling was universal.

"I'll show you right here what chums are John and Sam," said an enthusiastic American friend to me when I reached London; and within an hour we had seen two manifestations, dropping in first to the Empire, where the casual production of a bust of "Uncle Sam," in the regular course of a play, evoked a burst of cheering from every part of the house, while the band played Yankee Doodle thrice; and later, in the Palace Theatre, where the picture of President McKinley and the stirring strains of the "Star-Spangled Banner" called forth a spontaneous ebullition of enthusiasm, from the "full dress" to the "gods" in the gallery.

Seven days later I reached New York en route for Cuba. The full report of Dewey's victory in Manila on May 1 had just arrived, and it stirred the Americans as victory alone can stir a nation. The very sky was obscured by myriads of the stars and stripes, for "Old Glory" fluttered from every point of vantage. From the Hudson came the discordant screaming of a thousand steam sirens; bay-tug, ocean greyhound, and ferryboat joined to rend the heavens, while an immense crowd of patriots filled City Hall Square, before the Journal bulletin-boards, and sang the National Hymn to Fanchulli's band, while tears of effusive joy and gratitude ran down many a face. Amid this scene my thoughts

Under Three Flags in Cuba

reverted to Madrid, and it was easy to imagine our Spanish friends had shrugged their shoulders and prepared for Sunday's bull-fight, to celebrate the victory that officials had thrust on the credulous public. In the words of the Minister of Marine, "their losses had been severe; but they had the sublime satisfaction of knowing that the Yankees had not only been forced to withdraw (for breakfast), but throughout the day were compelled to manœuvre repeatedly."

CHAPTER XI

FORMING THE EXPEDITION FOR CUBA. — THE VOYAGE. —
LANDING IN CUBA.

REACHING Washington in May, I made preparation to cross the Spanish lines and re-enter Havana City on secret service. Finding however, that an army of invasion would leave for Cuba in a few days, I hurried to Tampa to join the Fifth Army Corps. The regular army was then mobilized, and outwardly all was in readiness for a forward move.

General Wesley Merritt, then the only West Point general officer in the United States Army, was named for commander of the invasion, and when his appointment to lead the Philippine expedition was announced, it was universally supposed that General Miles would take the army to Cuba. To the surprise of every one, General William R. Shafter was placed in command of the forming Cuban expedition. An officer weighing considerably more than three hundred pounds, and suffering from gout, seemed the last man to lead an army into a difficult country like Cuba, where the activity and intelligence of the leader could do much to overcome the obstacles of the country, and mitigate risks to the health and life of those exposed to such a climate.

Under Three Flags in Cuba

Various generals were nominated from civil life by the President; among them Fitzhugh Lee, and Joseph Wheeler the famed Confederate cavalry leader. Both these officers were " rebels " in the Civil War, and both had proved true as steel in defence of what they adjudged their rights. Their appointment and the spontaneous expression of loyalty from the South, betokened a new era in the history of the Union. The war touched true and great American principles, and the Blue and the Gray rose shoulder to shoulder in response to their country's call. To-day they are united by a fresh bond, stronger than the broken tie of '61.

The lack of system in the War Department was apparent at Tampa; confusion reigned, but that the army was increased sevenfold by a stroke of the pen, must be taken into consideration. Since the available transportation facilities under the Stars and Stripes could not have carried more than 25,000 men from the coast, the Administration is frequently blamed for not first devoting its entire energies to the equipment of a small army for service, before the vast resources of the National Guard were called upon, and the department paralyzed by the immense mobilization. But the hardly veiled animosity of certain powers toward the United States, and the possibility of foreign intervention on Spain's behalf, made an impressive display of military strength imperative.

Tampa, assuredly, was not an ideal spot for the prep-

The Expedition for Cuba

aration of an army of invasion. The white Florida sand made good camping-ground; but though drier, the climate is scarcely less enervating than that of Cuba. The great drawbacks, however, were the limited railway facilities and the monopolies enjoyed by the Plant Railway Company for everything.

The Plant System is but a single track, and in normal times runs but few trains, north and south bound passing each other by tedious side-tracking. The sudden rush of traffic overtaxed the possibilities of the railroad; the sidings became choked; heavy freights mixed with troop specials, and a constant tangle of trains meeting on the single line was the result. If it were necessary to mobilize the invading army in the far South, no Florida port was more desirable. The camp site at Miami was condemned as unhealthy by Colonel Curtis Guild; and by direct appeal to the President, the Seventh Army Corps was promptly moved to Jacksonville. Savannah and New Orleans boasted far greater embarkation facilities than either.

Everything in Tampa was expensive, and this entailed a great hardship on officers and men, who frequently were forced to purchase necessaries of food and clothing that the commissariat should have provided. Despite the exorbitance, however, the officers found life tolerable in the palatial Tampa Bay Hotel, the great winter resort which became army headquarters. Here the band played at night in the Oriental annex, under flourishing palms, and officers danced with bright-eyed Cuban "señoritas," a number of whom had fled from Havana.

Eager groups also discussed the war, the bronzed Indian fighters from the plains sharing the enthusiasm with the young subs just from West Point, and the civilian appointees, swelling 'neath their newly acquired rank and uniform, and anxious to do their duty, if they did owe both to the political influence of their respective papas. Yet it struck the stranger as hard to see gallant soldiers who had spent their lives in their country's service, wearing captain's bars, while unnotable sons of notables strutted around in colonel's stars and staff uniforms. Truly such is un-American; and it was distinctly refreshing when Colonel Roosevelt's Rough Riders arrived, to find the sons of millionaires and professional men of prominent families serving as troopers in the ranks with cowpunchers, packers, and "bad men" of the West, all actuated by the same patriotism, but deserving honor commensurate with their individual self-sacrifice.

Gathered in or around headquarters were considerably over a hundred war correspondents and artists, representing newspapers from every quarter of the globe. Evidently Lord Wolseley's young idea that the "drones of the Press" were the curse of modern armies (for which statement he has since humbly apologized) was not shared by the war lords of Washington. It was surprising to find that the vast majority of correspondents, even those representing

Press Censorship in Tampa

great New York dailies, had never seen a shot fired in anger, and were absolutely ignorant of military affairs. There were exceptions; and London sent some tried veterans, as Robinson, Wright, Sheldon, McPherson, Nutall, Hands, and Atkins; but many held passes who would never be permitted to accompany an army in the field by the British war office. The rigors of home camps soon proved too great for much of this "impedimenta," and it was a greatly diminished but very " fit " body of Press knights who finally landed in Cuba.

In Tampa a rigorous censorship was instituted, professedly to withhold information from the enemy; but a wrongful advantage of its restrictions was taken to prevent disclosures of disgraceful shortcomings. This muzzling of the press prevented the discovery and rectification of many evils that eventually cost dearly. A judicious censorship was necessary; the despotic gag was not. Mr. Bigelow, who pointed out the shortcomings of the invading army, was denounced as unpatriotic; but writers who had loudly cried " traitor " plagiaristically confirmed his statements, when proved by time, but too late for rectification.

Hundreds of expatriated Cubans living in Ybor City formed themselves into companies of volunteers; and swelled by natives from all parts of the country, three strong contingents were raised, commanded respectively by brave old Lacret, who had slipped over from Cuba a few weeks previously, and Generals

Under Three Flags in Cuba

Nunez and Sanguili. Colonel Janiz, the brave little doctor of Camaguey, was now his chief of staff, Karl Decker and Herbert Seeley were honorary members, and among other officers I was delighted to find young Mass, now a major, Frank Agremonte, Aguirre, and other brave fellows whose past services in Cuba and consequent sufferings in Spanish prisons had by no means deterred them from responding again to their country's call. General Nunez was joined by Colonel Mendez, two sons of the Morales family, and two New Yorkers, Thorne and Jones, all of whom did excellent service later in Cuba. Dr. Castillo took charge of the "Florida," and landed the expeditions safely.

General Shafter's force was ever sailing "to-morrow," until "mañana" had a Spanish significance, and the wait seemed endless.

The military authorities punctiliously enforced trivialities to the letter, and it was surprising to see the laxity and consequent disorder in more important matters. Sanitation and the water supply of the camps seemed a secondary consideration; the issue of rations and suitable outfits to the army would have discredited a staff of school-boys. The officers of the regular regiments smiled grimly, but could say nothing. Seven miles of freight cars were stalled in the sidings between Lakeland and the Port. The stores had been rushed forward indiscriminately, no manifests were provided, and no specific attempt was made at headquarters to evolve order from chaos.

A few details of intelligent non-commissioned

The Spy Farce

officers could have gone through the cars and tabulated their contents; but if beans were wanted, a search was made until they materialized, and the same cars would be overhauled by men searching for beef or tomatoes later in the day. Thus only the most necessary stores were brought to light, and tons of delicacies for the sick and medical stores were never unloaded. Great blame has been heaped upon the Administration for the want of everything in Cuba. The fault lay rather with the lack of administrative ability evinced by the authorities at Tampa. Supplies in abundance were shipped south to the army, but were never unloaded from the trains, though their inclusion in the equipment of an army on foreign service was imperative.

Extraordinary energy was shown at Tampa in hunting down spies.[1] This spy scare was a screaming farce save for the luckless victims caught in the toils. It is difficult to discover either the value of information that could be gained around the camps of the regular army or a method of transmitting the

[1] The arrest of the boy Garcia, son of Port Tampa's mayor, and the half-crazed Vanderbilt, just from a Spanish prison, were ridiculous. But the imprisonment of Mr. Castellanos for the heinous crime of receiving a letter signed " Bernabe," which many knew to be from his uncle, Mr. Bernabe Sanchez, British consul at Nuevitas, then in New York, but which the astute "secret service" decided might be from Señor Bernabe Polo, Spain's political agent in Montreal, and his incarceration for weeks in the filthy civil stockade with negro criminals, without a chance to clear himself, were an outrage adjudged impossible save in Spain. Emaciated and with a racking cough, Castellanos was finally dragged before a court-martial at Atlanta, and at once acquitted.

news to the enemy. The cable was useless; no one knew the date of sailing; everything else had been printed in the newspapers and magazines, so the quest of Spanish agents would be futile in Tampa.

The order for a general advance arrived on June 5. Its promulgation at 10 P.M. is history; it was war, not opera bouffe: it emanated from the commanding general, not Wilson or D'Angelis. "All who were not on board the transports by daybreak would be left behind."

In Liberia, President Cheeseman caused a rush of dusky admirals to the vaunted " Rocktown " by such procedure, and I had laughed at the ostentatious negroes, en route for hostile Kroos. In Tampa one could not laugh. Officers and correspondents dashed off to their quarters to pack, dress, and catch the 11 train for war. It arrived at 5 A.M. and we reached the embarkation pier at 6. Whole battalions were moved in the rush. Regiment after regiment had hurried down to the narrow pile dock, which was soon packed indescribably with men and baggage. Troops at the extreme end of the pier were afterwards assigned to transports moored at the shore end, and vice versa. The embarkation resembled the sailing of a vast excursion party rather than a military movement. With the capacity of each transport, and the roster of each regiment before him, the youngest officer could have made effective assignment and saved such dire confusion, which took two days to untangle, and entailed much sun-exposure

The Invading Army Sails

and hardship on the soldiers. But toward evening, June 7, all was ready.

Boom! went a saluting gun, and away went transport after transport, — the bands playing, the troops, relieved from the tedium of the wait, cheering as only such enthusiasts can cheer. But a gunboat, one time yacht, had sighted two tramp steamers, and from unexplained reason, taking them for Spaniards, showed a clean pair of heels to Key West with the tidings.

"Stop the expedition," cabled Washington, and the leading transports were headed off far down the bay and recalled after a long chase by the " Helena." A weary wait ensued,[1] the men, cramped on the vessels which were fitted and filled like cattle-ships, grew sick with the delay. The water grew stale; the lack of exercise, and the foul air of the crowded holds in the fierce semi-tropical heat, soon affected the troops; and the halt laid the foundation of many a subsequent death, beside the loss of a dry week in Cuba.

One week later we sailed. On the 13th the flagship "Seguranca" signalled the start; and with colors flying and bands playing, the vessels glided out to

[1] General Shafter's force consisted of 11,000, regular infantry, 2000 volunteer infantry, 2500 regular cavalry, and 500 volunteer cavalry, with four batteries field artillery, two batteries siege artillery, a battalion of engineers, and detachments of the signal and hospital corps, about 16,000 men all told.

The transports were coasting steamers subsidized by the Government, and showing every evidence of their rough conversion into transports.

Under Three Flags in Cuba

mid-stream and dropped down toward the sea. As the battery on shore boomed out a farewell salute, the soldiers swarmed to the deck and rigging, and the air was rent with a shout of triumph from sixteen thousand throats. The cheers were taken up on shore and echoed and re-echoed in pine forest and everglade. They were not evoked only by the usual zest for war shared by all men, the savage lust to fight which lies dormant in the piping times of peace. Those troopers knew they had a mission to fulfil. They remembered the blackened wreck in Havana Harbor, and the sailor comrades sleeping in that fœtid slough; they thought also of the women and children crying aloud for deliverance from starvation and despair, of the ragged patriots fighting for liberty as their own fathers had fought — but for far smaller issues — in the War of Independence. Upon the grimy coal-dock, a group of Cuban ladies, widowed and orphaned exiles, knelt, praying with tear-streaming faces for divine benediction on the liberating army.

Petty politicians have used the war for their own purposes, thimbleriggers have not been idle; but to the close observer it was evident that the war was a war of the people, the will of the multitude, inflamed perhaps by exaggeration and misrepresentation, but nevertheless exerted for a just purpose when unvarnished facts stand forth.

Twenty hours after the start was signalled we rounded Dry Tortugas, and in double column the

The Trip to Cuba

fleet headed Cubawards, flanked on either side by the guard of warships. The massive cruiser "Indiana" held to the shore side, while the aggressive torpedo-boat "Porter" dashed inshore at intervals, on the lookout for any lurking gunboat of Spain that might emerge on a forlorn hope, sink a transport, and meet the inevitable fate gloriously. The "Annapolis," "Bancroft," "Castine," "Helena," "Morrill," "Manning," and "Hornet" guarded the fleet of transports on the voyage, the "Detroit," "Osceola," and "Ericsson" acting as scouts.

The first land sighted was the sandy loam on Cayo Romano, and as the sun set in tropical suddenness, a fire flickered from the summit and was answered by a second flare on the distant heights of Cubitas: a message from the watchful guardia costa to the beleaguered Cuban Government, which has meted isolated justice in spirit rather than in letter, that the day of Cuba's triumph was at hand.

We had two alarms: two Spanish gunboats came up boldly, but dashed into Nuevitas when the "Osceola" steamed out to engage them, and later mysterious vessels sighted at night near Lobus, disappeared in the darkness as the warships raced to meet them.

The stoutly built British lighthouses fringing the Bahama Isles, alone broke the monotony of sea and sky after this, and as the three and one-half days' trip became lengthened into six days and seven nights, every one grew heartily sick of slow travel and cramped quarters. A call was made at Man-of-

Under Three Flags in Cuba

War's Bay, Inagua Isle, a little-known British possession lying midway between the extreme points of Cuba and Hayti. Passing through the Windward Passage, the mountains of Santiago loomed into view on the 21st.

Everything was quiet and peaceful, the transports lay to off Morro Castle, far out of range, and nothing but tiny clouds of smoke marked the presence of the blockading fleet, hidden below the dip of the horizon. For twenty-four hours we lay there. General Shafter joined Admiral Sampson, and they landed at Asseredo to hold conference with General Garcia.

On the 22d plans were perfected, and the transports headed to Daiquiri, sixteen miles east of Santiago. Here the Jaragua Iron Company own an iron pier for loading the ore, and at an early hour, as the warships drew near, a great column of smoke and flame went up: the Company's great storehouse and the township were fired by the Spaniards. As the garrison evacuated, the fleet bombarded the forts and road, checking the advance of some Cuban soldiers, mistaken for the enemy. At 10 A. M. boats were lowered and the first regiment, the 8th Infantry, landed without opposition. Horses and mules had to swim ashore, and all the men landed in a heavy surf in small boats, and not until the next evening had the cavalry and Lawton's brigade disembarked.

The landing of the army was picturesque and spirit-stirring. As the sun rose above the mountains,

Landing of the Army

a flood of lustre was thrown over the fleet of transports and massive warships, lying off shore on a sea of clearest blue. Away toward Guantanamo, the water shone like liquid gold, the waves washing over the base of the distant promontory in white cascades as the regular undulations were broken by the rocks. The appearance of the romantic shore was heightened by the debarking troops, forming up on the yellow beach, their arms glistening bravely in the sun, while just above them lay the little town backed by the lofty Sierras, the grim volcanic cliffs stretching westward, a dividing line between the expanse of sea and sky.

Our landing continued without molestation. On Thursday the 23d a distant rattle of musketry was wafted over Los Altares, six altar-shaped foothills, and huge columns of smoke crept up against the sky line. The Spaniards were burning the small towns and withdrawing into Santiago. General Lawton, with the 1st and 22d Regular Infantry, 2d Massachusetts, and detachments of the 4th, 8th, and 25th Infantry, pushed ahead into Siboney, finding it already occupied by Cubans under General Castillo, who had attacked the rear guard of Linares, as they were firing the town. The Spaniards fled, leaving stores and ammunition intact. They tried to destroy the railroad as they retired, but Colonel Aguirre and some Cuban cavalry followed them up, and the Imperial troops continued their flight. At Aguadores, which was strongly garrisoned, the railroad bridge over the creek was blown up with dynamite, to prevent our direct advance along the railroad.

The country within nine miles of Santiago was now in our hands. The base of operations was moved from Daiquiri to Siboney, a pretty little town, inhabited by the employees of the Iron and Railroad Company. General Linares had made preparation to vigorously oppose a landing here, and two almost perpendicular cliffs were terraced with trenches carefully masked from top to bottom. He hoped the troops would walk into this trap when they found the town seemingly deserted, and he could then open a hidden fusillade from either side with open country behind for retreat. A few searching shells from the fleet soon caused him to alter his decision, and the troops evacuated this stronghold, Comandante Billen being killed by a chance shell.

The warships continued bombarding Aguadores, and the Spaniards replied vigorously. One shell struck the "Texas," killing Ensign Blakeley, and wounding five others dangerously, and the gunboats that could be spared from the blockading squadron were unable to silence the coast batteries.

CHAPTER XII

THE FIGHT AT GUASIMAS. — THE ENEMY REPULSED. — DISEMBARKATION AT SIBONEY. — COMMISSARIAT SHORTCOMINGS. — GARCIA'S ARRIVAL. — A GENERAL ADVANCE ORDERED.

GENERAL SHAFTER remained on the Seguranca, with his plan of campaign. General Wheeler assumed command on shore, and conflicting orders resulted. General Chaffee's Brigade was ordered to form the advance in conjunction with Lawton's division, and reached Jaragua at dusk on the 23d. General Young's cavalry brigade, with General Wheeler, then passed these outposts and advanced to Siboney. The Cubans reported the enemy in force at Guasimas, and after General Wheeler had reconnoitred the position with General Castillo, he ordered the cavalry to attack at daybreak. At 4 A. M. the Rough Riders marched over the foothills by a thickly wooded trail, any section of which invited ambuscade and annihilation, had the Spaniards possessed initiative.

General Young, with the 1st and 10th Cavalry and four Hotchkiss guns, advanced along the main road. The enemy, neglecting to attack either force separately, held a position on a plateau where the trail

Under Three Flags in Cuba

and road converged. General Rubin intrenched his forces in a disused Barcardi distillery, with rough trincheras built at an angle obtuse to the approaches. Three companies of the Puerto Rico Battalion held his right, commanding the main road, while opposing the Rough Riders, Major Alcaniz commanded half a battalion of the San Fernando Infantry; two companies of the Talavero Regiment, a company of engineers, and two Plasencia guns held the centre.[1]

General Young deployed his men without discovery within 900 yards of the Spanish position. The Rough Riders, however, advancing down the trail, were met with a terrific fire, which checked them in some confusion; Captain Capron, Lieutenant Fish, and several men being killed and many severely wounded. The raw volunteer troopers, however, behaved splendidly. Colonels Wood and Roosevelt threw out their troops in skirmish order through the chapparal. The regular cavalry had extended their left flank, effecting a junction with the Rough Riders. A semicircular line of attack was thus formed, but owing to the dense undergrowth, the American fire could not be effectively maintained until a series of advances, in face of a hail of bullets, had brought the line to within 300 yards of the Span-

---

[1] The official reports show that the American generals have overestimated the strength of the enemy. From trustworthy sources, verified by a close examination of the ground directly after the battle, where the piles of expended shells showed the position of each soldier, I learned that only eleven hundred of the enemy held Guasimas; not four thousand, as claimed.

The Fight at Guasimas

ish position. Pouring in heavy volleys from their carbines, the cavalry then surged forward, the enemy's right flank falling back in good order before the Rough Riders, who were now enfiladed by Rubin's mountain artillery, and the infantry supports intrenched along the ridge. In a few moments the fire of the regulars drove back the Spanish left, and after Captain Alcaniz with the "Talaveros" bravely sought to cover the retreat of the guns and the wounded, the entire force fell back in confusion and withdrew to Santiago. They left but thirteen dead on the field, and removed their wounded, which were many.

At the supreme moment Captain Taylor, who had heard of the battle, came up with three troops of the 9th Cavalry. Several companies of the 71st Regiment also hurried to the front, but these reinforcements were not required.

Considering the disposition of the enemy, the American loss was extremely light. From a total strength of 964 men, sixteen, including Captain Capron and Lieutenant Fish, were killed, and fifty-two wounded. Majors Bell and Brodie, Captains Knox and McClintock, and Lieutenants Byram and Thomas were severely wounded. Mr. Edward Marshall, the war correspondent, was shot through the spine during the battle.[1] The Rough Riders gained unstinted praise for their bravery at Guasimas.

[1] Owing to the lack of bearers, the wounded fared roughly, and hearing that good treatment would prolong Marshall's life, Messrs.

Under Three Flags in Cuba

Colonel Roosevelt, after working incessantly to place the navy on a war footing, raised the regiment of cowboys for scouting in Cuba. But the antithesis of cowpunchers flocked to the corps, — tenderfoot dudes, first tolerated, afterwards beloved, by the ranchmen, — and an excellent camaraderie prevailed. Colonel Roosevelt has been charged with going to war to become Governor of New York. One of his men, replying to this, said, " If the Colonel was looking out for a prospective governorship, it must have been in Hades, for no one courted death more." I have seen Colonel Roosevelt gently soothing his wounded, fearlessly leading a charge, addressing meeting after meeting during his political campaign, and quietly resting with his family. His every act is characterized by a fearless sincerity, the sentiment of duty and principle of justice. The spirit of the man is even more than any series of his acts — a man the nation can trust.

The disembarkation of the remaining divisions of the army proceeded slowly, and many of the men, especially of the 71st New York, stood in the surf for hours in the tropical sun, seizing the approaching boats and dragging them on shore through the breakers. Such exposure in the tropics is a sure

Acton, Davies, Crane, McNichol, Howard, and Coffin carried him over the terrible trail, until they dropped from exhaustion. With the aid of Mr. Dinwiddie, he was safely carried over the hills to the " Olivette " and has since recovered from a precedented fatal wound.

Lack of Transportation

forerunner of fever. Perspiration poured off the men, as they unloaded stores on the burning sand, and their overheated bodies were repeatedly cooled as they plunged into the surf to drag the boats to shore. That labor was constant for fifteen hours per day for a week, and many a poor fellow unconsciously sowed the seeds of death, that soon stalked grimly through the ranks.

While the heliograph on La Galetta informed Linares of every move of the army on the coast, General Shafter ordered three transports to make a feint landing on the west of Santiago. Despite the obvious uselessness of this, the engineers were on board one of these vessels for four days, during which time the crazy pile dock at Siboney could have been repaired and strengthened by cribs, and the risks and exposure of a surf landing reduced to a minimum. Even suitable surf-boats were lacking, and the army and its commissariat landed in row-boats.

The soldiers were under the impression that tropical outfits would be issued for them in Cuba. They were still dressed in heavy serge, the old regulation equipment, and many had only thin civilian boots, which heat and salt water rendered useless. So few wagons had been shipped that there was no transportation for their effects, and as regiment after regiment was rushed to the front, the men, laboring in the sweltering heat, discarded articles mile by mile, until they had nothing but the clothes they stood upright in, and the route of the advance resembled the trail of a retreating army. Besides kit, rifle, and ammunition, the troops were ordered to carry three days' rations in their haversacks. They were marched at all hours, invariably during the heat of the day, and suffered severely; only the splendid physique of the American army made marches possible under such conditions.

The expedition landed just at the close of "el verano de San Juan" (the summer of St. John), and but for the unfortunate week of delay at Tampa, the advance could have been made in dry weather. The rains restarted on the fourth day and the difficulty of transport increased. Yet regiment after regiment was raced forward, when it was impossible to get sufficient supplies to the front. The Cubans and cavalry brigade, extended beyond Sevilla, made efficient outposts, and common-sense generalship would have mobilized the army first on the hillside near Siboney, where the men could have been easily fed, and the transport trains utilized to carry out supplies to an advanced base, protected by the cavalry. When all was in readiness, even the day before the battle, the army could have moved forward the eight miles toward El Pozo, and made the attack, well fed, and with an abundance of supplies on hand to sustain it.

It has been clearly demonstrated that for successful campaigns in the tropics troops must not be overloaded on the march, that a change of underclothing must be carried, and changed on alternate days, the

Commissariat Shortcomings

spare suit being exposed when possible to the sun, which acts as a powerful deodorizer. This simple hygienic precaution has been greatly conducive to the success of Great Britain's campaigns in India and Africa. It was impossible in Cuba, for even officers lacked transport for their clothes, and the health of the army was further jeopardized by the defective commissary.

While General Shafter was greatly to blame for not dispatching the fastest transports back to Tampa to bring forward additional mule trains and transport wagons, the supplies that were provided were utterly unfit for the climate, or for any army on active service. The staple diet, "hardtack," was of good quality, though whole-meal biscuit is more sustaining. But it was packed in wooden cases — it was soaked first in sea water, then by rain, the boxes lay around in thick mud which oozed into the badly made joints, and much of the hard bread was soon unfit for consumption. European armies use tin-lined cases for biscuit. Trained bakers could have built field ovens and issued a part ration of fresh bread. In the Soudan and West Africa the field bakeries covered themselves with laurels, and their equipment requires little transport.

The sides of salted "sow-belly" were of excellent quality, but were packed only in cheese-cloth. It was thus very difficult for the men to carry forward the slimy sides of bacon; it speedily became rotten, also, from sun and rain. But above all, only those who know the nausea of the stomach after exposure in a malarious clime can realize the repulsiveness of fat bacon in any form, while the torpid liver and impaired digestion inflicted by the tropics makes a fatty diet absolutely dangerous.

The canned meat was execrable — simply the offal of a beef-extract factory. It was possible to boil it for hours, and beyond the stringy substance at the pot bottom and grease on top, the water remained clear as before. Nutriment could not be extracted, and the men eventually preferred hunger as they gradually sickened. It was packed also in round tins, the most inconvenient for transport, and entailing much waste of space. I have eaten American canned beef in West Africa, in preference to the beef on the hoof procurable there. During the Ashanti campaign we thrived on it. In Sierra Leone and on the Gold Coast, in spite of an abundance of other canned comestibles, it forms the staple article of diet. Yet after weeks of semi-starvation in Cuba, and subsistence on the miserable Spanish-rancho during my deportation, I could not bring myself to eat the canned meat supplied to American soldiers by American contractors. This ration bore no resemblance to the me 'pplied to the British army. Besides excellent bouilli beef in portable cans, the Maconachie ration of canned beef-steak and vegetables is now issued with signal success to the English soldier on active service. In the United States, whose canned supplies rule the world, a similar ration could easily be prepared for the

Meat for the Army

American army: the meat retains its nutriment, and with the vegetables is palatable and sustaining. There was no excuse for the lack of fresh beef in Cuba. Grass was abundant; cattle could have been sent down easily, driven to the front in one day, thus saving transportation, and slaughtered in the lines. The contention of General Shafter that meat killed in the tropics will not cool, I venture to contradict. If the beasts are slaughtered at sundown, meat in Cuba is perfectly fresh for consumption on the ensuing day. Marching across Camaguey with General Roloff, we drove before us cattle captured from the Spaniards, and slaughtered them as required. In the pestiferous environs of Equatorial Africa cattle are scarce, but I have seen them slaughtered successfully. Even an occasional issue of fresh meat to the troops would have proved a great boon, and would have been greatly conducive to health. Yet when I left Santiago, six weeks after the capitulation had placed an open port in our hands, only a meagre supply of frozen meat had been sent to the army of occupation and the men were still existing on the old ration.

Excellent canned tomatoes were provided, but it has yet ɘ proved that they contain the qualities of a staple diet. Dried beans, an excellent ration, were shipped in large sacks and could not be sent forward. The canned beans were soaked in pork fat and were nauseating even to the Massachusetts troops. The coffee was good, but unground, partially roasted, and packed in paper. The men had no appliances for grinding in the trenches, and the beans were laboriously broken up between stones, and a miserable concoction without milk or sugar was the result. A cheap, refreshing beverage of cocoa-paste, containing both milk and sugar, is easily obtainable, but was not included in the Santiago menu. Saccharine was not used.

"Boil and filter all water before drinking," read one wise clause of instruction and advice to soldiers in the tropics, issued by the War Department. There was no transport for camp kettles, and no filters were provided. The drinking water was thus one of the most serious menaces to health and life. Modern armies provide the portable Pasteur filters for each regiment; and the soldier's charcoal filter and drinking tube, costing eight cents, and which can be slung on the frog or water bottle and used with ease, has yet to be included in the equipment of the American soldier.

Lack of fresh meat and vegetables is a serious danger to health, and lime juice or preserved vegetables are essential to prevent scorbutic disease. A German firm has perfected a ration of dried vegetables that have been used with excellent results in recent military and exploring expeditions, though it was not adopted in Cuba. A regular ration of lime juice should certainly have been issued, but only a few bottles could be purchased at the base.

A small ration of rum is an excellent nightcap for men exposed to miasma, and it is issued as an evening

Commissariat Disabilities

ration to British and German troops in tropical service. A huge store of excellent Bacardi at Siboney was poured on the ground, and barrels of red wine also, by order of the Commanding General. A few days later, when dozens of brave fellows lay panting for breath, their frothing mouths a harbor for flies, the glassy eyes silently pleading for an indescribable something, one's thoughts would revert to the rum and wine poured on the ground to prevent its abuse, regardless of the fact that its use would now save lives. A teaspoonful poured between those blue lips could alone have revived, and the hardtack and fat pork available would but hasten the approaching end.

Consolidated extracts and soups for an emergency ration are portable, but were lacking. The Medical Comfort box, containing beef tea and other delicacies for the sick, was also unknown before Santiago; if plain beef tea were shipped for the hospital, it was not unloaded. Emergency rations have been experimented with on the Plains, but were not adopted in Cuba. A concentrated combination ration, weighing three ounces and costing six cents, can be obtained, and would have proved a universal boon at the front during the starvation days of battle.

An impending attack of fever may be warded off by a dose of quinine, but there was none supplied save the scanty store among the medical supplies. Quinine, or its excellent substitute " Kreat Halviva," which contains all its properties and has none of its after effects, should be issued almost as a ration in the

Under Three Flags in Cuba

tropics. In hundreds of cases in Cuba, the fever was in far advanced stages before the patient could obtain the drug, and it was then too late.

From the first day of landing, there was a shameful neglect of simple sanitary precautions. This was especially noticeable at the base of Siboney. No sinks were dug there for many days, and when thousands of refugees crowded in from the hills, conditions became worse. They were chiefly negroes from the ruined coffee estates, who had precariously existed in the woods and were reduced to mere animals. Yet they were allowed to mix indiscriminately with the soldiers, and no sanitary regulations were enforced. The whole environs of the town were defiled to an indescribable extent; there was no quicklime, indispensable even for small camps; and erelong Siboney became a fœtid plague spot, and they wondered why yellow fever raged.

"Success is a bad word; its false resemblance to merit deceives mankind" was a favorite epigram of Victor Hugo. It makes an admirable text for this chapter, since the overwhelming success to American arms is invariably quoted, as a vindication of what is now called Algerism, and it is used as a shield of defence for the officialdom that failed to accomplish what the brave officers and men won by a miracle, despite disabilities and their shameful treatment.

The army went to Santiago to accomplish a stupendous task. A landing had to be effected on a hostile coast, artillery and supplies moved forward

Strategical Blunders

through ten miles of difficult country, open at all sides for surprise attacks from the enemy. Siege had to be laid to a considerable city, well garrisoned, naturally intrenched with steep ridges, and with a powerful fleet to assist in its defence. By negligence and blunder, the land operations from first to last were a series of mistakes, any one of which might have proved fatal to American arms. Victory was snatched at heavy cost, but a victory that can be attributed alone to Providence; for had the morale of the enemy been less impaired by starvation and disease, or had the fleet remained in Santiago Harbor, the amazing valor of the American soldiers must have gone for naught, and a reverse been entailed.

Owing to the unaccountable delay in road-making during the dry days and the subsequent employment of improper measures in repairing washouts and ruts with brushwood and sand without fagots and corduroy, to withstand the periodic downpours, even the light mortars could not be brought to the front before July 9, and not one of the siege guns was landed. What General Shafter hoped to accomplish with an army thus equipped and moved against the city, it is impossible to say. What would have been the result, even if Santiago City had been carried by assault, if the Spanish fleet had turned its heavy guns against the invading army, it is easy to foresee.

Ostensibly the army was to go to Santiago to attack and destroy the batteries and Morro in rear and thus enable the navy to enter the harbor, remove the mines, and co-operate with the army on land in destroying the fleet and capturing the city. To accomplish this, an advance should have been made along the coast railroad under cover of the guns of the navy. Aguadores could then have been captured, leaving only a short march across the foothills between El Morro and Santiago. The shore batteries at the harbor mouth would have been isolated and captured, and a combined advance made on Santiago by sea and land, the army covered by the guns of the navy. General Shafter, in the "Century," says: "I regarded this as impossible." Yet on July 2 he wrote a note to General Wheeler, asking if it were not feasible to capture the forts on the bay to let in the navy, and on July 6 he still talked of it to his staff.

The army was sent up the most difficult approach, against the strongest defences of the city ; by superhuman exertion the outlying positions were captured, but without sufficient artillery the army could go no farther. They had the city surrounded, but must have withdrawn or faced decimation by disease, without a chance to expel the fleet or assist the navy in gaining entrance, had not the enemy steamed out to escape, and brought on, from our point of view, the coveted result.[1]

[1] It is openly charged by many that jealousy of the navy alone caused General Shafter to act independently and attempt the course he did, thinking he could capture the city and snatch the glory while the warships did the blockading outside. He succeeded in gaining nothing and narrowly escaped defeat. But it is and ever

Injustice to the Cubans

After the fight at Guasimas, Siboney presented a busy sight. From sunrise to sunset the work of disembarkation and unloading of stores was pushed forward. Mule trains were being despatched to the front, while thousands of starving pacificos came into town from the hills.

Castillo moved his Cubans forward to El Pozo, where, under De Coro and Gonzales, they did efficient outpost work a mile beyond the American lines, thus relieving the soldiers from much arduous guard duty. Garcia brought 2000 insurgents, his negro regiments of Cambote and Barracoa, from Assedero, in government transports. Thoughtful Americans felt a thrill of pity when they saw the unkempt and emaciated insurgents, who had steadfastly endured three years' campaigning. Their march to the coast had been terribly trying, and for several days they had existed on grass soup. Can we wonder, then, that these ignorant negroes were demoralized at the sight of hard tack and bacon "ad lib."? They broke open the boxes and devoured the first square meal of three

will be impolitic to deal with this question. The Commander-in-Chief was but carrying out the orders of the War Department, and he should not now be made a scapegoat for this. The very knowledge of the unpreparedness, the weighty sense of responsibility, so preyed on the general's mind that his physical condition was pitiable. His gouty foot pained him considerably, and those who for political reasons intrusted the care of an army and national honor to an officer of such disability are morally responsible. Awaiting his orders, no practical reconnoissance of the country was made. He had no personal knowledge of the local topography, or the disposition of the enemy. "How can a man decide what he should do if he is ignorant of what his enemy is about?" says Jominie.

years, with so much gusto that certain gentlemen looked on with disgust and called them pigs, and energetic pressmen were speedily making copy on the "lazy Cubans' hate of work and love of eating." The Cuban soldiers marched to the north of Santiago, and had few transactions with the army for food or orders.

Along the now disused trail between Daiquiri and Siboney, overcoats and blankets were rotting by the wayside, and some of the "boys" told the ragged pacificos of this discarded treasure which was useless to the army. The poor wretches soon appropriated everything, but unfortunately they applied this permission universally, and on subsequent marches, when the men laid their packs by the roadside to collect later, they frequently found them rifled. Ragged and ignorant as were Garcia's soldiers, they did not steal and loot as charged, for theft is religiously punished with death in the rebel camps. The negro pacificos, many of whom were armed with rifles shipped down at the time but were absolutely without discipline, had no such scruples, and pilfered at every opportunity. It is impossible to fix any standard of judgment for people in their condition. But they were not insurgents, they were not Cubans. One-third only of the population of Cuba before the war was colored. Weyler killed off many of the whites in the West, but the negroes we saw around Santiago were no more typical of the Cuban race than are the ignorant colored squatters and

To the Outposts

cotton-workers of the Georgia backwoods representative Americans. Unfortunately, by the action of these negroes, the American troops soon lost the reverence they felt for the patriots' struggle for liberty, since they had neither time nor opportunity to form a broad and charitable judgment. Some of the very writers, who in Havana had misled the public with faked stories of victorious insurgent armies sweeping the Island, now found material at the expense of the Cubans in the exposé of the phantasms created by their own imagination. The sage Housas say, "If you find a cup and show it as gold, don't smash it as worthless, when it is proved brass, for the fault is yours, not the cup's."

Pressing forward to the outposts on June 26, with Bengough the artist and two servants who had previously served on the Nictheroy during the Brazilian trouble, we camped just above El Pozo, in a snugly thatched hut considerately erected by the Cubans. The rains had restarted, and miasma hung over the valley like a heavy pall, but toward evening the misty curtain was suddenly drawn aside, the skies turned blue as if by magic, and a most glorious panorama lay revealed to our wondering gaze. Santiago lay on a gentle ridge, alarmingly close, the minarets of the ancient cathedral and the blue walls of the San Cristobel convent, peeping over the graceful palms covering the valley. The sun was dropping behind the heights of El Cobre, and shed a golden radiance over the peaceful scene. The military hospital, carcel, and barracks, standing at the edge of the city, were plentifully bedecked with Red Cross flags, while before them, separated delusively by an invisible valley, were the forts and blockhouses of San Juan.

The light uniforms of the soldiers lounging around the blockhouses showed up plainly; they were apparently oblivious of the approaching army. A few distant booms to seaward — the navy exchanging courtesies with Morro — were the only evidence of war. The tinkling of the hammered pots in the belfry, calling to vespers, was wafted across the valley, and only the battened vultures that swarmed the trees could have divined the coming scenes of carnage. Sunset was first heralded by the Cuban bugler, but his puny notes were soon drowned by the harmonious burst of trumpets, as the beautiful "retreat" of the American army was sounded by the various regiments encamped at Sevilla, about a mile behind. Then their bands burst into the "Star-Spangled Banner;" and stretched across the heavens — silver stars shining from a sky of blue, the crimson glare of the setting sun intersected by white fleeced bars of cloud — the very spirit of Old Glory was typified. It seemed that a spiritual hand had thus emblazoned the heavens in omen of the flag so soon to float over that benighted land.

The army was camped near Sevilla. Despite the rain and the sorry rations, the spirits of the soldiers were sustained by the thought of battle. The light batteries were up, but we still looked across at the

Plan of Attack Formulated

enemy working on the defences before Santiago, while our guns were parked, and the men worked on the roads. General Shafter arrived at the front on July 29, cursorily viewing Santiago from El Pozo. On the following afternoon General Castillo and several American officers made a reconnoissance from the war balloon, and in a pouring rain at 3 P. M. a general advance was ordered.

Santiago lay to our direct front. General Lawton was to advance to the extreme right, with the Second Division, comprising the brigades of General Chaffee, the 7th, 12th, and 17th Infantry, General Ludlow, 8th and 22d Infantry and 2d Massachusetts, and Colonel Miles, 1st, 4th, and 25th Infantry, and two field batteries. After capturing El Caney, a fortified town menacing the right flank, Lawton was to swing round and invest the north side of Santiago. The First Division, General Kent, comprising the brigades of General Hawkins, 6th and 16th Infantry and 71st New York, Colonel Pearson, 2d, 10th, and 21st Infantry, and Colonel Wikoff, 9th, 13th, and 24th Infantry, and the Cavalry Division, General Wheeler, comprising the brigades of General Sumner, 3d, 6th, and 9th Cavalry, and General Young, 1st and 10th Cavalry, and the Rough Riders, with three field batteries, were to capture the advanced positions of Santiago at San Juan, and invest the city on the east. General Duffield, with the 9th Massachusetts and 33d and 34th Michigan and a force of Cubans, was to advance along the coast and join the navy in a combined

Under Three Flags in Cuba

attack upon Aguadores, menacing the left flank. If possible, he was then to move on Santiago from the south. A semicircular cordon would thus entirely compass the city. Garcia and his two thousand Cubans were expected to cover the entire western edge of the bay and the extreme north, to prevent reinforcements or supplies entering through either the Condella, Cristo, San Luis, or other passes leading to the city.

It is inexplicable why a general advance should have been ordered on the 30th. Lawton had seven miles to march to the right, but the centre divisions had less than two. The sudden movement of the army corps into the narrow trail retarded Lawton for several hours. The remaining divisions might have remained in camp until daybreak, and marched the short distance to the Pozo, dry, fed, and fresh for the assault. So congested was the trail that darkness supervened before many regiments had advanced at all, and at midnight the drenched troops lay down in the muddy road and rested on their arms until daybreak.

CHAPTER XIII

THE ATTACK BEGINS. — THE ARTILLERY DUEL. — A RECKLESS ORDER. — THE STORMING OF SAN JUAN. — AGUADORES. — CANEY FALLEN.

REVEILLE on July 1 roused a wet, bedraggled army from unrefreshing sleep. The troops lit fires with difficulty, and the centre divisions roundly "groused" at the spoilt night that they might have spent comfortably in camp. But the boom of Capron's first gun at Caney sent a thrill through the ranks; discomforts were forgotten, and the tension of anxious anticipation, the exultant, undefinable something of approaching battle, dominated each one of us. With Creelman and Armstrong, I moved down toward Caney, and turned to view the shelling of the citadel from the Ducrot. This citadel resembled a French château rather than the Moresque forts of Spain; but the guns made little impression upon it, and I rode back to El Pozo, where Battery A, Captain Grimes, was intrenched on a ridge opposing San Juan.

Directly behind the guns the cavalry were at ease, preparing a sorry breakfast. I remembered, at certain examination manœuvres at Aldershot, that a field-

Under Three Flags in Cuba

officer was disqualified for halting his men some distance in rear but directly behind a battery during an artillery duel. Seeing the guns about to open, I had the temerity therefore to warn one officer of the danger, should the enemy's artillery reply. "We have our orders and cannot move," was the answer.

By the guns Captain Grimes and Lieutenants Conklin and Farr were ranging, the cannoneers stood by their pieces, the high numbers at the caissons. At one minute to eight, No. 1 and 2 guns were loaded with common shell.

"Range 2500 yards!"

The breech block was closed with a snap, the trail of No. 1 gun was swung into position, the layer looked over his sights, depressing the piece a trifle. The sight of No. 2 gun was adjusted in readiness.

"No. 1! Fire!"

The report rang out — a shell went screaming over the peaceful valley and burst at impact just beyond the ridge, amid the cheers of the soldiers.

"Too much elevation! No. 2 at 2450. Ready! Fire!"

"Still a little high!" No. 3 gun sent a shell crashing below the blockhouse. No. 4 missed fire through defective pricking; but in the second round each gun sent a shell hurling against the blockhouse, and the enemy could be seen scampering to cover. The range fixed, shrapnel was resorted to. To the thirteenth round there had been no reply, though we looked instinctively across the valley after each discharge.

The Artillery Duel

Suddenly a tiny ring of bluish smoke circled through the air, and with a vicious scream a shrapnel hurtled over the battery and burst just above the heads of the crowd behind the hill. Men fell on all sides, and before the surprised soldiers had recovered from their astonishment, another shell exploded. With marvellous direction, shrapnel burst regularly just over the battery, among the troops so wickedly exposed there. A group of Cubans were literally blown to pieces, horses were killed, and then a shell burst before No. 3 gun, killing two gunners, Helm and Underwood, instantly, fatally wounding Roberts, and injuring every man in the vicinity. As I turned, blinded with dust, with Scovel and Bengough, to seek a less exposed place, the grimy figure of Corporal Keene loomed through the smoke, and with blood pouring from two wounds he returned to his gun, which Michaelis, the son of a brave officer, and the only one uninjured in the detachment, was coolly working as if on parade, while Brown, a Harvard man, carried ammunition from the caissons.

There was a subtle fascination in watching the three devoted officers, and the men of Battery A, standing exposed to the sure and deadly fire, and answering shot by shot. Colonel Ordoñez, the Spanish inventor and artillerist, succeeded Colonel Melgar, commanding the artillery, and had personally ranged the position with fearful accuracy. The enemy used smokeless powder, and their battery could not be located, while the black powder of our guns made a perfect target. After nine minutes of this effective shelling, the Spaniards fortunately held fire, and thus the crowded troops behind the ridge were able to move from their perilous position. Grimes fired thirteen more rounds, and failing to evoke reply, he also ceased fire, and his men fell, exhausted by their efforts in the hot sun. Below the hill Surgeon Quinton worked heroically under fire with Dr. Church of the Rough Riders.

When the artillery duel had ceased, though there was no indication that the enemy's guns had been silenced, the regiments started to pour down the trail leading through the thickly wooded valley intervening between El Pozo and the enemy's position on San Juan. Lieutenant-Colonel McClernand, A. A. G. to the Fifth Corps, had ridden up with orders from General Shafter for Generals Kent and Sumner to move their divisions forward through the valley to the edge of the woods and there await orders. The trail led down to the San Juan River, walled in on either side by impenetrable bush. Just beyond the last ford the woods ended abruptly and a gentle grassy slope led to the foot of the San Juan ridge, which is like a huge rampart thrown up to defend Santiago. Extending along its whole length were trenches, intersected with blockhouses, while below strong barbed-wire barricades were stretched along the base of the hill. San Juan was the strategical key to Santiago. Beyond was an intervening valley, with a gradual ascent leading up to the plateau on

Tactics at San Juan

which the city stands. It commanded the succeeding rows of trenches on the hillside and the strongly fortified and barricaded outskirts of the city, that rose like a wall along the next crest.

One moment's consideration of the topography of this position will show that an attacking force marching down the wretched trail to San Juan would be forced to form line of battle at the edge of the woods, under a sweeping fire from trenches and forts, and after thus deploying, the depleted force must advance across the open, against the fences, and storm the hill. Such a course could but court extermination.

There are defined, strategic rules for capturing such a position. Preparatory action holds infantry to cover with artillery at the front, until the shelling has produced sufficient effect for a general advance. The configuration of the ground seldom admits guns remaining far in rear of the advance, but there is no justifiable hope in advancing strong masses of troops against an intrenched position without preparatory artillery action, and no assault should be ordered until the artillery duel has silenced the enemy's guns and shaken the defending forces. A few hour shelling would have demolished the blockhouses and cleared the trenches along the ridges. Then, with rough trails cut branching from the road through the trees to the edge of the wood, several columns could have emerged simultaneously in the valley, formed line, and charged the hill with small loss, ready to face the enemy's main position. During the war of

Under Three Flags in Cuba

'70 Moltke advised his generals that frontal attacks on a position usually failed, unless means had been taken to engage the enemy's flank simultaneously.

During the struggle to expel the usurper Joseph Bonaparte and his brother's army from Italy, one of Massena's columns advanced down a narrow wooded road. At the head of the track a handful of loyal Calabrians sheltered behind rocks on a low eminence, swept the opening with their rifles. In vain the column strove to press forward and charge the position — the French soldiers emerged from cover, only to be shot down by the unerring mountaineers, and a sorry remnant alone escaped by retreat. The position resembled San Juan, only the head of the Santiago road was held by regular soldiers, intrenched, armed with repeating rifles, and with artillery that could shell the road long before the attacking force reached the open valley. One regiment of infantry and a single battery from perhaps any modern army but Spain's, could have held San Juan against the entire force of Shafter advancing without artillery support.

General Shafter intended that the columns should advance quietly through the woods, and stand ready to make the charge when the artillery had prepared the way and Lawton's Division had swung to flank the position on the right. Possibly he thought the enemy would sleep in the interim.

Into the unknown jungle the cavalry and infantry advanced. The road was muddy, and in places but

The Battle Precipitated

three could march abreast, so that when the advance guard reached the first ford, the road was choked with closely wedged men for considerably over a mile. The Spanish pickets concealed in palm-trees in the valley, soon saw blue uniforms advancing, and gave the alarm. Not certain of the strength of the force, the Spaniards fired only a few desultory volleys, but as the vanguard came unseen down the road, the captive war balloon was sent bobbing along in the very advance, just over the tree-tops. It developed the fight, the moment it drew within range.

Every rifle from fort and intrenchment blazed at once at the silken globe; the artillery reopened, and bullets and shells poured through the tree-tops, dealing death and destruction among the men in the crowded trail. By this time the cavalry were starting to deploy along the creek; but when the wretched balloon had finally received its quietus, and sunk amid the curses of the men stricken through its agency by an unseen fire, the enemy had exactly ranged the line of the road, and were apprised that a general advance was taking place. A withering fire was directed against the angle where the balloon had disappeared and along the edge of the wood.

In a moment the insanity of the tactics dawned upon the American army. "Not though the soldiers knew some one had blundered . . . Theirs not to reason why. Theirs but to do and die." The whole command would have been withdrawn, and the artillery allowed to prepare the way, had not the trail been so packed that a retrograde movement would have cost hundreds of lives, besides demoralizing the survivors. A modern army, composed of the finest material in the world, had been moved recklessly into a death-trap, to be decimated by what proved to be a handful of half-starved Spaniards.

Generals Kent, Hawkins, and Sumner held a hurried consultation. Lieutenant Ord climbed a tree and viewed the enemy's position far more effectually than a hundred balloons. General Hawkins crossed the ford, and glanced upward at the ridges. In a few moments the leaders of division, seeing retreat impracticable, decided to rush the position.

Lieutenant Miley, representing headquarters where the commander-in-chief should have been, concurred in their view. Grimes Battery had reopened, and as there was imminent risk from our own shells falling short, he sent orders to the artillery to cease firing while the troops deployed. A heroic figure of six feet three, Miley stood at the ford, encouraging the men, who moved over the stream into a hell of fire. Cavalry and infantry were mixed, but the former deployed to the right, the latter on the left. The men were ordered to reserve their fire and to lie flat on their faces as they formed line. The San Juan River ran streaked with blood, for the dead and wounded fell from its slippery bank into the water repeatedly.

Hawkins's Brigade, the 6th and 16th Infantry, extended first; the 71st New York, who had suffered

The Forces Deploy

severely, being ordered to support. Through misunderstanding these volunteers [1] were halted and lay down in the road beneath a galling fire, and Wikoff's Brigade, 9th, 13th, and 24th Infantry, passed over them. Colonel Wikoff was killed as he reached the head of the road. With magnificent coolness Colonel Worth of the 13th stepped forward to lead the brigade. He was shot down instantly. Colonel Liscum of the 24th sprang into his place and fell delivering his first order. The leading company, seeing the three officers shot in succession, faltered; but Colonel Ewers of the 9th heroically took the lead, and the brigade, steadied, deployed on the extreme left.

General Wheeler, through sickness, had that morning been relieved of command of the cavalry by General Shafter. General Sumner took his place at the head of the division. Colonel Wood had assumed charge of Sumner's Brigade, Lieutenant-Colonel

---

[1] The leading companies of the 71st were thrown into confusion by stampeded mules, and halted under the stream of bullets aimed at the collapsing balloon by their side. The men became panic-stricken, being unable to realize their distance from the unseen foe, and while temporarily disorganized, the regulars swept through their ranks and to the front. Numbers of the volunteers followed the regulars, and participated in the charge; Companies F, Captain Rafferty, I, Captain Meeks, M, Captain Goldsbury, with Lieutenants Williams and Olin, going forward intact. Major Keck brought up his battalion to support. This regiment performed very arduous duty throughout the campaign, and as a close observer at San Juan, I can positively state that a combination of circumstances rather than inefficiency or cowardice caused the failure of New York's popular regiment at the critical moment.

Under Three Flags in Cuba

Roosevelt leading the Rough Riders, Colonel Diel the 1st Cavalry, and Colonel Baldwin the 10th. General Young had sickened after heroic service at Guasimas, and on the previous day, he was invalided home. Colonel Carroll assumed charge of his brigade, with the 3d Cavalry, Major Wessells, 6th, Captain Kerr, and 9th, Colonel Hamilton. They deployed steadily on the right under a terrific fire.

When General Wheeler heard the firing, he rose from his cot and journeyed to the front in an ambulance. Finding wounded by the roadside, he insisted on mounting his horse, relinquishing the hospital wagon for their use. Thin and wan, and shaking with fever, the ex-Confederate rode slowly down the lines, followed by his son and aide, Lieutenant Wheeler, and the men could scarce forbear a cheer. As senior officer he assumed command, and virtually directed the action for the remainder of the day.

The men were suffering severely while deploying, and as I crawled partially along the line, the dead and wounded were thickly strewn down the fringe of the wood, and it seemed that disaster had come. Lieutenant Mitchie, aide to General Hawkins, lay dying beside the creek. Benchley was killed delivering an order. Captain O'Neill fell dead just before the line broke cover. Lieutenants Devereux and Haskell were wounded and apparently dying. Captain Henry was shot from the saddle as he crossed the creek. Lieutenant Roberts lay beyond mortally wounded, with a dozen troopers around him

Line of Attack Formed

dying or dead. Captains Swift and Steel, also of the cavalry, had both fallen, and dead or wounded officers and men lay in all directions.

I waited for a few minutes with the 9th Cavalry. Many of the colored troopers were praying aloud with negro familiarity, but their supplications were constantly broken by the flight of bullets, when a volley was fired in our direction, and they continually responded in kind. It was a relief to join in and pump a Winchester at the hidden enemy; but the order was soon passed down: "Cease firing! Load magazines!"

Alsop Burrows and Basil Rickets, society men, serving in the Rough Riders, had charge of the dynamite gun, and had moved it forward. It became jammed after the first discharge, and the valuable adjunct had to be relinquished. The gunners, however, sprang to a machine gun, and worked that manfully. Lieutenant Parker rushed his Gatlings up and swept the crest, private Sine working the crank of one until the lead melted. He was killed ere his gun cooled.

Pearson's Brigade, the 2d, 10th, and 21st Infantry, had now crossed the ford. Colonel McKibben led the 21st to support Hawkins. The others swept away up the valley to the left. Our loss was considerably over a thousand, before the lines for attack were formed through the chaparral on the fringe of the woods. At the supreme moment thirteen-inch shell, fired right over the city by the Spanish fleet,

Under Three Flags in Cuba

thundered into the lines like rushing trains. Then the stirring "Charge!" from Hawkins's bugler rang through the trees, and the cavalry trumpets repeated it. The men had long scrambled through torrent and thicket under a galling fire; the sight of comrades falling acted as an incentive, and, like a series of waves, the companies surged forward, the platoons irregular, commands mixed. As the line broke cover, the Spaniards blazed down with Mauser and machine gun, and their fire resolved the assault into a series of short rushes. There was a murmur of hoarse commands, bugle-calls rang out, while the roar of artillery, incessant crash of rifles and bursting shells, drowned the imprecations of the soldiers and the agonized cries of the wounded. On the right of the line Colonel Roosevelt spurred his horse forward, and with a cheer the Rough Riders started toward an eminence to the right front, Marianje, now Kettle Hill. The whole cavalry division moved forward rapidly. Colonel Hamilton was shot dead; his senior, Captain Taylor, and Adjutant were severely wounded as they advanced. Colonel Carroll fell as the Spanish outposts ran back, Major Wessels was wounded a few moments later, Captain Bigelow received three bullets before he relinquished his company, Captain Mills was shot through the head. The grassy ascent was soon covered with dead and dying, but the troopers swept upward, and captured the fort and trenches, the enemy retreating with loss to the woods beyond. Turning slightly to the left, the cavalry

MELGAR'S HALF BATTERY OF PLASENCIA'S, LOADING AT SAN JUAN, JULY 1, 1898, AS THE BATTLE OPENED.

The Defenders of San Juan

then charged the main line of intrenchments, soon extending until they touched the centre division, assaulting San Juan.

In the centre General Hawkins, his white hair flowing loosely in the breeze, led forward his infantry brigade. Barbed wire fences barred the way, but Lieutenant Wise, of Military Kite fame, and other officers smashed the posts with logs. A fraise of barbed wire was negotiated with loss, and as the cavalry joined hands with the infantry right, it was an individual race from the extended lines to the top of the hill. "Les épaulettes en avant!" was the cry that led the raw armies Gambetta's enthusiasm had raised. At San Juan every officer was an individual leader, and the terrible percentage of officers who fell is an eloquent tribute to their worth.

The San Juan Heights were held by Colonel Baquero of the Simanca Regiment, and but three companies of the Puerto Rico Battalion. Carefully intrenched, and hardly touched by our artillery fire, this small force, aided by machine guns and two nine-pounders, had torn up their assailants in the valley below with no appreciable loss. But they were disconcerted by the steady American advance, and redoubled their volleys as the thin blue line crossed the valley and commenced to climb the steep ascent. They leaned over their defences to fire at the stormers almost directly below them, and being suddenly exposed, received volley after volley from our reserves, and were swept by the Gatlings. The brave Baquero was killed, vainly attempting to rally his men; and as the leading files of the almost exhausted Americans clambered over the ridge, and prepared for the crash of hand-to-hand conflict, a straggly line of pale blue rose against the sky, as the Spaniards sprang up from their trenches, evacuated their fort, and fled precipitately into the intervening valley before Santiago.

Ere twenty of "ours" had clambered over the ridge, "Old Glory" fluttered proudly on the hill, the cavalry guidons were planted on the ridges to the right, and many a stricken and dying soldier raised his bleeding body and gave one cheer of exultation and defiance.

For perhaps two minutes there was a lull in the firing; then our shouts of triumph were drowned by a crash as of thunder, as every fort and house on the outskirts of Santiago, and the main lines of defence extended in three rows before the city, opened up on the outworks it had cost us so much to storm.

Wounded and dead Spaniards were strewn along the ridge. The hard clay of the hill had made revetments unnecessary, but the perpendicular trenches, backed by a fausse-braye before the fort, had impeded their retreat and caused the only serious loss from our fire. On the berm of the trench Captain Venancia Raga lay shot through the hips. As our first line passed over the ridge, Lieutenant Ord, pointing at the Spaniard with his revolver, shouted, "Carry that officer to the rear." Mistaking the action, Raga

The Position Captured

threw up his pistol and shot Ord through the head. Thus died the most conspicuously brave officer of the war. The soldiers, enraged at the unintentional treachery, poured a volley into the Spaniard as they passed on. The Spanish flag was torn down from the fort by Agnew of the 13th, and the guidons of the 6th and 64th Infanteria were captured by the 6th Cavalry. The 16th, 6th, 9th, 13th, and 24th Infantry formed along the captured ridge, while Pearson's Brigade, 10th, 21st, and 2d Infantry, which had extended on the extreme left, swept over a succeeding ridge, driving in a second outpost of the enemy.

Despite the terrible fire raging from Santiago, the eager soldiers passed beyond San Juan, clinging to available cover, and shooting with little fire discipline, at the trenches dug in the hillside leading up to the city. In reserve behind the trees Colonel Sierra had two squadrons of the King's Light Cavalry. Noticing the weakness of the American line, now greatly depleted by wounded and their helpers, and the scattered formation of the various companies that had advanced wildly beyond the ridge, General Linares ordered the cavalry to charge down the road and flank the lines in the valley. Such an onslaught would have proved disastrous to our advance. But their uniforms showed through the trees as they mounted, a volley was fired into them, and despite the efforts of Major Irles and others, they wheeled and galloped into the city, losing very heavily from the spent bullets that made both rears more dangerous than the respective firing lines. So thick was the cover that the American officers knew nothing of the foiled charge, though I followed the line of retreat later by the carcasses of accoutred horses and torn clothing and equipment.

At this juncture General Linares fell wounded, and Toral assumed command of the Spanish army. The San Juan fort was now the objective of the enemy's fire, and their well-placed shells drove out the occupants. The volleys along the whole front grew more steady and regular, and General Hawkins, realizing the uselessness of irregularly facing the entire Spanish army, ordered the "rally" sounded. The eager soldiers then fell back to the ridge they had captured, and intrenched themselves along the crest. The cavalry had also advanced impetuously beyond the hill, and retired reluctantly to its shelter. As they hurriedly intrenched, the enemy poured from the woods, and finding cover behind rocks and along hedges, fired steady volleys that would have proved terribly effectual when the troopers were beyond the hill, and probably have driven the American lines back demoralized.

With Nicholls and MacDowell, I had lain behind the disused sugar-kettles at Marianje, against which bullets rang incessantly. The engine-house there was turned into a temporary hospital, and a terrible fire was soon raging against it. Crawling along the advanced ridge, I could see the Spaniards creeping forward, and the recapture of the position

The Defence of Santiago

from our thin lines seemed imminent. General Sumner and Colonel Wood both sent to General Kent for infantry reinforcements, and the gallant 13th was moved to the right to support the cavalry. At this time an advance was also made against San Juan, the enemy having the advantage of a gentle slope and excellent cover. But as we watched the straw hats bobbing, and an occasional swarthy face, the whole cavalry division reverted from individual firing to rapid volleys, a machine gun turned loose, the infantry on our left were responding strongly, and the enemy withdrew to their first line of intrenchments with loss.

Opposing us on the hillside forming Santiago's outskirts, the chain of forts, blockhouses, and fortified houses, and succeeding rows of trenches were held by the 1st Battalion Asia Regiment, 1st Puerto Rico Provisionals, 1st San Fernando, historic with Serrano's charge at San Pedro; 1st Constitucion and 2d Talavera Regiments, two companies of Heavy Artillery, one battery of light artillery, and two companies of engineers. Two companies Guardia civil, a battalion of Irregulars (Guerillas), nineteen hundred volunteers,[1] and three hundred enrolled firemen formed the reserves, and with the Caballeria del Rey brought the force up to eight thousand men. The centre was augmented by twelve hundred marines from the fleet and four machine guns.

[1] After the capture of San Juan the volunteers, with the exception of Pratt's famed and bloody veterans of '69, left the trenches

Under Three Flags in Cuba

The intrenchments extended from Dos Caminos on the north to Punta Blanca on the coast. These lines were strengthened by thirteen forts surrounding the city: Forts Cruces, Gasometro, and Nuevo on the south, Beneficencia, Canadas, San Ursula, Guayabito, Canosa, and Santa Inez on the east front, and Cuabitas, San Antonio, Yarazo, and Barges at the north and head of the Bay. Fort San Antonio boasted three bronze guns, and Santa Inez one. Two of the three guns at San Ursula were doing effective shelling under Colonel Ordoñez, wounded during the afternoon. Four bronze Sevillian guns at El Sueno were poorly worked through lack of gunners, and the three guns at Fort Nuevo, which almost enfiladed Pearson's brigade on the left, fired few shots effectively. During the afternoon one Hontoria also was mounted under fire before the city. Toral had little ammunition for his guns, and at Canadas rusty chain shot, piled as relics on the Plaza, were utilized.

As I crawled along the ridges, I was surprised to find so few of the enemy's dead at San Juan, which had cost so terribly to capture. I saw but sixteen — the highest estimate was thirty. Some wounded begged pitifully to be spared when one approached,

and refused to fight. As shown in Chapter III., these braggart loyalists have caused Cuba's misrule. Toral dared not order them back to the trenches, and he afterwards told me bitterly: "We came here as soldiers to fight for Spain, whom these men had embroiled with the Cubans. They cried for war with the Americans and then left us to bear the brunt."

Defeat Closely Averted

but the dead were comparatively few. Having gauged direction from the balloon, the enemy had poured down their merciless fire without exposure from volleys returned from two hundred feet below. Had the impetuous Latins waited in their position, they could have swept off the exhausted Americans as they gained the summit, and the victory evolved from the egregious blunder of July 1 would have had a different sequel.

The capture of San Juan cannot form a demonstrative precedent in modern tactics. Ordered into an untenable position, the striking individuality of the American soldier, criticised by some as undiscipline, rose superior to the occasion. A technical defeat was turned to victory when the tactics of Shafter had failed. It was eminently a soldiers' battle. Invidious praise has been heaped on certain regiments; equal credit is deserved by every officer and man participating in the assault. "It is pardonable to be defeated, but never to be taken by surprise." The army at San Juan knew the enemy was before them; but owing to the lack of orders, no officer knew what to anticipate. The first intimation of battle was a shower of bullets crashing through the tree-tops from an unseen foe. The commanding general, when he ordered the advance through the valley to Bloody Angle, overlooked Marmont's text of elementary tactics, — "Marches in the vicinity of the enemy cannot be made with too much precaution and prudence."

Under Three Flags in Cuba

The massed formations, dear to the heart of the Great Frederick, are no longer possible in these days, when the inventor is the master of the hand that slays; and mere valor can now seldom prove the deciding factor in warfare. In Cuba the Mauser proved superior to the Krag Jorgensen for rapidity of fire and penetration. It was pitiful to see the American troops extracting, with difficulty, single cartridges from their sodden belts, while the Spaniards pressed home the pentacapsular clip in their Mausers and had five shots ready. A clip adjustment and a cartouche box should certainly be adopted by the United States. The enemy also had smokeless powder, and neither battery nor trench could be located; while the United States Artillery and the Springfields of the National Guard made a continual smoke target, and obscured the view. In the confusion of the battle fire discipline was not maintained, and I heard no ranges given during the day.

The fighting, by four o'clock, had resolved itself into an offensive defence by both armies, neither of which were in a position to advance. In taking the ridges our losses had been: First Cavalry Brigade, strength 1054, lost 2 officers and 9 men killed, 12 officers and 114 men wounded; Second Brigade, strength 1468, 4 officers and 31 men killed, 18 officers, 185 men, wounded. The Infantry loss in Kent's Division was First Brigade, strength 2052, 5 officers, 39 men killed, 14 officers, 263 men wounded, and 49 missing. Second Brigade, strength 1557, 1

Feint at Aguadores

officer, 17 men killed, 10 officers, 118 men wounded, 5 missing ; Third Brigade, strength 1416, 6 officers, 31 men killed, 11 officers, 187 men wounded, 9 missing: an aggregate loss of 1140 officers and men in taking a position that artillery alone could have made untenable.

The firing on the extreme flanks at Caney and Aguadores continued, though news soon reached the centre that Duffield had retired to Siboney, the fleet continuing the attack from the sea. The 9th Massachusetts and 33d and 34th Michigan, and a force of Cubans, had moved along the coast, their advance protected by the fleet. At the ford of the Aguadores River they found the enemy in ambush, and drove the Spaniards back to the town, despite the heavy fire of a battery, which caused great loss to the 33d and the Cubans. The "Newark," however, silenced the battery, and Admiral Sampson, from the "New York," after signalling to Duffield on shore, led the attack with the Flagship, assisted by the "Suwanee" and "Gloucester." The old fort was speedily demolished, and the enemy were driven from their trenches. Unfortunately, the Aguadores River was so swollen by the rains that it was impossible to ford it; pontoons or engineers were non est, and the troops returned by rail to Siboney. As a diversion the demonstration was a success; but the attack was a failure as a flank movement against Santiago.

Seeing the San Juan ridges were now completely invested, I caught a stampeded troop horse in the valley below, and strove to ride through the bush to the extreme right. The rude path across country, however, was infested with sharpshooters, a number of fugitive soldiers from Caney were lurking in the trees, and the trail was so difficult that I soon abandoned the attempt. From a wooded hill beyond Marianje I could see that Lawton's Division was still hotly engaged, and he was apparently suffering from the want of artillery that cost so many lives.

General Vara del Rey at Caney had barely 600 of the Constitutional Regiment, and no artillery. They were strongly intrenched round the town itself, however, and in the heavy stone citadel on an eminence at the southern outskirts. Five smaller forts — Rio, Cemeterio, Yzquierdo, Matadero, and Asia — held the approaches on the north and west.

At first the guns had accomplished little; but as the infantry closed in on the citadel, several well-planted shell burst within. Our infantry had little cover, and the enemy's machine guns, finally located in the church tower, played sad havoc. The American lines advanced slowly, the attacking force dashing across open spaces and seizing every bit of available cover. As at San Juan, they had moved into range before the artillery had paved the way, and they suffered severely in consequence. Colonel Haskell fell early in the day, wounded in three places, and Chaffee's Brigade, the 7th, 12th, and 17th, lost heavily as they advanced against the citadel under a heavy fire from the

Attack on Caney

town, besides the direct resistance from the fort and surrounding trenches. Colonel Miles, with the 1st, 4th, and 25th Infantry, closed in on the west, coming up on the other side of the hill; and after Capron, with a few excellent shots, had crushed in a bastion and carried away the roof in a dozen places, a united charge took place, both brigades storming the hill. The soldiers in the trenches escaped into the town, however, and only eight privates and a corporal were captured.

The first man to reach the fort and tear down the colors was James Creelman, the war correspondent. Speaking in Spanish, he told the survivors of the garrison to surrender, reassuring the poor wretches, who begged for quarter. Seizing the flag, he waved it triumphantly to the oncoming troops. When they saw their colors had fallen, the enemy opened heavily on the fort from the town. Creelman sank with a bullet in his shoulder, which tore its way through the blade, making a gaping wound three inches in diameter. The 25th Infantry suffered severely, ascending the hill; and though the citadel was the key to Caney, its capture had by no means ended the fight. Chaffee and Miles now led their forces against the town. General Ludlow's Brigade, 8th and 22d Infantry and 2d Massachusetts, moved against the defences on the northwest. The 1st Infantry extended, cutting off retreat to the hills, and a detachment of Cubans engaged the blockhouses on the north, but made a poor showing, having expended their ammunition recklessly before closing in. Being unable to obtain more, they could not drive out the enemy.

Ludlow's brigade, afterward supported by the 11th Infantry, captured the blockhouses holding the highroad; and flanked by Cubans under Sanchez, they drove the enemy from an intrenched trail within fifty yards of the town. The enemy, realizing retreat impossible, and expecting no quarter, still resisted desperately, fighting from trench to trench. Ludlow's horse was shot under him. Colonel Paterson was wounded. Lieutenant McCorkle, 25th Infantry, Lieutenant Wansboro, 7th Infantry, and Lieutenant Field, 2d Massachusetts, were killed.

Lieutenant Dickeson, 17th Infantry, under a heavy fire, nobly went to aid Colonel Haskell when he fell, and received two mortal wounds. He was struck a third time in the leg, just before he died. Captain Jackson, Lieutenant Lefferty, of the 7th; Lieutenants Dore and Churchman, 12th Infantry; Lieutenant Neary and Hughes, 4th Infantry; Captains Jones and Mosher and Lieutenant Godfrey, 22d Infantry; Captain Warrener and Lieutenants Meyneham and Hapgood, 2d Massachusetts, and many other officers were wounded, encouraging their men under heavy fire.

Vara del Rey meantime was apprised of a way of escape, and, seeing the day was lost, he hurriedly mustered the garrison in the town and prepared to evacuate, leaving the depleted defenders in the out-

Death of Vara del Rey

works, to check the attacking force. Mounting his horse, he galloped across the plaza, but fell, pierced with two bullets. The garrison retreated, unseen, through a narrow path in the woods, dragging the general's body with them. Watchful Cuban scouts notified General Sanchez of the move, and he hurried De Coro over to head the Spaniards off. The veterans of the battalion "Constitucion" fought desperately, however; and though they relinquished Vara del Rey's body and lost many men, they cut their way through the Cubans, and reached Santiago at night. Vara del Rey's body was found next day.

As the main body of the enemy withdrew, the whole American force were led at the charge against the town. The barricades were torn down, the outworks stormed; and though a few desperate soldiers fought from house to house, Caney was soon in our hands.

Lawton's division lost: killed, 4 officers, 74 men; wounded, 36 officers, 562 men; missing, 62. Bates's additional brigade, 5 killed, and 2 officers and 26 men wounded.

CHAPTER XIV

THE AFTERMATH OF SAN JUAN. — THE WOUNDED. — THE SIEGE OF SANTIAGO. — HORRORS OF CANEY. — CAPITULATION OF TORAL. — SANTIAGO AFTER SURRENDER. — CLOSE OF THE CAMPAIGN.

"DEATH on the battlefield is a glorious thing," said General Von Francois, as his life blood gushed forth at Rothe Berg. After the flag waved over San Juan, and reaction from the excitement enabled us to realize the sad realities of victory, there seemed little glory for the silent forms that lay on the field where they had fallen; or the hundreds of wounded who were helpless in the thicket, or crawled to the rear, with blood spurting from their wounds, to the dressing-station improvised in the creek bed.

By Army Regulations, each soldier carries into action a first-aid dressing, — the Esmarck bandage and two antiseptic pads. Through negligence, perhaps of the men themselves, many were not supplied with this simple but indispensable adjunct. Medical supplies at the front were absolutely lacking in the Shafteresque confusion, save for the hospital pouches the surgeons had carried on their own shoulders. Thus the single surgeon apportioned to each regiment not only found before him the work of six, but he had

The Hospital Service

nothing save the first-aid packages intended for application on the firing-line, to stay the life-blood that gushed from the rows of men awaiting attention. It is not for me to impute the blame. General Sternberg had provided ambulances and an abundance of medical necessaries; but ambulances were left in Tampa by General Shafter, and the stores that were taken were loaded beneath the unlanded siege-guns, and could not be reached.

No field hospital was equipped within specified distance, and the wounded were placed under shelter of a sand-bank, in the San Juan creek, and lay for hours awaiting cursory attention. Distracted surgeons tore up shirts and requisitioned handkerchiefs, underclothing, anything, in lieu of bandages. The patients, if they could move, then crawled down to the divisional hospital four miles back, where Colonel Pope and Major Wood had hastily erected hospital tents and two operating-tables. I saw but one ambulance along the trail; there were the necessary stretchers for the heat prostrations and casualties attendant on peaceful summer manœuvres, and the badly wounded were either dragged over the soggy road in a blanket or lay at the creek until the next day.

Diagnostic tabs, which facilitate the work of the surgeon, were wanting at the front, and to save time and confusion, Major Pope took in patients in the order of arrival, — American, Cuban, or Spaniard in turn, — greatly to the surprise of the wounded enemy awaiting execution with becoming patience.

Under Three Flags in Cuba

Beyond the Rio Seco, near El Pozo, there was an admirable site for the field hospital, which was speedily utilized as a temporary station by Dr. Bell of the 71st. Its limited capacities were soon exhausted, and a long line of suffering men wended their way through the mud to Sevilla.

At the San Juan dressing-station, the bullets of the enemy, passing over the ridge, fell like hail in and around the stream. To make room behind the bank, we carried poor Mitchie and several other dead across the ford to await burial. When carrying one poor lad over, a bullet passed through the lifeless body, and a number of wounded were killed by sharpshooters in the trees, despite the Red Cross flag that was hoisted over the station. Quiet heroism abounded on all sides. Wounded officers lay at the front, refusing to be moved until privates had received attention. I offered an arm to one of the 13th, shot in the side. "There is a man there that wants help more than I," he said, pointing into the trees. He plodded down toward the station, leaning upon his rifle, and hearing a moan, I turned to see him fall on his face, shot through the throat. I joined Chaplain Swift a few minutes later. A spent ball had struck him in the knee, which had swollen considerably; but he continued aiding the wounded, under fire for two days and nights. He searched the dead also, taking charge of personal effects, and attempting to establish the identity of each, before the vultures commenced their work or the burial detail was sent out. This action

Lack of Identification

of Chaplain Swift, and Dr. Vandewater of the 71st, led to an infamous charge, made by certain cowardly volunteers, that the two chaplains had robbed dead bodies as they lay on the field.

It was extremely difficult to establish the identity of the dead. Identification slips, which should contain in tabulated form the name, rank, regiment, and next of kin, of the wearer, were not supplied to the troops. Singularly, also, the individual regimental kit number, which in European armies must be stamped on every article of the soldier, was not in general vogue in the American army. It is a simple regulation, invaluable in peace, essential in war. By its use, the misappropriation of kit, a common form of recruit hazing, would be impossible, and the possession of a full equipment by each soldier easily assured. In Cuba it was frequently impossible even to discover the regiment of a wounded or dead man, countless mistakes arose, and for weeks families at home endured a terrible suspense, when some loved one's name was posted as missing, whose body had probably been buried without identity by a fatigue party.

The charges for the dynamite gun had been left at the dressing-station. Several shells burst near by, and an explosion of the dangerous ammunition was imminent, when Basil Ricketts, of the Rough Riders, and two troopers hurriedly dug a trench for the boxes. Bullets were falling around in all directions, and the enemy's sharpshooters also opened upon the little party. We had lifted the cases into the pit, when

Under Three Flags in Cuba

Ricketts fell, shot in the groin. "Cover them up; never mind me," he cried, as I stepped to aid him. I managed to drag him half-way over the river toward a place of shelter; but he turned in the water, with his wound bleeding and the bullets splashing around, and instructed the men to place logs and stones over the pit-top for further protection. When this was done by Glackens the artist and two troopers, Ricketts consented to be carried out of range.

The battle subsided into a desultory picquet fire at sunset. For an hour after dark, details scoured the valley for wounded, and surgeons worked on all night in the moonlight, while guerillas took pot-shots at them from the trees. Several attempts were made to dislodge sharpshooters in the woods, but screened amid the pinnated foliage of royal palms, and using smokeless powder, they were difficult to locate. Near the angle, two troopers pointed out a suspicious something in a palm-tree, and creeping along the creek bank, we fired several shots, until first a rifle, then a body, fell crashing out into the bush. Two days later, two Cubans cut their way through the tangle to the place I indicated, and found the body of a Spanish sergeant. They brought out his coat with the red chevrons pinned on the sleeve and a Cross of San Fernando on the breast. Several Rough Riders also brought men down, and guerilla soon ceased to trouble. These guerilla had fired indiscriminately at wounded and litter-carriers far behind the firing-line. One band even fired into

Underestimate of Losses

headquarters and at the field hospital in the next potrero, four miles behind San Juan. The enraged soldiers soon ceased to discriminate, and several harmless pacificos were shot plucking mangoes, and many insurgents were killed at night by picquets, for not answering the foreign challenge promptly. Garcia's men grew wary of carrying despatches after dark, and gave our lines a wide berth, though starving negro pacificos hung round the camps in hundreds, and pestered the soldiers, who berated Cubans in general in consequence.

Late at night, General Shafter cabled Washington that his aggregate losses were "above four hundred; of these not many are killed." Later he weakly admitted that he had underestimated the casualties, and asked for forty surgeons and a hospital ship. The anxiety caused by this despatch in the United States was aggravated by a silence at headquarters until July 3, when an urgent demand from the War Department elicited the fact that the city was well invested.

The army worked far into the night intrenching, and then sank supperless in their muddy trenches to wait for daylight. A tired and hungry group gathered in a disused drying-yard, — Crane, Harding Davis, Burr McIntosh, Hare, Glackens, and myself. Then Nicholls rode up and generously disgorged his saddle-bags. Sir Brian Leighton of the British African Service joined us, and we supped royally on hardtack and canned bacon. We slept where we could, Sir

Under Three Flags in Cuba

Brian securing two discarded blankets, with which we bivouacked in the sopping grass with some degree of comfort. At midnight the artillery moved to San Juan, and then the silence was broken only by groans of the wounded and hoarse challenges from the guards.

At 4.30 A. M. the first glimmer of dawn was heralded by a volley from the enemy, that drove in our outposts and started the battle raging along the whole line. Major Dillonback's batteries opened well, but every Spanish rifle was soon directed against the guns, which were barely intrenched, and in great confusion the pieces were dragged from the ridges, that were absolutely untenable at such a range. Thus again the worn-out cavalry and infantry were without artillery support, in a country topographically a gunner's paradise had reconnaissance been made for the selection and preparation of suitable sites. The artillery officers had awaited the formulation of a plan of campaign, and several told me that they received no definite orders until late on July 2, when the guns were moved laboriously through the woods, to a ridge on the left of El Pozo, too late to be of effective service. The failure of the artillery in Cuba may be chiefly attributed to the lack of mobilization manœuvres in the American army. Numbers of officers, absolutely proficient in every branch, had never had practical experience with combined branches, mobilized as an effective whole. An army is like a machine, and in the war with Spain the component parts were placed together for the first time, and the

The Staff of the Army

working lacked harmony. Constant practice in the field with every corps on a war footing, the commissariat working with the line, can give the desired result. The United States has now adopted an outside policy. Obviously the army must be adjusted to that policy, or the policy to the means of its defence. The blunders of the Santiago campaign proved the weakness of the system, and undoubtedly the object lesson will prove valuable, and should leave the army in the hands of trained soldiers rather than politicians.

The staff of a modern army should be composed of officers who have been qualified by an exhaustive course in the staff college. In Cuba, men absolutely ignorant of military affairs held staff positions, and while they proved their courage and patriotism, the youngest line subaltern was better fitted for the work, and the staff duties fell heavily on the few attached regular officers. The staff appointments of several Cuban gentlemen, notably Señores Maestre, Mendoza, Munoz, and Diaz, proved wise. They were all mentioned in despatches, and received commissions for their services. Señor Munoz was shot through the jaw, but continued on duty. Lieutenant (now Colonel) Miley,[1] who represented headquarters at the front, made superhuman effort to sustain relations with the various brigades, fearlessly exposing himself in the performance of the work of a full staff.

[1] Colonel Miley died of typhoid fever in Manila, September 21, 1899.

Under Three Flags in Cuba

General Bates's Independent Brigade, after reinforcing Lawton at Caney, moved over to support at San Juan. Lawton also moved his division on the night of the 1st, but, through a mistake in the road, he was forced to march through by El Pozo, extending and strengthening the lines on the right early on July 2. They were soon heavily engaged, receiving shells also from Cervera's fleet. This division marched and fought continuously for sixty hours, with nothing but hardtack and one ration of coffee.

During the battle on the 2d our losses were much lighter, but the creek bed and road were choked with wounded. In lieu of ambulances a few transport wagons were utilized to take them to the rear. General Shafter, who has not learned the Pythagorean precept of silence, has stated that he left ambulances at Tampa, since army wagons bedded with straw make efficient transport for the wounded. At Santiago the straw failed to materialize. When wagons were sent to the front, the semi-naked wounded were laid in rows upon the rough bottoms and jolted back to the hospital. The springless wheels on the rough road made torture enough for the stricken men, but at the so-called rivers, mere streams that four hours' labour with the timber growing on the banks would have bridged, the teams first jolted down the steep banks, throwing the wounded in a bleeding, groaning heap at the head of the wagon. The rear wheels bumped into the water, throwing the human mass rudely apart; and as the

Bloody Angle

wagon was dragged laboriously up the opposite bank, the inmates slid toward the tailboard, shrieking and groaning in their helpless agony. Bandages became loosened, hemorrhages re-started, and men who had gone forth to bravely fight for their country a few hours previously, begged piteously to be killed to end the agony entailed by official negligence.

The communication with the front was difficult and dangerous. Bullets and shells from Santiago fell behind San Juan in continuous hail. Several men wounded at the front were killed when going to the rear. When helping a wounded Rough Rider to the dressing-station, a shell buried itself in the ground at our side and exploded, killing my Cuban mule and blinding us with dirt and splinters. As we hurried to the creek bank, Captain Danforth, the surgeon of the 9th Cavalry, whom I had previously met as physician to the Cuban Government, turned to greet us, and fell shot through both temples. Two wounded men were again hit, and two horses fell writhing over on the Hotchkiss gun to which they were attached. It seemed that the Spaniards purposely directed their fire at this place, protected by the Red Cross, though I believe the configuration of the ground caused the bullets to drop there. Poor Danforth had been a great exponent for Cuba libre; and as we gently lifted his quivering body to shelter, I remembered his former prognostication, "I shall die for Cuba."

There was no lull in the firing all day, and one instinctively worked among the wounded, for "the harvest was plenteous, but the laborers were few." During the afternoon the first attempts were made to bury the dead. Chaplain Brown conducted a service under fire over the grave of Captain O'Neil, and later assisted Chaplain Swift with a general burial in the valley. It may console the friends of many who fell during those terrible days, to know that their dear ones were not thrust into unhallowed graves when they fell on the battlefield, thanks only to these devoted chaplains, who stood bareheaded, motionless, the target for sharpshooters, in the path of spent fire, and who emerged scathless through divine protection. The dead were shrouded in blankets or tentes d'abri, and were laid in reverse rows in a large pit. There were but four mourners, — two negroes, a corporal of the 71st, and myself. Erelong bullets began to whistle around, but neither chaplain recked it. "Ashes to ashes! Dust to dust!" Dr. Brown's voice broke; his colleague finished the service. Then each chaplain seized a spade and filled the grave.

At sunset General Shafter started to the front for the first time. Cowardice is certainly not one of his attributes, for as he rode across the Rio Seco, a party of guerilla opened down the ford. The sentry at the crossing fell dead, but the commander-in-chief rode coolly on, a few cavalrymen emptying their carbines into the trees. The general did not ride out to the lines, and few knew of his excursion. The firing died away with the daylight, and

Night on the Battlefield

having secured my horse, I started to ride toward Caney, hoping to aid Creelman. I pressed on, guided only by the stars, but soon became hopelessly entangled in a swamp. At the De Crot House, I learned from Follingsby that a stretcher and bearers were imperative. There were no litters at the front, though the Cuban officer at the Pozo offered me six men as carriers. So I decided to ride in to Siboney, and returned to the firing-line to collect any letters or despatches that officers might care to send down.

As I crossed the battlefield, the full moon poured down a lurid glare that made the country light as day. Dark objects lay silently in the valley, stark and stiff; uncanny vultures blinked like owls in the moonlight, so emboldened by the carnage that one's advent disturbed them little; over all rose the indescribable odor of blood and death. In the trenches above, the worn-out supperless troops had sunk in the mud in troubled sleep.

I had collected several letters, when a light flickered toward the Cobre Road, and a distant skirmish fire was heard. Then a second fire appeared on the hill to the west, and finally a third blaze appeared behind Estrella Point. Rabbi, under cover of the darkness, had taken Cubans round to the west shore and fired the Spanish blockhouses, which were evacuated as he approached. At the same time he opened fire against the Spanish ships and on the trenches at the head of the Bay. The Spaniards, thinking the expected assault on the city by land and sea was to take place, were terror-stricken. At sword point, officers drove their men to form outposts to check the expected onslaught. This movement stampeded a mule, which galloped toward the American lines. Our picquets challenged and fired, and the Spaniards turned to run back to the city. Their jabbering, and the attempt of Toral's staff officers to stay the retreat, broke the stillness as our worn-out troops were aroused by the picquet fire. The alarm spread: our startled men opened a wild fire; the outposts came tearing in. The alert defenders before Santiago responded heavily; their outposts in the valley, falling on their faces to escape the fire of friend and foe, also commenced to shoot. The opposing lines were marked by successive sheets of flame, and though the advanced Spaniards suffered heavily, no American was killed or wounded. The fight soon subsided, as if by mutual consent. Brilliant word painters have described this "night attack" in thrilling language, artists never in Cuba have painted desperadoes congruent to Sidonia's caravels, storming our trenches.

Since in places but three hundred yards intervened between the opposing lines, the outposts advanced on either side were very close, and each side accuses the other of attacking and being repulsed. Minds worn by strain and fasting readily conjure phantasms, and the cries of the Spanish outposts and the sudden awakening led many of our men to believe that the enemy resolutely charged the line, and, as such, it will perhaps go down to history.

A Needless Night Alarm

The alarm caused a deplorable stampede at the divisional hospital. Some frightened volunteers dashed into headquarters, shouting that the enemy had broken our line. Some of the staff lost their heads; their needless panic spread to the hospital, where rows of wounded lay in the grass awaiting attention. Some pleaded to be killed rather than left to the enemy; several, with blood spurting from their wounds, started to run through the mud; others called for rifles, swearing that they would die like men, not like dogs. It was several minutes before the panic was stayed.

The alarm over, I was asked to carry a requisition for field dressings to Major Lugarde at Siboney; Miley also had been reported killed, and wished a cable sent to his wife. As I splashed over the ford, flashes and reports rang out as the guerilla took ridiculous pot-shots at me in the dark, revealing their position. Replying with a couple of shots, I rode on across country to the coast, overtaking Scovel on the road. Our horses sank to the knees in the swamp, rivers were swollen with heavy rain, and at a late hour we reached Siboney.

At the base hospital there, with the navy and fleet of transports in the offing, there was a lack of everything, and men were virtually dying for the want of nourishing food. So few hospital supplies had been unloaded that before July 1, when the army was buoyed against sickness by the prospect of the combat, the wounded from Guasimas alone overtaxed the hospital facilities.

Under Three Flags in Cuba

Hay spread on the ground and covered with blankets formed the bed of the patients; land crabs, scorpions, and tarantulas worried the men repeatedly, and they bitterly resented the treatment of the country they had bled for. Miss Barton and her staff on the Red Cross ship "State of Texas" were waiting at Guantanamo, with tons of supplies for the Cubans. Just before the San Juan battle, Mr. Davies ran his despatch boat down to the "Texas," and informed Miss Barton of the dire need of the hospital at Siboney. Regardless of red tape, Miss Barton moved the "Texas" down the coast, and finding a lack of cots, clean linen, cooking utensils, medical supplies, and suitable food at the hospital, she landed her entire staff and the necessary stores, just as the hundreds of wounded began to pour in from San Juan.

Little did the generous Americans who sent the "Texas" for the Cubans realize that their donations would providentially succor their own soldiers, whose lives were imperilled by incompetent officialdom. With Dr. Lesser, his devoted wife, Sister Bettina, and Sisters Anne, Minna, Isabel, and Blanche, and Mrs. Trumbull White stood for hours by the operating-tables, assisting the tireless surgeons and soothing the suffering men with the divine influence God has bestowed on woman. The army had provided little beyond hardtack and field rations for the wounded, and had no facilities for cooking. The Sisters prepared rice and gruel over braziers, and thus only did the wounded obtain the food they could

Hospital Shortcomings

assimilate. Day and night the devoted Sisters slaved, with brief respites of sleep on sides of packing-cases covered with a blanket; and it is small wonder that they all sickened and were removed in a dangerous condition to the hospital ship.

Ice is imperative in a hospital in the tropics. During the Ashanti and Benin campaigns half-civilized Houssa soldiers in the British service found ice in the hospitals in the West African jungle; but in Cuba, an island adjacent to their own shores, the American army moved without an ice-machine or arrangements for manufacture of ice on one of the forty transports. Mr. Hearst, from his yacht "Sylvia," sent several tons to the hospital ship "Olivette" and to Siboney, and thus by private ministration fevered wounds were kept cool, and dangerous complications averted. The correspondents from the despatch boats spent their spare time in nursing, Davies, McNichol, Root, Anderson, and others assiduously working. Mumford turned the Journal headquarters into a ward, in which he personally tended all the officers he could accommodate until he fell with yellow fever contracted by exposure at the front and the long hours he devoted to this work. Self-sacrifice was thus rewarded in Cuba.

When I arrived at Siboney, the surgeons were still busy at the tables, and Major Lugard, blood-stained, and weary from lack of sleep, turned patiently to hear my story from the front. He gave me all the dressings he could spare, and after talking with Miss

Under Three Flags in Cuba

Barton, she arranged with Dr. Egan, Dr. and Mrs. Gardner, Dr. Hubbell, and Mr. Kennon to take a wagon-load of stores to the front. Miss Barton was joined by Mrs. Horace Porter at the field hospital, and they worked for many days at the front.

I stepped softly between the rows of suffering soldiers that night at Siboney; fires outside and flickering lanterns lit up the gaunt faces, some stamped with approaching death. Amid all the anguish, few groaned; some raved in delirium, one boyish lieutenant again urging his men forward in the historic charge. Some wounded that I had assisted at the front gave me a faint smile of recognition; a corporal watched with anxious eyes for his brother, taken to the table, and when they gently told him the soldier had answered a higher call, he gave up hope and died, sobbing quietly. His name I never learned, but in a blood-stained wallet we found the picture of the sweet-faced mother who had given both her sons to her country. May they all be united at the great Reveille!

Snatching three hours' sleep, I obtained a litter for Creelman and started back to the front before sunrise. Branching off by a side trail to cross the hills to Caney, I rode some distance up the spur of the Condella to locate my position. Below stretched the glorious country. The sea shone like a polished mirror framed by the ironstone coast; the white houses and drying-yards of coffee-estates, nestling peacefully in the undulating valley, strongly con-

Cervera's Fleet Destroyed

trasted with the sea of variegated foliage below. Before Santiago lay the two opposing armies, — an artillery duel in progress between Shafter and Toral.

As I gazed on this scene, I remembered it was Sunday. In America thousands, saddened by the news of the two days' battle and its sacrifices, were praying for their army in the field. In Spain the people knew little of the straits of their forces, and celebrated their "impending victory" by fiesta and bullfight. At that time the American troops were depressed. They realized the inability of their line to withstand combined onslaught of the enemy. The army could go no further: it could do nothing to expel Cervera's fleet or capture the city; heavy rains and increasing sickness made the prospect dark indeed. And at that moment the God of battles hearkened to his people's cry and placed victory in their hands.

Scanning the Bay, I could see no trace of the Spanish squadron. Then also I noticed an unusual roar of guns to seaward. Morro was wreathed in smoke, the shore batteries also, and I decided that Sampson was trying to force the harbor and Cervera had moved down the Bay to meet him. The narrow entrance and the sea beyond was hidden by the foothills, and I was all unconscious of the decisive action being fought below them.

I found Creelman later, but at headquarters. The field hospital at Caney had been stampeded by the night alarm, and the wounded had crawled six miles through the mud to the centre division. He was in a raging fever, and we carried him to the hospital. His shattered shoulder-blade was dressed, and Bengough and Stoddard aided him to Siboney. Truce was declared that morning to enable the burial of the dead. During the afternoon, as I talked with Lieutenant Wheeler before his father's tent, a despatch arrived for the general announcing the destruction of Cervera's fleet that morning. The news spread down the line from brigade to brigade, and the worn men raised themselves in the trenches and gave a cheer that sent the enemy scuttling back to the trenches they had left.

General Shafter had realized the seriousness of the position to which his army had plunged with such loss. Without sufficient artillery he could do nothing, and just as the fleet steamed out and accomplished for itself the main object of our expedition, he cabled the following despatch : —

SECRETARY OF WAR, Washington, — We have town well invested on north and east, but with very thin line. Upon approaching it, we find it of such a character and the defences so strong that it will be impossible to carry it by storm with my force, and I am seriously considering withdrawing about five miles and taking up a new position on the high ground between the San Juan River and Siboney, with our left at Sardinero. . . .

SHAFTER, Major-General.

This message reached Washington at 11.44; and Secretary Alger, in reply, advised, for the sake of the

An Altered Situation

effect on the country, that San Juan be held if possible, and promised reinforcements.[1]

The news of Cervera's defeat changed everything. General Shafter sent in a demand of surrender to General Toral, informing him of the loss of the fleet. But a few hours before, the Spanish general had cabled Blanco and Madrid that Cervera had escaped, and General Aguirre at Cienfuegos was ordered to receive the squadron with ostentation, and General Correa cabled his congratulations to the Admiral. One can but sympathize with unhappy Spain, whose jubilation was turned to despair when they learned the absolute loss of the squadron.

Toral, however, staunchly declined to capitulate, but did all in his power to prolong the truce until reinforcements, marching from Manzanillo, should arrive to aid him in repelling the assault he hourly expected, but which Shafter was powerless to carry out. Thanks to the Cubans, daily reports of the relieving column from Manzanillo reached headquarters. Garcia with two thousand men was holding the extreme right, cutting off the San Luis valley and the five thousand men garrisoned there within sixteen miles of the beleaguered city but kept in ignorance of Toral's straits by the vigilance of the insurgents holding the intervening valley. Garcia, realizing the impossibility of

[1] General Shafter has not explained why so many men were sacrificed and the army moved into the position before he discovered the fortifications too strong to storm. Intelligent reconnaissance could have informed him of this a week before the battle.

Under Three Flags in Cuba

holding the entire west of the Bay against six thousand Spaniards, who might advance at any point of his scattered lines, asked and received permission from Shafter to ship half his men, under Rabbi, down the coast a few miles to Assedero, where, in conjunction with Colonel Estrada at Contre Maestre, they could hold a pass at the Aguacate River through which the Spaniards must march. In that position only could the insurgents stay the advancing force supposed to be under Pando, though Escario subsequently proved to be in command.

After the destruction of the fleet General Shafter decided that the Rabbi expedition was unnecessary. He believed the city would surrender, and said that if Escario gained entry there would be the more prisoners to his credit. Garcia stated that he would do his best to hold them out, but realized that it was impossible with his thin line. Escario had a column of thirty-three hundred infantry, two hundred and fifty cavalry, two field-guns, and sixty transport mules. The insurgents had harassed him on the march to Contra Maestre, where Colonel Estrada and six hundred of the Maceo Regiment made a strong stand. Both the Spanish battalions, Isabel la Catolica and Andalusia charged the position, but were driven back; and had Rabbi and his force been sent over, Escario admits that the Spaniards must have been routed. Finally, however, Estrada's meagre ammunition gave out, and flanked by the Chasseurs of Puerto Rico, the six hundred Cubans fell back.

Escario's Entry

The enemy crossed the Cobre Hills at daybreak, and skirting the bay, entered the city during the truce. The Cuban outposts there had been given explicit orders not to fire without orders, pending which the Spaniards gained the city. General Garcia keenly felt the unjust charges made against his forces, and those officers who knew his position exonerated him entirely. General Ludlow, who was on the extreme flank, eulogizes the Cuban forces in his report, mentioning Sanchez and others by name, and no other officer was brought into closer contact with the ragged patriots. To judge them beside trained American soldiers was, of course, impossible. Three times they intrenched, though without tools, and cheerfully relinquished the result of their labor to the Americans, when the lines extended to the right.

They carried wounded, drew rations but twice; and the reports, inspired by the conduct of starving pacificos and exaggerated by irresponsible correspondents, that credited the Cuban rebels with laziness and theft, are not only unjust but absolutely false. The stories of atrocities upon Spanish prisoners were palpable fakes. The insurgents in Santiago rendered much service to the army unostentatiously, and have gained nothing but abuse. Had Shafter given Garcia definite orders, they would have been carried out. In General Miles's words, "Our requests were as commands to the brave Cuban."

On July 5 a second demand for the surrender of Santiago under threat of bombardment was rejected by Toral, and non-combatants were advised to leave the city. The inhabitants had suffered terrible privations, and on the 1st and 2d they were terrorized by shells from the warships that fell in all parts of the town. The consuls drew up a letter of protest to Admiral Sampson, against shelling the place without due warning. The guns, however, were directed against the defences behind Aguadores at great elevation, and unintentionally overreached the mark. Cervera on the 1st had threatened to shell the city should the Americans gain entrance, and gave notice to that effect. Rather than face this, the French consul and his subjects went to Cuavitas and entered the Cuban lines. The British consul, Mr. Ramsden, cabled for a warship to remove the people under his care. The panic was indescribable, when Shafter's ultimatum was delivered.

The consuls passed out to see General Wheeler, pointing out that the destruction of Santiago would not harm Spain materially, since the city was looked upon as doomed; it could only destroy the homes and drive out the inhabitants to starve in a country devastated by Weylerism. The effect of their appeal was the grant of one day longer for the people to move out. H. M. S. "Alert" and "Pallas" removed British subjects, and twenty thousand people moved out beyond our lines, little recking that Shafter's threat was backed only by a few field-guns. Toral, pointing out, ironically, that since he had now several thousand less mouths to feed, he had plenty of supplies for his

Shafter Implores Naval Aid

troops, then positively refused to surrender. Without siege-guns or mortars, Shafter was unable to follow up his ultimatum, and his strategy gained nothing and rendered thousands of women and children homeless.

Having acted independently of Admiral Sampson, by not advancing against Morro Castle and the shore batteries, the commanding-general now turned helplessly to the navy, demanding that they should force an entrance to the harbor and attack from the Bay. Since it would assuredly have resulted in the loss of one or more vessels, the sinking of which would have closed the channel, Admiral Sampson declined to make the attempt. On July 4, the commander-in-chief cabled to Washington as follows: —

ADJUTANT-GENERAL, Washington: In the Field, near San Juan River, 4. — I regard it as necessary that the navy force an entrance into the harbor of Santiago not later than the 6th inst., and assist in the capture of that place. If they do, I believe the place will surrender without further sacrifice of life.

SHAFTER, Major-General.

This message he supplemented by a further appeal one hour later, stating that the sure and speedy way to take the city was through the Bay, otherwise he would require 15,000 more men speedily, and doubted if they could be landed, since it was getting stormy; and during the afternoon he repeated his first message. Secretary Alger wrote to Secretary Long, asking him to order the navy to force the Bay at once; but since the War Department had sent the army into its precarious position, disregarding the only feasible plan of co-operation with the fleet for joint attack, Secretary Long refused to overrule Admiral Sampson. Adjutant-General Corbin then sent the following despatch to General Shafter:

"Your telegram concerning the navy entering Santiago Harbor received, and your action thoroughly approved. The Secretary of War suggests that if the navy will not undertake to break through, take a transport, cover the pilot-house in most exposed points with baled hay, attach an anchor to a towline, and if possible grapple the torpedo cables, and call for volunteers from the army — not a large number — to run into the harbor, thus making a way for the navy. Before acting, telegraph what you think of it. One thing is certain: that is, the navy must go into the harbor, and must save the lives of our brave men that will be sacrificed if we assault the enemy in his entrenchments without aid. This is strictly confidential to you."

The insanity of advocating baled hay to shield an unarmored transport from modern projectiles that had ignited the wood lining of Cervera's ironclads, is obvious. The certain sinking of the burning steamer in the tortuous channel of the harbor would have effectually barred out the navy, completing the work attempted by the enemy with the "Reina Mercedes."

On July 6 the truce was extended for the exchange

Nonæ Caprotinæ

of Lieutenant Arias and fourteen privates for Lieutenant Hobson and the crew of the "Merrimac." The exchange was conducted by Colonel Astor, Lieutenant Miley, and Captain Maestre, and Comandante Irles and Captain Rios who conducted Hobson and his men from the city. The heroic sailors received a profuse welcome from the army as they crossed the lines, and at night they were all back on the flagship. During the afternoon Captain Chadwick of the "New York" and Lieutenant Wood of the "Gloucester" visited headquarters. The captain pointed out the impracticability of the navy forcing the harbor.

The Junta of defence met in Santiago. Several officers advocated surrender, the clerical party advised it, Linares wavered, and the brave Toral was in a quandary. Irles sprang to his feet and in an impassioned appeal reminded them that they were custodians of Spain's honor; that Shafter showed no disposition to end the truce and bombard. As soldiers, they must resist to the last ditch; as cowards, surrender. The effervescible Latins were roused again, though three officers and several privates deserted in the night and entered the Cuban lines.

During the protracted truce the formation of our lines completely changed, and nightly the troops closed in, drawing the cordon tighter. But the soldiers grew dispirited with inaction: exposure and army rations were beginning to tell, and finally yellow fever broke out. On July 7, Nonæ Caprotinæ, a frightful storm raged, and, wondering at the general inaction, a classical trooper suggested that the commanding-general had emulated Romulus, and disappeared in the midst of it. Other storms followed, swamping the trenches and adding to the difficulties and discomforts of the army. Had injudicious censorship allowed news of the plight of the forces to reach Madrid, and had Toral been notified to hold out longer, the army, sent unequipped to face fever, famine, and Spain, must either have hurled its depleted strength against the city's defences, to save a national disgrace by assault at frightful sacrifice, or faced annihilation by disease and privation.

The banks of the three rivers crossing the line of communications were steep and well wooded. A few hours and palm-trees would have effectively bridged them. A tie-block trestle or single-lock span would not only have allowed the passage of light artillery and transport trains, but would have saved the constant immersion of the troops, who were forced to wade or swim across San Juan several times each day. During the whole campaign the men thus lived and slept constantly in wet clothes; and there were many victims of latent malaria thus developed by negligence that even France was not guilty of in her disastrous Madagascar expedition.

Foreign attachés were amazed to find officers faring the same as their men. I frequently messed on pork, hardtack, and poor water with cavalry officers. Their men had coffee, but they explained apologetically, "We do not sponge on their ration, for they need it

Self-Sacrifice of Officers

more than we." Colonel Evan Miles was told by the doctors that his life was endangered by lack of food, and that he must be invalided home. He could not assimilate hardtack, and he had no tent at the front, though commanding a brigade. But he stayed resolutely with his men, and, too ill to stand, I have seen him wrapped in his cape and propped above the mud and water by ammunition boxes, directing operations night and day. When the city surrendered, he consented to be invalided home. Heroism and self-sacrifice existed along the whole line, and such officers can lead men anywhere and to do anything.

But the sufferings of the army were as nothing compared to the privations endured by the unfortunate non-combatants from Santiago. They were huddled in thousands in El Caney; every house was so crowded that none could lie down, but squatted on the floors of the rooms and on the piazzas, unable to move.

Delicate wives and daughters of merchants, prominent residents of the city, were herded in with dirty negroes and the scum of the population. There was no privacy. Food was unobtainable, though the woods were scoured for mangoes, which were fortunately plentiful and alone staved off starvation. The town resembled a vast reeking pigsty, — there were absolutely no sanitary observances; the streets were littered with filth; in the one stream that provided the refugees with drinking water, the people washed their clothes and themselves, and it was polluted by surface drainage.

Under Three Flags in Cuba

The emaciated survivors of the reconcentrados, whose pudicity had departed through force of circumstances, thought little of the lack of privacy; but the delicate Cuban ladies from the city felt their position keenly until they also sank into the apathy of starvation. In single rooms fifty persons were sheltered, ladies in silken robes and beggars in rags. Money availed nothing, and on several occasions, when I rode out with the few tins of beef and the hardtack I could secure for special cases, I saw the fortunate recipients offered and refuse gold pieces for a single biscuit, and one man produced twenty-five dollars to buy a can of beef. Most of the wealthier class left Santiago before the blockade, especially the families of the Spanish merchants, and the officers' wives stayed in the city; but there were Spanish and Cuban ladies in silks and satins abjectly starving in Caney.

The most pitiable sights were to be seen in the Plaza and the side streets, where thousands of people were unable to obtain shelter and lay exposed to sun and storm, the former perhaps the more trying. Two loads of food were sent out on the fifth day, but these supplies were as the ten loaves and fishes for the multitude, with no miracle of increase. Then the Red Cross workers arrived, and Dr. Elwell did what he could to relieve, but "No transport available" was the answer to his entreaties to headquarters, and tons of food spoiled at Siboney, while hundreds starved but thirteen miles away.

One could not fail to notice the wagons that daily

The Hungry at Caney

arrived at headquarters with forage for the horses of the general and staff and his cavalry escort, when vast potreros of Parana grass in the valley guaranteed food for the animals. One of those wagons filled with food each day would have saved much suffering to the men at the front and to the refugees, for whose plight we were morally if not legally responsible. Each day caldrons of soup were made, and this distribution led to fierce riots, in which weak buffeted with strong in a struggle for the precious decoction that was exhausted before one-fiftieth of the crowd had been served. Frail women and children were trampled under foot in the mad rush; men forgot their chivalry in the fight for food, which they usually wanted for their own little ones, and few but the most resolute, and therefore the least needy, ventured into the seething crowd. In the scenes of suffering and misery women were reduced until they priced their honor for a morsel of food for their dear ones.

The more intelligent class roundly berated General Shafter, when his threat of bombardment was postponed from day to day. "How dare he," they argued, " drag us out to this misery and then make no effort to bombard the city into surrender? All these days of truce we might have stayed at home." Rumors reached the people later of supplies ad lib. at Siboney, and then a steady stream of fugitives started through the muddy trails to make one effort to reach the land of plenty. They had to carry their effects or discard them. The streams were swollen, the roads quagmires; and it made one's heart ache, to see the helpless women and children wading and stumbling down that fearful fifteen miles to the coast, hundreds falling by the way from sheer weakness. Many died from exhaustion; but the majority either gave up in despair and returned to Caney, or managed to reach the main road from Siboney to Santiago, where the passing troops, touched by the mute appeal on those despondent faces, devoted the greater part of their own scanty rations to aid them on the way. It took the people three days to reach the looked-for Mecca, which then turned out to be a plague spot of yellow fever, quarantine enforced, and no shelter or rest for their weary bodies.

The Red Cross, however, soon opened a relief depot, and finally many were housed in the coffee storehouses on the hillside, the residue existing as they might in the woods.

On July 10, Toral, receiving prompt rejection of his offer to capitulate if allowed to march out with full honors of war, requested that cable operators might go to the city, to transmit to Madrid the terms of unconditional surrender demanded. General Randolph arrived with additional field batteries, and the 1st District of Columbia and 3d Illinois Volunteers also marched to the front. Despite these reinforcements, Toral, that afternoon, sent out a defiant letter to Shafter, stating that he could sustain a long siege, and reiterated his refusal to surrender, save with a safe conduct for his army with full honors.

The Bombardment Opens

To this Shafter sent a terse reiteration for unconditional surrender, and the Sunday quietude was broken by a scattering volley and a shell from the Spaniards, as they defiantly dragged down the white flag. Our artillery were at extreme range, and opened at 4 P. M. The suffering soldiers, sick with inaction, tumbled into the trenches, and the fighting restarted. With Armstrong and Bengough I rode out to the advance ridges, to witness the effect of the bombardment. The mortars threw bombs, rather ineffectually, against the hillside leading to the city, and the field-guns did little damage. One shrapnel, however, struck Fort St. Inez, killing three privates, and wounding Colonel Pascual, Lieutenant Diaz, and fifteen men. Alsop Burrows also planted a shot from the dynamite gun right below a bronze cannon just mounted by Melgar. The piece was hurled from its carriage, the gunners blown to atoms, and the escarpment torn up for thirty feet. The Spanish reply was badly directed, and shells hissed and screamed over our heads, bursting in the woods in rear. Their Hontoria planted three shells at the foot of our outworks, and one, tearing its way through the military crest of the ridge, burst under a bomb proof, killing Captain Rowell and Nelson, and wounding Lieutenant Lutz and several privates, all of the Second.

The shells from the fleet were more effective, though fired at very great elevation over the foothills, and ranged by mathematical calculation. Several houses were demolished; but with such precedents

Under Three Flags in Cuba

as Sebastopol, Strasburg, and Paris, it was easy to realize that Shafter's threat to knock Santiago to pieces with his puny field-guns was futile; even aided by a powerful navy, it might take long to force surrender.

At night General Ludlow moved his brigade round at the extreme right, his tired forces occupying trenches voluntarily erected with stupendous difficulty by Garcia's men. At daybreak on the 11th, firing was resumed; but the Spaniards replied weakly. Our left was but three hundred yards from the enemy's position; and from the trenches of the 21st Infantry a very clear view of the enemy was obtainable. Colonel McKibben turned a round hill into a redoubt, and, with Captain Ebstein and Captain Cornman, commanding battalions, a continuous fire was directed against the enemy's guns. But the position was far from comfortable, and it was a terrible ordeal to lie hour after hour, behind scanty cover, while a frontal, oblique, enfilade and cross fire was poured against the position, with seven-inch shells thumping over into the centre of the hill at intervals. With Lieutenants Mullay and Martin I squirmed through the brush clothing the ridge, and viewed the batteries erected directly opposite. The judgment of these officers — that several "guns" the enemy had mounted were but logs of wood — proved correct. We could plainly see large shells from the "Brooklyn" dropping among the intrenchments on the hillside.

At 2 P. M. the bugles rang out "Cease firing!" as

Arrival of General Miles

a boyish-looking "alvarez" stepped fearlessly up on the enemy's earthworks and planted the white flag. General Wheeler then rode out to meet General Toral, who now asked for time to consider "unconditional surrender." Our men again sank apathetically into their trenches, cursing their plight, and urging that it were better to die like men in assaulting Santiago than like dogs in a ditch.

On the following day General Miles [1] and General Henry arrived with reinforcements, and at 9 A. M. a flag was sent, asking General Toral to meet the commander-in-chief. Generals Shafter, Wheeler, and Gilmour, Colonel Morse, and aides, moved out beyond the lines to attend the conference, and Toral manifested that his desire to surrender was only outweighed by the fear of blame in Spain. But the advent of the general-in-chief and reinforcements had a marked effect: Toral retired to consult Sagasta and Blanco over the cable. Blanco at once acquiesced, and several hours later the Spanish Cabinet accepted the inevitable, on condition that the garrison should be repatriated.

[1] Landing at Siboney, General Miles was horrified to find the terrible defilation; and learning of Major Lugard's futile appeals to headquarters for men to police the base, he sent an order to the front. Next day the 25th Infantry marched into Siboney; the town was burned by night and the defilation covered. But the recognition of the subtle enemy in rear, far more to be dreaded than the Spaniard at the front, was too late. Several cases of sickness were recognized as yellow fever, and as victim after victim fell in its ravages, the men who had fought so fearlessly, blanched at the foe no man can combat. A few days' prolongation of the siege, and the army was doomed.

Under Three Flags in Cuba

With graceful tact General Miles did not stay to share the triumphs of the victory he had done much to consummate. Before sailing to Puerto Rico he sent Shafter instructions as to army camps, to which the latter querulously replied that he had understood that he was not to be superseded in command. In quiet irony General Miles replied that he had the honor to command the United States Army, of which Shafter's force was a part, and the incident closed.

A commission consisting of General Wheeler, General Lawton, and Lieutenant Miley, met General Escario, Colonel Fontan, and Mr. Mason, British Vice-Consul, to arrange the terms of capitulation. The Spaniards finally agreed to surrender the whole division of Santiago; *i. e.*, the portion of Cuba east of a line drawn through Aserradero, Dos Palmas, Cauto, Tanamo, and Aguilera; the United States to transport all troops in the command to Spain; officers to retain their side arms; the forces to march from the city with honors of war, laying down their arms at a given point, it being understood that the commissioners would recommend that the Spanish soldier return to Spain with the arms he so bravely defended.

Sunday, July 17, — the day assigned for the closing scene of the campaign, — dawned auspiciously. At ten o'clock church call rang out. The chaplains led their regiments in divine worship and thanksgiving for the cessation of hostilities. It was a memorable service, and as the strain "Praise God from

The Closing Scene

whom all blessings flow" rose through the trees from voices softened by the gratitude and emotion of men brought by the scenes of war to a nearer realization of mortality, the finite and the Infinite, many a sick American boy sobbed aloud, as his thoughts reverted to the distant home where prayers were rising for the loved one in the field. General Shafter, the gen-

FACSIMILE OF SIGNATURES ATTACHED TO THE ARTICLES OF CAPITULATION BY THE SPANISH AND AMERICAN COMMISSIONERS.

erals of divisions and brigades, and their staffs, and an escort of cavalry rode beyond the lines at ten o'clock, to receive the capitulation of Santiago. War correspondents were refused permission to witness the surrender, in language coarse if emphatic, though the reason for this suppression of one of the great chapters in American history seemed inexplicable. In striking unfairness, a favored few, myself included, received permission to witness the ceremony.

In the Canosa valley, below San Juan, the American officers halted. A few moments later, General Toral and his staff, and an infantry brigade marched out from the city. Victor and vanquished shook hands. The duty of surrendering is only worse than receiving surrender, and the American officers by every courtesy strove to lessen the humiliation of the defeated foe. The Spanish bugles played a pitiful "retreat." Our cavalry carried sabres; the Spaniards presented arms, and then marched in column, depositing their rifles in a heap. Several of the Spaniards were weeping bitter tears of mortification, and though for months I had joyously anticipated the end of their brutal sway in Cuba, now one could but feel pity for Toral and his staff, who at least had fought bravely for their country and had won respect.

The generals rode into the city, but I recrossed the lines to borrow a camera, and was unable to again pass the guards. I was amply rewarded, however, for the distant view of the occupation of the city. As I rode out to the advanced outposts, the whole army moved up into line along our entire front. The midday chimes from the cathedral were wafted across the valley. The regiments sprang to attention. Every eye was fixed on a faint black line marked against the sky — the flagstaff of the Governor's palace. Something fluttered up the pole: a thrill of

Old Glory over the City

exultation dominated each heart, for "Old Glory" was waving over the city. Unmanly? Perhaps! But those who had endured the campaign are the better judges. At the sight of the flag great lumps rose in our throats. We strove to speak, but choked. Santiago suddenly seemed enveloped in mist, and strong men turned away and wept as children. Capron's battery was booming in salute, every band burst into the "Star-Spangled Banner;" and as the fourth gun reverberated in the hills, voices were regained, and from five miles of throats rose the beautiful refrain, —

> "The Star-Spangled Banner, oh, long may it wave,
> O'er the land of the free, and the home of the brave."

Then three prolonged cheers of triumph ran down the lines, like a *feu de joie*, mingled with a hoarse shout from the Cubans, "Viva los Americanos!"

As the flag was raised, the general representing the dignity and honor of the American nation addressed Scovel in language so coarse and action so threatening that he lost self-control, and struck the man, forgetting he was thus striking the rank of General of the United States Army.

Knowing Santiago well, I was asked to go in with the Signal Corps. I finally received a joint permit with Armstrong, and we rode in at midday. We were politely received by the Spaniards, who were greatly relieved by the termination of the war, and whose condition was pitiable. A death-like

Under Three Flags in Cuba

stillness reigned throughout the city; the streets were deserted, and the houses closed, save where residences of Cubans had been sacked by the guerilla, or the walls smashed in by our shells. We rode along the outer edge of the city, where the streets were barricaded like Paris in Commune, the walls loopholed, trenches cut across the highways, and so formidable a line of defence formed that an assault on the city would have proved costly. Nine succeeding rows of trenches must first have been captured on the slope leading from San Juan, the terrible barricade of barbed wire, protected by the forts and blockhouses, surmounted, before the stormers could reach the city and its immediate defences. The place was practically impregnable from infantry attack.

Close behind the trenches the Spanish dead had been hurriedly covered with earth, and the road to the city was strewn with dead horses, marking the cavalry retreat of the First. Above all rose an intolerable stench which seemed heightened by the vultures and wild curs we disturbed from gruesome feasting. Two field-guns were mounted directly before the hospital, covered by the Red Cross flag, and one gun had been run out and fired from an annex which gave excellent shelter for loading. The hospital itself was in a deplorable condition: the lawn beyond, covered with old dressings, excrement, and refuse of all kinds, must necessarily have proved a terrible plague spot. The cots were chiefly filled

In Santiago

with sick, and by verified reports the Spanish loss in killed and wounded was very much less than ours, though much greater if the number of Americans needlessly sacrificed before San Juan be deducted from those lost in actual battle. The entire Spanish loss at San Juan, Caney, and the succeeding fighting before Santiago was: General Vara del Rey, one colonel, three comandantes, twelve subalterns, and ninety-eight men killed; General Linares, two colonels, six comandantes, thirty-nine subalterns, and three hundred and ninety-two men wounded; seven officers and one hundred and sixteen men missing or prisoners.

Late in the afternoon a long line of emaciated non-combatants commenced to stream back to the city. Before they were settled in their homes the "State of Texas" had risked submarine defences and entered the harbor, and tons of supplies were soon being distributed by Miss Barton and her staff. But the exposures and privations at Caney had left their mark. For three weeks the death rate in Santiago averaged over a hundred per day, among less than thirty thousand people; and for three months the deaths were abnormally high. It is estimated that over three thousand people lost their lives through the humanity that allowed non-combatants to escape the puny bombardment which destroyed but a dozen houses.

General McKibben was appointed Military Governor. The 9th Infantry garrisoned the city. During

Under Three Flags in Cuba

a trying period the officers of this regiment showed great tact in dealing with the various factions. Colonel Ewers was afterwards promoted, and assumed charge at Guantanamo. He and his aide, Lieutenant Frazer, arranged for the passing of Spain, and won the gratitude of Cuban and Spaniard.

The garrison of Santiago surrendered 14,892 rifles, 1247 carbines, 84 revolvers, 267 sabres, 692 machetes, and 4,652,200 cartridges. Of this ammunition one million rounds were for the Argentine Mauser, though the garrison had but 800 rifles of that pattern.

After the city had fallen, our sick list increased enormously. Nostalgia, assured by tedious inaction following strenuous exertion, is invariably augmented by fever. Despite the exodus of invalids, shipped North on dirty transports supplied with hardtack, canned meat, and foul water, to become an object lesson to the American people of the effect of Cuban climate and official negligence, 4122 soldiers were on the sick list in Cuba on July 24. The generals held a conference, and signed a petition to the Secretary of War, urging that it was imperative that the army be moved North at once. General Shafter concurred in this; his army had not even cooking-utensils; and since no intelligent attempt was apparent from Washington to ship either suitable food or shelter to the stricken army, the officers plainly saw approaching extermination. The President promptly decided to move the army North, and dur-

The Army Withdraws

ing the first two weeks in August, the regiments were moved to Montauk, Santiago being garrisoned by immune troops mobilized through the South.

The army that had landed but seven weeks before, in the flush of health and strength, crawled back to the transports in regiments of gaunt spectres, to return to the country whose readiness and anxiety to do everything possible for its defenders had been negatived by the unfortunate officialdom and chaos in Washington. The horror and sadness of it — that Americans should have died for lack of medicine and food in a land adjoining their coasts, and within reach of a generous people willing for any sacrifice that the troops should have need of nothing! A glorious campaign, that attained stupendous results? Yes. But inward history will prove that those results might have been attained with, practically, no sacrifice.

CHAPTER XV

SANTIAGO AFTER CAPITULATION. — A RETROSPECT OF '99. — CONCLUSION.

FIFTEEN months have elapsed since the flag was hoisted over Santiago; ten months ago Spain relinquished her sovereignty over Cuba, and the Island passed under the military rule of the United States. After many weeks' delay, negotiations for peace between the two nations ended satisfactorily; the Spanish army folded its tattered banners, and withdrew from the land that would soon have proved its grave. They left a desolate desert, a monument of ruin, despair, pestilence, and death, to the magnanimous victor morally pledged to stand sponsor to the Free Cuba that is to arise on the blood-soaked ashes of the Island.

In this mundane age the heroes of Washington's day are apt to be forgotten, but the aspirations of 1776 are dominating the war-worn Cubans of '99, and desire for betterment of this people, ragged and ignorant as some of them are, has been actuated by the influence and example of the great Republic at their doors. Only those who know the Cubans intimately, realize the price they have paid for liberty, and appreciate the misgivings they have to-day for

Reprehensible Misunderstandings

the future. This mistrust is the direct result of a series of grave mistakes made by military rulers, the effect of which must retard the redevelopment of the Island, and the tranquillity and content so necessary for the well being of any country.

After the inhabitants returned to Santiago, many families looked with joy for the reunion with dear ones, long absent in the field. But General Shafter, for no substantial reason, prohibited Cuban soldiers from entering the city that many of them had been born in. At the capitulation the Cubans were not represented, despite the aid they had gratuitously given. When the British saved Bekwai from Prempeh, the king furnished contingents to General Scott for scouting and transport. Every one of those savages was enrolled at once, and received regular pay and rations, and after due warning against looting, the king and his followers were given a place of honor in the ceremonies when Kumassi capitulated. By such tact England rules some millions of savages just emerged from cannibalism, by a few companies of native soldiers and a score of white officers. She has learned by bitter experience that firm kindness is cheaper and more efficacious than a battery of Gatlings. If Aguinaldo had been invited to enter Manila with his body-guard, and received due recognition for the fighting his men did in Luzon, he would have been in a reasonable frame of mind to accept the inevitable. He could undoubtedly have aided in the formation of the liberal autonomy intended by the United States, and from personal knowledge of some of his adherents, I believe he would have proved a worthy ally rather than a relentless enemy, without diminution of American power or prestige in the Islands.

The same lack of tact nearly proved costly in Cuba. "By the exclusion of our leaders and flag from to-day's ceremony we feel as the patriots under Washington would have felt had the allied armies captured New York, and the French prohibited the entry of the Americans and their flag," remarked one Cuban. Garcia withdrew his forces and marched against Holguin, and the bitterness among the people in the city was increased by the arbitary orders of Shafter, and the conduct of the rough element of one or two regiments. Kissing women on the street may be harmless horse-play, and mere curiosity prompted the soldiers to enter private houses and roam around, but Latins do not understand these things.

Señor Ros, the autonomist civil governor of Santiago Province, was asked to retain his position after American occupation. A moderate Cuban, for years a resident in America, trusted by all parties and factions, he was the one man likely to aid the United States in the reconstruction of eastern Cuba. His first act was to discharge from office some notorious Spanish officials of the old régime. Perhaps he exceeded his authority: General Shafter thought so. Sending for the governor, Shafter, in the presence of a crowd, coarsely berated him as a —— presumptuous rascal.

Dangers of Unjust Criticism

Mr. Ros, in quiet dignity, turned and tendered his resignation. Representative of the conservative element of the Cubans, the breach was serious, and only the withdrawal of Shafter and the appointment of General Wood averted disorder and a threatened rupture.

The unjust attitude of a section of the American press caused dangerous irritation in Cuba. The action of a few negro desperadoes during the war were taken as texts for wholesale condemnation of the Cuban race. I well remember sitting in a Cuban camp one cool August night, talking with the officers, educated gentlemen to a man. A copy of the "Army and Navy Register" of July 23 was produced, and in English, which three-fourths of the officers there understood, a captain read: —

"The insurgents felt, when Santiago capitulated, that they should be privileged to sack the city and gratify their lust for robbery, greed, and generally riotous living. They have been refractory since General Shafter refused them the consummate gratification of their dreams, the slaughter of the Spaniards and seizure of everything Spanish. . . . Pursuing a barbarous system of unholy indifference for the lives of those they capture, inured to the worst sides of life," etc., etc., etc.

At the close of the article no one spoke. Then one officer sprang to his feet, and in an impassioned harangue called all to swear to fulfil their oath, "Independence or Death," and face the latter before submitting to American intolerance. "This is the official organ of their army," he went on; "this is American justice. Have we not two thousand Spanish prisoners living in idleness at Cambote, while we are starving here? Have we not punished by death all those who violated our commands to respect prisoners?"

Slights and insults General Garcia met calmly. "We did our best," he would say sadly, "and time will show that my ragged, hungry soldiers have endured with the resolute sincerity of the Americans of Saratoga or Yorktown." The past nine months have proved that the Cubans are magnanimous, and desire only the return to peaceful industry. After the continued cruelty of Spain, they have evinced no desire for reprisals, Spaniards have been respected as no Tory was respected during the Revolution, and the Cuban to-day stands ready to join the Spaniard in the building of a mutual country. When Pinar del Rio and Sancti Spiritus surrendered, the insurgents took charge of the cities on behalf of Americans, and not one outrage or injustice was reported.

General Wood soon perceived the danger and injustice of treating the Cubans as a conquered people. His kindly tact and firm discrimination then had a marked effect. Calling in the insurgent leaders, he asked for their co-operation. They were completely won over by his genuine Americanism; their men had soon stacked their arms, and showed their ability and desire to work, being employed at road-making and sanitary

Conditions during the Siege

improvement. Deserving Cubans were placed in all public offices, schools were reopened, and in a few weeks the filthiest, most distracted corner of Cuba was as clean and orderly as an American city. The avidity of the younger element to attain the education so long debarred was surprising, and all the schools were soon filled to overflowing. By the latest report of General Wood, the regularity of attendance has been sustained, the Cuban officials have without exception proved satisfactory. Official dishonesty has disappeared, and the administration of the Eastern Department shows positive proof of the ability of the Cuban for self-government under the guidance of the United States.

Through the blockade, and during the weary negotiations for peace, when anarchy reigned in Cuba, the residue of the reconcentrados and hundreds of the lower classes in the cities succumbed to privation. During the first seven months of '98 there were 17,760 deaths in Havana, against 2224 births, from a population of little over 230,000. With such a death-rate the extinction of the Cuban race would soon have been assured. When the Evacuation Commissioners had completed their work, and the Army of Occupation was moved to western Cuba, the aspect grew more hopeful. General Blanco returned to Spain, Castellanos assumed command, and as the Spanish troops were mobilized in the large cities, the smaller towns, freed from restraint, invited the insurgents to enter. Thus dozens of towns practically

Under Three Flags in Cuba

came under Cuban administration. At this time four-fifths of the people in the cities were starving.

When the insurgents had disbanded, I realized, as never before, how the Cuban male population had disappeared during the war. To-day the Cubans are being criticised as a mongrel race. The best blood in the Island is soaked in the soil; the backbone of the Island, the white farming class, has disappeared. Cuban women are nursing the offspring they have been forced to bear to their hated oppressors. Thousands of the people are so reduced that they can scarcely crawl. As the Spaniards withdrew, I travelled through the districts they evacuated. Space forbids the horrible details of the trip, which was cut short in Matanzas by an impromptu duel with a Spanish colonel. I was forced into this brawl by Carchano, courtmartialled by Blanco for flogging naked reconcentrados, and Escalante, and received a ball in the chest, which was extracted by a Spanish surgeon, who showed me much kindness.

The military government in Cuba has accomplished much during the past year: as far as the restoration of Cuba is concerned, it has accomplished little. The return of the rebels to their homes was necessarily the first step toward regeneration. The Cuban Assembly, a body politic, elected by the army, and representing every division in the Island, sent envoys to Washington to ask for a loan guaranteed by Cuba's revenue. This commission was not received, and the Administration, overlooking the

The Assembly Ignored

Assembly, sent Mr. Porter direct to Gomez, offering a loan of $3,000,000, provided the Cubans would give up their arms to the United States military authorities. Gomez accepted these conditions, forgetting that he held his commission only by appointment of the Assembly, who had sole control over the army.

Incensed by the slights, resenting the demand that the patriot army surrender its arms to another power, the Assembly rejected the President's offer, and deposed Gomez from command. The deadlock thus caused delayed the disbandment of the Cubans for many weeks; the lack of security thus caused hindered important investments of capital, and was only removed by the diplomatic compromise of Capote, who arranged that Gomez should represent the Assembly in the distribution of the loan, and the arms be stored honorably.

After all these months the census, so vital for revised franchise and popular government, is not yet complete; no organized effort has been made for the rehabilitation of the country, and the Cuban looks wonderingly for the freedom he so long has craved. With this indefinite policy of indecision and procrastination, capital for interior investment has been withheld, and redevelopment seriously retarded.

It is difficult for a country to formulate its first colonial policy, and the experimental colonists are to be pitied, but procrastination cannot lessen the difficulties to be faced. The military government of

Under Three Flags in Cuba

Cuba should have ceased with the necessity for it. The appointment of ex-Cuban generals as provincial civil governors was wise; but their power is nominal, and popular voice is dead. A civilian, as Mr. Hannis Taylor, placed at the head of affairs in Cuba, would have accomplished more in a month, with tact and discretion, than the military rule of Cuba will ever accomplish. The army officers have done splendid work, but it has yet to be proved that a military training fits men for the reconstruction of a system of jurisprudence suitable for a Latin people, the administration of the revenue, and intricate economic and financial problems and the adjustment of currency, to be faced in Cuba.

But if political reconstruction has been slow, the vast improvement in sanitation accomplished by the army will prove of lasting benefit to Cuba. General Ludlow has carried out a crusade against disease and dirt in Havana, — undoubtedly the filthiest city in the world, — and the accumulated offal of ages has been removed from the towns and cities, and sanitary regulations enforced for the first time in history. The work of cleansing the capital was aided by the unfinished system of drainage and the splendid water-supply. The bulk of the houses, built in Moorish style, boasted a fœtid cesspool under the centre courtyard, from which all rooms open. Numbers of these lacked connections with the main sewers, which emptied through open culverts into the harbor and sea. During the war many houses contained a fam-

Improvement of Sanitation

ily in each room, with no sanitary appliances: the offal and refuse were thrown into the street beyond. Hundreds of tons of waste have now been destroyed, new sewer connections put in, and the worst quarters of the city demolished entirely.

This cleansing has reduced the death-rate to regular proportions, yellow fever during the past summer has been unprecedentedly scarce, and when the projected canal is cut, to flush out the vast cesspool, Havana harbor, the city, quaint and beautiful despite the dirt, will become a Mecca for winter tourists.

Despite the abolition of the preferential tariff and the reduction of duty on necessaries, the Cuban Custom House now shows an increase on the revenue paid in by Spanish officials after peculation. The exports from Havana during the past eight months of American occupation were valued at $18,958,570. The United States took $13,423,417 of this, $5,535,153 going to other countries. Of the above amounts $12,899,033 was merchandise, $530,374 gold coin. $875,040 in merchandise, and $1,803,429 in gold went to Spain. France took $973,960 in merchandise and $513,950 gold coin. This report is highly satisfactory, but the vast shipments of tobacco practically cover the merchandise. The sugar industry will need much capital for revival and increase. Of the one hundred and fifty-nine sugar estates in central Cuba, but forty-one factories are operating. Fruit and coffee raising will prove fields for the foreign investor, vast timber concessions are idle, but until roads are improved little can be done save on the coast. Farming is at a standstill for the want of seeds and implements. The construction of the railroad from Santa Clara to Santiago will open up the richest districts in the Island, which as yet are untouched.

Capital and labor are alike needed in the Island. Maso's project of inducing restricted immigration from the Canary Islands and northern Spain will solve the latter difficulty, if placed into effect. While American capital is cautious, English capitalists are obtaining options and making effective arrangements for aggressive investment. The commercial instinct and energy of the Spanish merchant will retain him the control of mercantile trade, as the gachupine of Mexico. But since transoceanic nativity no longer insures preferment, political and commercial, the united power of these men, so long Cuba's curse, will exist no longer. The notorious carpet-baggers have returned to Spain: by the Paris treaty Spaniards residing in the Island are to have equal rights with Cubans for one year, after which they must proclaim their citizenship or become aliens.

For the future one can say little. The United States is morally pledged to give the Cubans independence. To-day Cuban obedience is enforced by a power too strong to be resisted: enforcement creates resentment. That obedience will be willingly given to the acknowledged superiority of America, if the Cuban realizes that the betterment of his Island, not the selfish wishes of financiers and the greed of car-

Annexation

pet-baggers, is concerned therein. Forcible annexation the Cuban will not hear of; it will precipitate insurrection. But tactful administration to-day, sustained by Cuban officials elected by the people, will assuredly foster the desire of the people to become an integral portion of the United States. The Cubans desire the right to live, and a voice in shaping their destiny. The revival of industry is so slow that the Cuban fails as yet to appreciate altered conditions, and he knows nothing of his political future.

Time will work all these things, but revival of industry cannot come until the future policy of the Government is definitely settled. The intelligent Islander to-day desires independence under American protection, and realizes ultimate annexation inevitable. Annexation by force he will resent; with Cuban institutions founded, and the Island pronounced free and independent, he will desire the closest ties with the United States, if not admission in some form to the Union.

THE END

16

www.ingramcontent.com/pod-product-compliance
Lightning Source LLC
Chambersburg PA
CBHW030426300426
44112CB00009B/869